Specific Targeted Research Project on the Formation of Europe:
Prehistoric Population Dynamics and the Roots of Socio-Cultural Diversity

Institute of Archaeology
Jagiellonian University

The First Neolithic Sites in Central/South-East European Transect

Volume I

Early Neolithic Sites on the Territory of Bulgaria

Edited by

Ivan Gatsov
Yavor Boyadzhiev

BAR International Series 2048
2009

Published in 2016 by
BAR Publishing, Oxford

BAR International Series 2048

The First Neolithic Sites in Central/South-East European Transect, Volume I

ISBN 978 1 4073 0624 7

BAR Publishing is the trading name of British Archaeological Reports (Oxford) Ltd.
British Archaeological Reports was first incorporated in 1974 to publish the BAR
Series, International and British. In 1992 Hadrian Books Ltd became part of the BAR
group. This volume was originally published by Archaeopress in conjunction with
British Archaeological Reports (Oxford) Ltd / Hadrian Books Ltd, the Series principal
publisher, in 2009. This present volume is published by BAR Publishing, 2016.

Printed in England

BAR
PUBLISHING

BAR titles are available from:

	BAR Publishing
	122 Banbury Rd, Oxford, OX2 7BP, UK
EMAIL	info@barpublishing.com
PHONE	+44 (0)1865 310431
FAX	+44 (0)1865 316916
	www.barpublishing.com

From the series editor

The modelling of the process of Neolithization – one of the basic tasks of the FEPRE project – requires to built a complete database i.e. not only the register of radiocarbon dates but also the inventory of the FTN sites: both those excavated as well as those recorded in the course of surface surveys. In view of the fact that in the Neolithization of Europe the axis running from the Balkans to the Carpathians is of essential importance we have decided to make up the inventory of FTN sites along this axis. Within the territory from 41 to 51 degrees latitude north the following sheets have been taken into account: I – Bulgaria, II – Romania, III – Eastern Hungary, IV – Eastern Slovakia, V – South-eastern Poland (see map). The result are five volume catalogue of FTN sites with the following contents:

1. General information about cultural evolution at the onset of Neolithic in a given territory: taxonomic definitions, stratigraphic sequences, seriations, basic data on settlement, material culture, subsistance economy
2. Additional data on cultural and economic problems specific for a given region
3. A list of radiometric dates
4. A catalogue of sites in alphabetical order.

Site catalogues are made up of the following data categories:

Identification and location of sites

Name of a site (and number on the map)

1. Administrative unit appropriate to a given site
2. River basin
3. Geographical coordinates
4. Geomorphological situation (river basin, location in relation to the land relief)

A. Information on excavated sites

1. Name(s) of researcher(s) responsible for the excavation
2. Date of excavation (years)
3. Bounded research area: excavated and surveyed
4. Type and number of features
5. Relative chronology based on archaeological seria- tion and absolute chronology; number of settlement phases

B. Information on sites recognized on the basis of surface finds

1. Area of occurrence of portable finds
2. Taxonomic attribution and – when possible – chronological framework of sites

C. The most important references

Each volume deals with a different taxonomic unit representing FTN in a given territory:

Volume I – Bulgaria – sites of the Monochrome and the Early Painted Pottery Phase (Karanovo I type);

Volume II – Romania (Transilvania and Banat) – sites of the Early Phase (with white-painted pottery) of Criş- Körös Culture;

Volume III – Eastern Hungary (Tisza basin) – sites of the Körös-Starčevo Culture;

Volume IV – Eastern Slovakia – sites of the Early Phase of the Eastern Linear Pottery Culture;

Volume V – South-Eastern Poland – LBK sites.

The database and the analysis of archaeological records provides the most up-to-date groundwork for the construction of the model on Neolithization of Central Europe within the framework of the FEPRE project; it is also aimed at any other modeling of these processes.

Janusz K. Kozłowski

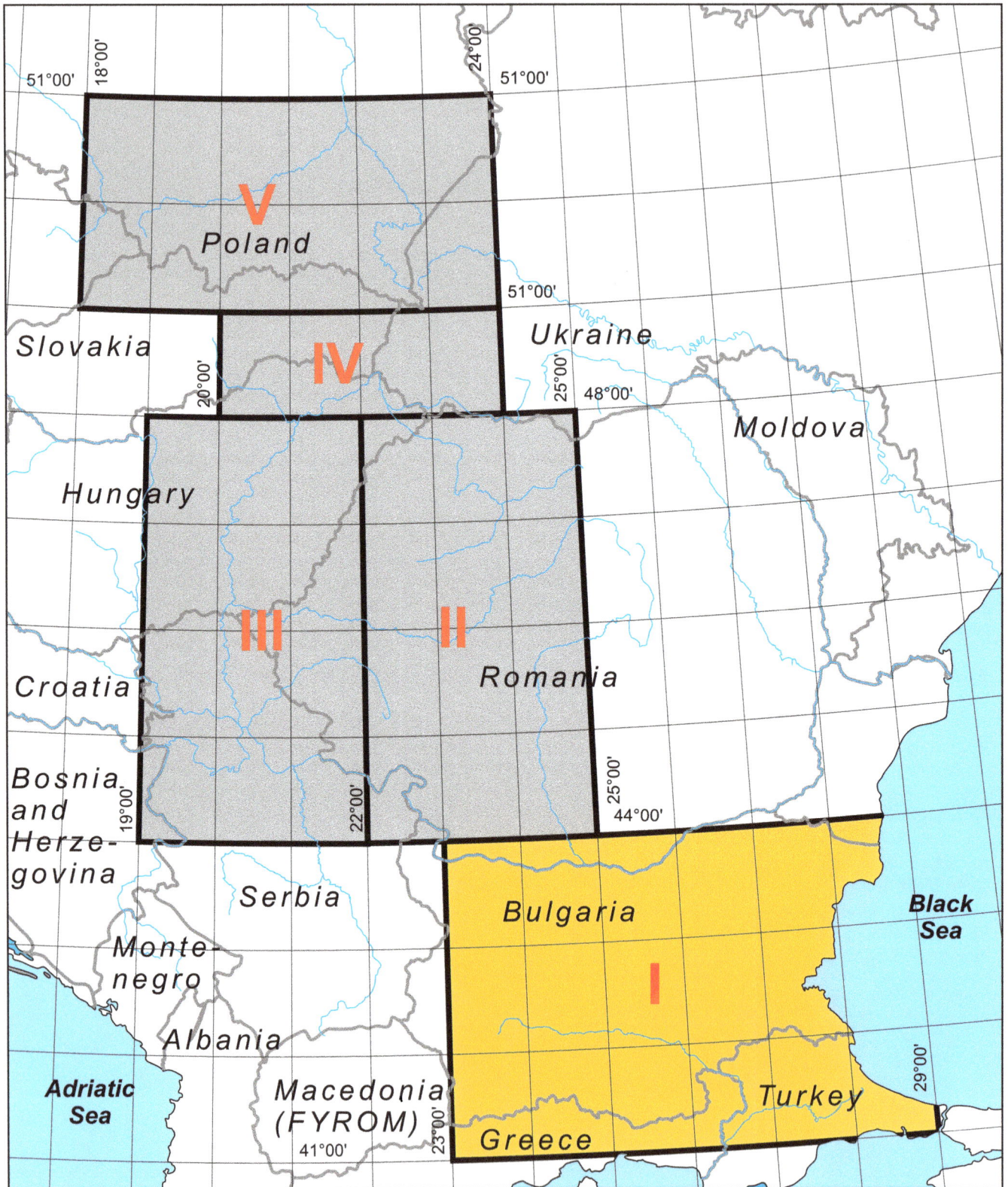

CONTENTS

7–43.

EARLY NEOLITHIC CULTURES ON THE TERRITORY OF BULGARIA

Yavor D. Boyadzhiev

National Archaeological Insitute and Museum, Bulgarian Academy of Sciences, 2 Saborna Str. BG-1000 Sofia, Bulgaria

EXISTING PERIODISATIONS OF THE EARLY NEOLITHIC PERIOD ON THE TERRITORY OF BULGARIA

Studies of the Neolithic period on the territory of Bulgaria have been held for over a century. They have been especially intensive since the second half of the XX century when a great number of settlements have been studied and great quantities of empirical material has been accumulated. The major Neolithic cultures have been differentiated. However, there are still discrepancies with reference to the main periodisation of the Neolithic period (see Tab. 1).

In Bulgarian literature, the three-segmented periodisation has been widely applied – namely Early (EN), Middle (MN) and Late (LN). In different periods though, different authors have implied different content in it. V. Mitkov defines the EN as purely hypothetical period suggesting that the high quality painted pottery of Karanovo I Culture could not appear accidentally without any prior development. To the MN are related layers I and II at Karanovo (= Karanovo Ia and Ib after V. Mikov) and to LN – layer III (= Karanovo II after V. Mikov) (Mikov 1958, 48–50). The same periodisation was accepted also by P. Detev (Detev 1963, 13, 16, tab. II; Detev 1978, 59). G. Georgiev includes into EN the cultures of Karanovo I and II, to MN – Karanovo III, and to LN – Karanovo IV (Georgiev 1961; Georgiev 1974). That periodisation was accepted and complemented by H. Todorova who included in the Karanovo system also the cultures outside Thrace (Vajsova 1966; Todorova 1981). For more than 30 years it has been the widely accepted periodisation among the scientific circles in both Bulgaria and abroad. It was not until the recent years that the periodisation of G. Georgiev of the Neolithic period was reconsidered and the idea of replacing the three-segmented periodisation with a two-segmented one was promoted. H. Todorova unites the Neolithic cultures (both those on the territory of Bulgaria and those of the neighbouring countries on the Balkan Peninsula) into two blocks – a block of the Balkan Early Neolithic (BEN) and a Balkan block of the Late Neolithic and Early Eneolithic cultures (BLN-BEE) (To-

dorova & Vaysov 1993, 74–83). BEN is divided into four phases. To the first phase (BEN-M) belongs the phenomena of the so called "monochrome" pottery; the second phase (BEN-A) covers the phenomena of the white painted decoration on pottery; third phase (BEN-B) – two cultural settings are associated with it – of the cultures with dark painted pottery and of the cultures without painted pottery; the fourth phase (BEN-C) was defined as a time for transformation during which the BLN-BEE block was formed. The block of BLN-BEE is also divided into four phases where the first two of them – BLN-A and BLN-B are associated with the LN.

A combination of three and two-segmented periodisation of the EN (in particular for Thrace) was suggested by V. Nikolov. According to him, the development in Northeastern Thrace went through three phases – EN (Cultures Karanovo I and II); MN – Group Karanovo II-III and LN – Cultures Karanovo III and Karanovo IV, and the development of Western Thrace – through two: EN – Culture Karanovo I and LN – Cultures Karanovo III and IV (Nikolov 1989; 1993a; 1998, 4).

New studies continuously provide more and more grounds to assume that the Neolithic period in Bulgaria should be divided into two major periods – Early Neolithic to which the cultures with painted pottery belong and Late Neolithic which covers the Cultures of Karanovo III and IV and their synchronized phenomena.

In archaeological science, however, there is no consensus either regarding the differentiation of Early Neolithic cultures on the territory of Bulgaria, or on the phases of their progression. It results mainly from two factors. The first is the still insufficient examination of the period, the second – the lack of clear criteria when defining the concept "archaeological culture". The differentiation of cultures is usually based only on ceramic materials and even sometimes only to single elements of pottery. Consequently, for every region on the territory of Bulgaria there are a number of existing periodisations which reflect both the phases of development of prehistoric research and also of the views of different researchers.

Table 1

Periodization of the Neolithic period on the territory of Bulgaria

	V. Mikov	G. Georgiev	H. Todorova	V. Nikolov	
				NE Thrace	Western Thrace
Early	?	Kar. I Kar. II/Azm. version.Kar. I Kar. II	BEN[1]-M BEN-A BEN A/B BEN-B	Kar. I Kar. II	South-Western variant
Middle	Kar. Ia = Kar. I Kar. IB= Kar. II	Kar. III	BEN-C BLN[2]-A	Kar. I-III/ Kar.II-III	of Karanovo I
Late	Kar. II=Kar. III (after Georgiev)	Kar. IV.	BLN-B	Kar. III Kar. III/IV Kar. IV	Kar. III/IV Kar. IV (Kapitan Dimitrievo Group)

[1] BEN – stands for Block of Early Neolithic period
[2] BLN – an abbreviation for Block of Late Neolithic period

The main problem that led to essential disagreements in different periodisations and synchronizations and also to constant changes in them has been the overestimation of the role of pottery as a chronological indicator. In practice, all former synchronizations and periodisations have been based exclusively on the analysis of ceramic material. The logic behind that is the following:
– pottery with common features is synchronous[1];
– differences in the ceramic material (and more specifically of the chosen "dating" element) mean chronological discrepancies of corresponding sites.

Both principles are not specific enough. Every cultural phenomenon has its own centre of origin, a period of affirmation, directions, routes and rate of spreading. The larger the territory of penetration, the greater the chronological interval between the moment of origination and its acceptance in the most distant point of spreading would be. Various subjective factors could exercise influence on the penetration of a specific cultural phenomenon and in it is impossible to account for them at present. As a result, between the appearances of one and the same phenomena in two separate settlements there could be a significant chronological difference. That circumstance was especially significant exactly during the period of Neolithisation of the Balkan Peninsula (i.e. during the Early Neolithic period) when the contacts among separate settlements were still very poor and thus the "colonists" could have kept their "native traditions and methods" even at times when at the point of origin they had already changed. It is also quite possible that in one and the same geographical region, colonists from separate origin "centres" to have settled and consequently to have brought different "traditions and methods". In order to assess and describe most objectively (at least at the current state of archaeological research) the dynamics and tendencies of the processes occurring during the Early Neolithic period it is necessary to collect and make comparisons not only of all types of artifacts found, but also of the results of modern physics-chemical dating methods.

There are enough ^{14}C dates for the Early Neolithic cultures on the territory of Bulgaria so that different phases could be dated well. Of exclusive significance is the availability of series of dates from successive horizons in

---

1   It should be taken into consideration that most often synchronizations are made on the ground of separate elements of pottery (usually of the fine pottery), and comparisons with the entire ceramic setting is missing (in fact there is no single site in which all the ceramic material to have been studied/published statistically).

Table 2

Correlation of ^{14}C dates according their stratigraphic position in multi-layer settlements in Southern Bulgaria – II and III stages of Early Neolithic Period

Karanovo	Stara Zagora	Azmak	Slatina	Kovachevo	Galabnik	Kremenik	Cavdar	Cal. BC
Hor. 1 7110± 50 7090±90 6955±45 6810± 65 6710±55				Ia 7180±45 Ia/b 7090±70	Hor. 1 7220±80** 7030±70** 7120±70 6950±70 6790±80 Hor. 4 7070±180 7020±60		Hor. VI 7208±52 7202±55 7195±65 7070±50 7020±45 7003±45 7000±60 6994±55 6820±50 6550±50	6000
Hor. 2 7130±70 Hor. 3 7110±50 6730±80	Hor. 1 7139± 65 6814± 65 Hor. 2 6939±60	Hor. I-1 7303±150 7158±150 6878±100 6768±150	Hor. 1 6970±60 6960±60 6940±60 6890±60 6860±50 6840±60 6840±60 6830±60 6810±50 6780±60	Ib 6975±50 6990±45 6980±65	Hor. 6 7140±80 7020±50 6760±80		Hor. V 7120±80 6840±50 Hor. IV 7040±100** 6680±100** 6997±100 6985±100** 6930±100** 6852±100**	5820
Hor. 4 6760±50 6750±50 öîd. 5 6785±60 Hor. 7 6910±60 6850±60 6780±60 Hor. ? 6807±106	Hor. 3 6918±45 6844±100 6820±100 6750±60 6744±100 6720±100 6668±150	Hor. I-2 6779±100 6720±100 Hor. I-3 6880±100 6812±100 6758±100 6675±100 6652±140 6540±100		Id 6830±85 6760±160	Hor. 8 7100±80 6760±60 6710±60 6670±70	Hor. 2 6620±100 6460±60	Hor. 3 7045±120 6990±150 6870±100 6815±100 6760±100 6760±100 6720±100 6655±100** 6555±100** Hor. 2 6720±100	5740/5720
6540±100 6490±100		Hor. I-4 6483±100 6426±150				Hor. 3 6840±60 6660±60 6530±50 6480±60 6475±40 Hor. 1 6550±60 6450 ±100 6350±60		5640/5600
		Hor. I-5 6279±120						5460/5400

Legend:
- White Painted Pottery
- Dark Painted Pottery
- Karanovo II Pottery

multi-layered settlements. It allows tracing the changes of dates in time (based on strata succession) and the comparison of that particular modification to the calibration curves.

That way, a much greater accuracy when defining the chronological place of separate horizons is achieved than by direct calibration of different dates or series (Boyadžiev 1995,

9

150–160). Most important in that respect is the series from tells Karanovo, Galabnik, Chavdar, Azmak, Okrazhna Bolnitsa-Stara Zagora (Tab. 2).

Together with dates for the EN on the territory of Bulgaria, I am going to examine also the dates from neighbouring areas so that the place of EN in Bulgaria could be clearly defined in relation to that of the neighbouring to the Balkan Peninsula regions. The currently known ^{14}C dates for sites from the beginning of the Early Neolithic period in the Balkan Peninsula region could be divided into 6 groups (Boyadžiev 2006, 8–9, tab. I). The differentiation of separate groups is made both according to the very estimates of ^{14}C dates and also according to their distribution in separate series, based on the dates in proceeding and subsequent strata series. When defining the absolute age of the sites, data from archaeomagnetic dating have been considered.

In those cases when ^{14}C or any other dates are missing, some objective (even though not always very accurate and precise) strata data could be of great assistance. Above all things, such data is the number and thickness of cultural layers in a given settlement, especially when it is multi-layered with a well defined vertical stratigraphy. To reason the applicability of that criterion as a chronological indicator, I have proceeded from the assumption of the following principal prerequisites:

– a specific chronological period is related to a corresponding number of human generations;

– under the same natural-geographic conditions and way of life, those generations would leave almost the same number of settlements – that is approximately with the same thickness and structure of cultural remains.

The series of ^{14}C dates from successive horizons in multi-layered sites provides an opportunity to date with comparatively great accuracy the beginning and ending of existence of the corresponding site – that is, its time duration, and therefore the average life span of an undestroyed horizon (layer), as well as the average rate of debris accumulation of the cultural layer (Boyadžiev 1995, 152–160). For the EN on the territory of Bulgaria the above mentioned indicators are correspondingly 50–70 years and about 7–8 mm per year. The life span of a prehistoric house of approximately 60 years is confirmed not only by the established in some houses more than 50 floor plasterings (Nikolov 1992, 33), but also by the precise dating of the house in Slatina on the ground of series of dates from the various periods of its existence (Boyadzhiev 1994).

PHASES OF DEVELOPMENT OF THE EARLY NEOLITHIC PERIOD IN BULGARIA

The process of Neolithisation on the Balkan Peninsula had begun in the second half of the VII millennia BC. It occurred under the influence and direct participation of the peoples of Anatolia. The first Neolithic settlements appeared in Thessaly about 6500/6400 cal. BC. Approximately about 6400/6300 cal. BC in that region began the Early-ceramic Neolithic period. From Thessaly it gradually had spread in northern direction and in about 150–200 years reached Southern Macedonia region. The penetration of the

Neolithic peoples in the central areas of the Balkan Peninsula had happened mainly along the river valleys which cross the Peninsula in the direction North-South.

Until the present though there is no existing consensus among researchers on the routes and stages of peoples' penetration. Regarding the process of Neolithisation of the Eastern part of the Peninsula and in particular of modern Bulgarian lands, there are three main hypotheses. According to the first one, it had occurred along the valleys of the rivers Struma and Mesta under the influence of the bearers of the Culture of white painted pottery. Its beginning was about 6000 BC. Initially, Southwestern Bulgaria and the Rodopa Mountains region were settled, followed by Thrace and finally by Northern Bulgaria. Supporters of that theory considering that the so-called "Monochrome Neolithic period" spread mainly in Northeastern Bulgaria developed synchronously to Culture Karanovo I in Thrace (Stefanova 1996, 19; Nikolov 1998, 4; Lichardus & Iliev 2000, 80).

According to the second theory, the process of Neolithisation of the Eastern part of the Balkan Peninsula began around 6400/6300 BC and had occurred along the courses of the rivers Vardar and Struma, and later – along the South Morava and the Danube Rivers. Its bearers were representatives of the so-called "Monochrome Neolithic period". Initially, the regions of Shumadia (Šumadia) and South Banat (the region around the "Iron Gates") went under the process of Neolithisation, and from there, following the course of the Danube River, groups of Neolithic peoples had reached the river of Rusensky Lom on which they had penetrated into Northeastern Bulgaria. Thrace went through Neolithisation around 6200/6000 BC caused by the representatives of the Monochrome Neolithic in Northeastern Bulgaria who had migrated South due to climate cooling (Todorova & Vaisov 1993, 59–63).

The third hypothesis assumes that the settling of central Northern Bulgaria happened from the south, most probably along the valleys of the river Maritsa and its tributaries Tundzha and Sazliyka (Stanev 1995, 59; Boyadžiev 2006, 9; Gatsov 2009, 121).

In order to clarify the ethno-cultural picture during the early Neolithic period and the processes occurring then it is necessary to consider the main archaeological cultures – their spreading and development, as well as their juxtaposition – territorially and chronologically – with the rest. At the same time, all available data should be juxtaposed – data on the material culture; stratigraphy; dating by means of physics-chemical methods.

Early Neolithic period – Stage I (? 6200/6100–6000 cal. BC)

That stage is related to the appearance of the earliest Neolithic people on the territory of modern Bulgaria. Evidences for that culture are still scarce and most of them come from a comparative distant geographical region – Central Northern Bulgaria. All previously established expressions are combined under a common term – "Monochrome Neolithic period".

Monochrome Neolithic period (MnN) – Phase I

The term was introduced by H. Todorova to differentiate what was discovered on the site of Polyanitsa – Platoto cultural phenomenon from the Early Neolitihic cultures of painted pottery (Karanovo I and WBPC[2]) (Todorova 1989, 10–11; Todorova & Vaisov 1993, 75). That term, however, is not very precise. On one hand, there is also some painted pottery associated with that culture. On another, the spread of monochrome pottery is established in various cultural phenomena both during the second half of the Early Neolithic (Group Karanovo II in Thrace; Culture Ovcharovo in Northeastern Bulgaria) and during the Late Neolithic (Culture Karanovo III, Hotnitsa, Vincha (Vinča). For that reason it seems more appropriate to apply the term Early-ceramic Neolithic period which term is used for other neighbouring cultural phenomena on the territory of Thessaly. In the current paper though we will continue to use the term "Monochrome Neolithic period"=MnN as that has been already widely accepted in relevant literature.

Most of the uncovered settlements of MnN so far have been in Northern Bulgaria and they were concentrated mainly in Central Northern Bulgaria – on the river valleys of the Yantra and Rusenski Lom: the sites Belyakovets-Plochite; Dzhulyunitsa-Smardesh; Hotnitsa-Peshterata-Iztok; Koprivets, Pomoshtitsa. Near to that area is also Polyanitsa-Platoto. In Southern Bulgaria there only one settlement that is definitely associated with that culture – the lowest horizon with house traces in Kraynitsi. The culture is differentiated on the ground of the ceramic material found. It appears very similar within the setting and at the same time distinct in its main parameters to that of the Karanovo I Culture and WBPC.

The clay is abundantly mixed with organic temper – in most settlements chaff, but in Kraynitsi – excrements. That temper is especially common in raw pottery. It is also badly baked. Its surface in most cases is only smoothed; the colour is basically in various nuances of brown – from bright to dark. In single cases there is red slip or the surface is polished. Fine pottery was made of better refined clay, with temper from quartz particles or a combination of sand and chaff. It is also baked better. In most cases it has a wine-red or brown slip polished until shining. There are rare cases of grey-blackish polished surface. The shapes are relative limited: carinated dishes, semi-spherical bowls or dishes where there are some bi-carinated ones – with a sharp or blunt curve; open or closed spherical pots with cylindrical or curved upwards mouth; deep spherical jars with tall cylindrical or turned upside conically neck sometimes blown up very much in their lower part (Fig. 1). Specific are the slightly slanted "tubular lugs" (Fig. 1: 11, 13). Widely spread was the lugs. Among the vessel bottoms, specific are the thickened low solid stumps where they could also be slightly differentiated or concave. The decoration most often is impresso – pinches and nails impressions; plastic decoration; dotted decoration. In Dzhulyunitsa-Smardesh is established also a distinctive type of painting with dark-brown and black paint (Fig. 1: 1). Actually it is a very fine paint layer which is embedded into the surface of the vessel. The

decorative motives found are oval spots in negative or positive and wide horizontal bands (Elenski 2008, 97).

Two sites are associated to the first phase according to ^{14}C dates – Polyanitsa-Platoto and the lowest layer in Dzhulyunitsa-Smardesh. The series from the Polyanitsa-Platoto is the earliest for the Neolithic period on the territory of Bulgaria. The ^{14}C dates from Dzhulyunitsa-Smardesh[3] are very close to those from Polyanitsa-Platoto. Dates with estimates mainly between 7400 and 7200 BP correspond approximately to the period of 6200–6000 cal. BC. Dates with similar estimated have been registered in Achilleion II and Sesklo phase EN II (Culture Proto-Sesklo); Nea Nikomedeia – on the transition between EN I and EN II, and Hoça Çeşme IV – MnN (Boyadžiev 2006). The two series are earlier not only in comparison to dates for the Karanovo I Culture in Thrace, but also to dates for Protostarchevo (Protostarčevo) Culture in Serbia. That dating disproves the hypothesis of synchronicity between the appearance of MnH and the Cultures of white painted pottery. In addition to radio-carbonated dates on the chronological priority of the MnN with relevance to the bearers of the white painted pottery, there are also stratigraphic data from Southwestern Bulgaria. The situation is best defined at the settlement of Kraynitsi where the horizon of MnN is covered by 0.75–1.20 m layer without any cultural remains separating it clearly from the above found two horizons with white painted pottery (Tchohadjiev & Bakamska 1990, 53–56; Chohadzhiev *et al.* 2007, 182). The situation is similar at the settlement of Slatina-Gradini. The stratigraphic situation there is the following (from top to bottom): layers from the Late Neolithic period; layer of grey-ashy soil (with 0.65 m thickness); 0.30 m thick layer with pieces of clay plastering and pottery painted with black and red paint; 0.50 m thick slimy layer; under the slimy layer – rubble layer. On the bottom of the slimy and rubble layer, fragments of raw pottery some of which decorated with nailed ornaments have been found in addition to other archaeological materials (Petkov 1961, 70–71). The settlement was studied more than 50 years ago when the existence of MnN was still unidentified and therefore the significance of the discovered cultural phenomenon remained unrecognized. Its stratigraphy undoubtedly suggests that the so-called "pile-dwelling" is earlier than the layer of painted pottery. It also cannot be associated to the white painted stage at the Slatina settlement (dwelling) because of two reasons. First, it is the lack of pottery painted in white paint. And second, the presence of a 0.50 m thick slimy layer suggests a flood and continuous marshing of the terrain. Such a natural phenomena could not have happened without effects on the settelement of white painted pottery stage lying close to the MnN settlement. Among the previously conducted research, however, traces of flooding or discontinuity of life in the settlement of white painted pottery had not been established. Consequently, its emerging happened significantly later and far away from the most humid (and lowest) area – the area of Gradiny. The available data, no matter how scarce they are, give ground

---

2   WBPC stands for West-Bulgarian painted pottery horizon.
3   The dates are still unpublished. Thank you to N. Elenski for the information provided.

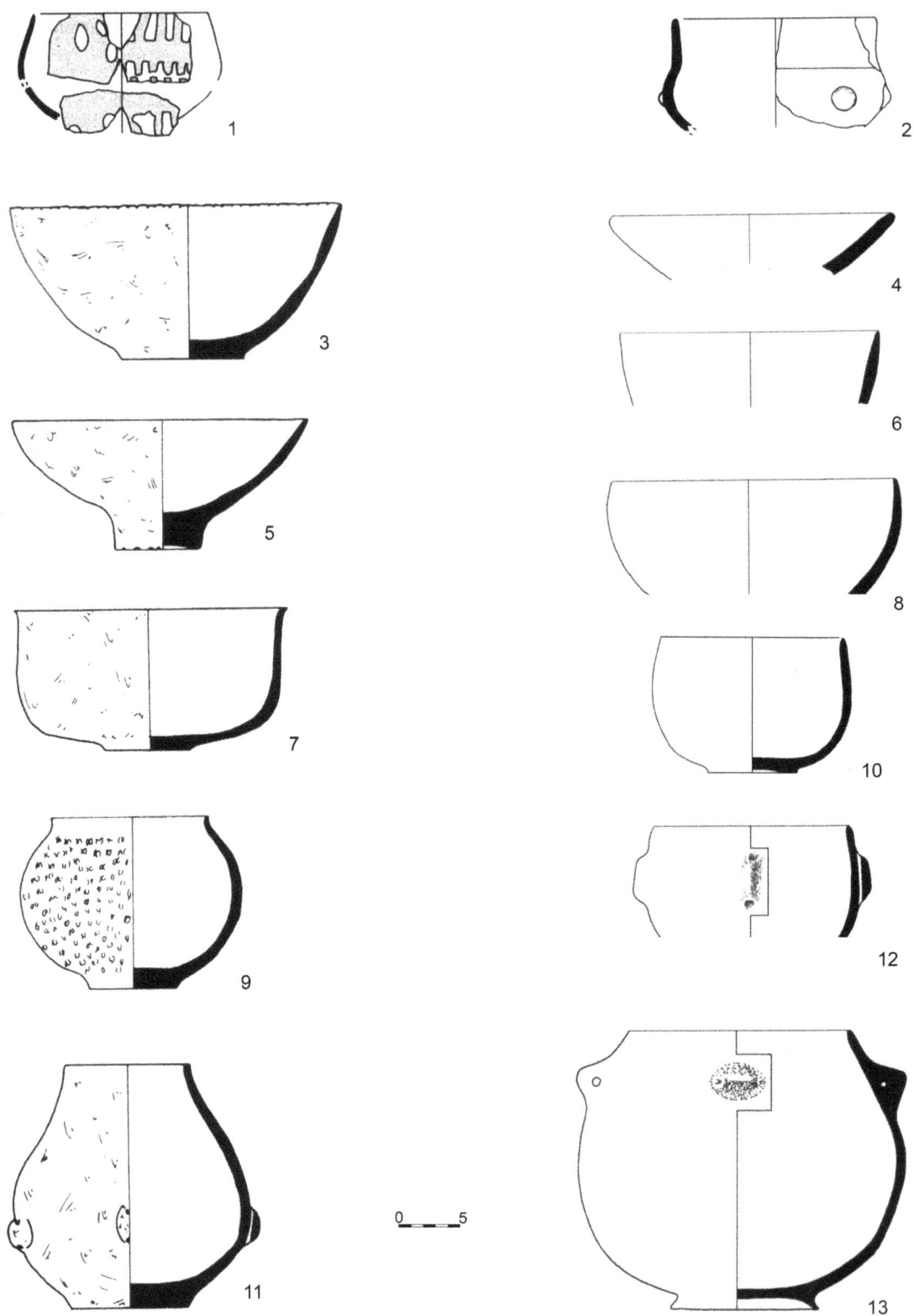

Fig. 1. MnN, phase I: 1, 2 – Dzhulyunitsa – Smardesh (after Elenski 2008, fig. 4: 1, 9); 3, 6, 8, 10, 12 – Polyanitsa-Platoto (after Todorova 1989, taf. 2); 4, 5, 7, 9, 11, 13 – Kraynitsi (after Chohadzhiev *et al.* 2007, fig. 3: 5, 7; 4: 5; 5: 2; 7: 1, 4).

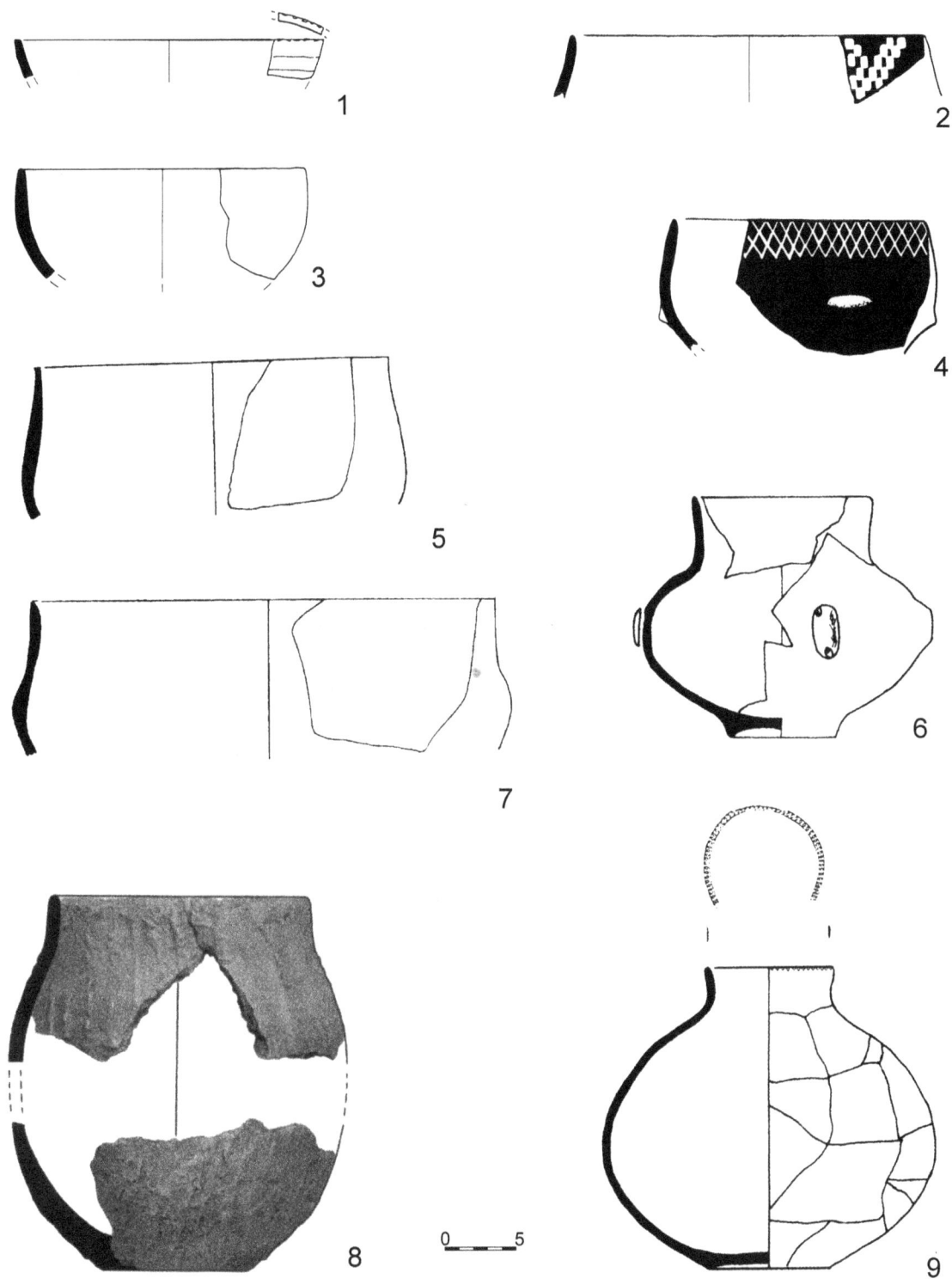

Fig. 2. MnN, phase II: 1, 3 – Pomoshtitsa (after Stefanova1996 tab. 7: 2, 3); 2, 4, 6, 9 – Dzhulyunitsa – Smardesh (after Elenski 2008, fig. 9: 9, 3; 8: 12, 10); 5, 7 – Koprivets (after Popov 1996, fig. 21: 4.4, 4.3); 8 – Ohoden (after Ganetsovski 2007, tat. 1-4: 2).

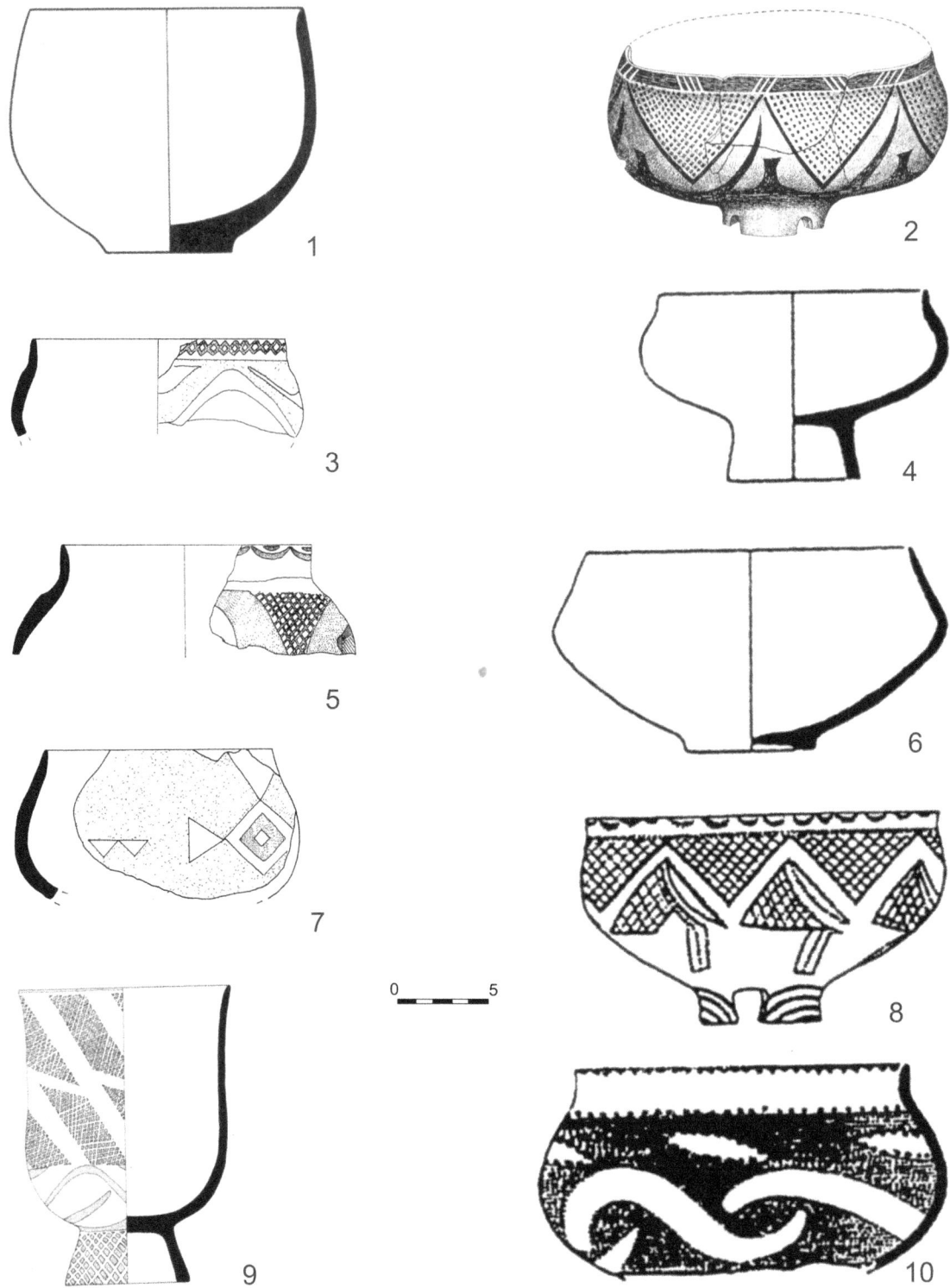

Fig. 3.   Karanovo I, phase I (white painted): 1, 4, 6, 8, 10 – (after Tao 2000, Fig. 1: 13, 5, 4, 1, 2); 9 – Karanovo (after Hiller & Nikolov 1997, taf. 67: 1); 3, 5, 7 – Rakitovo (after Macanova 2000, taf. II: 6, 1; III: 5); 2 – Kremikovtsi (after Petkov 1962, fig. 6).

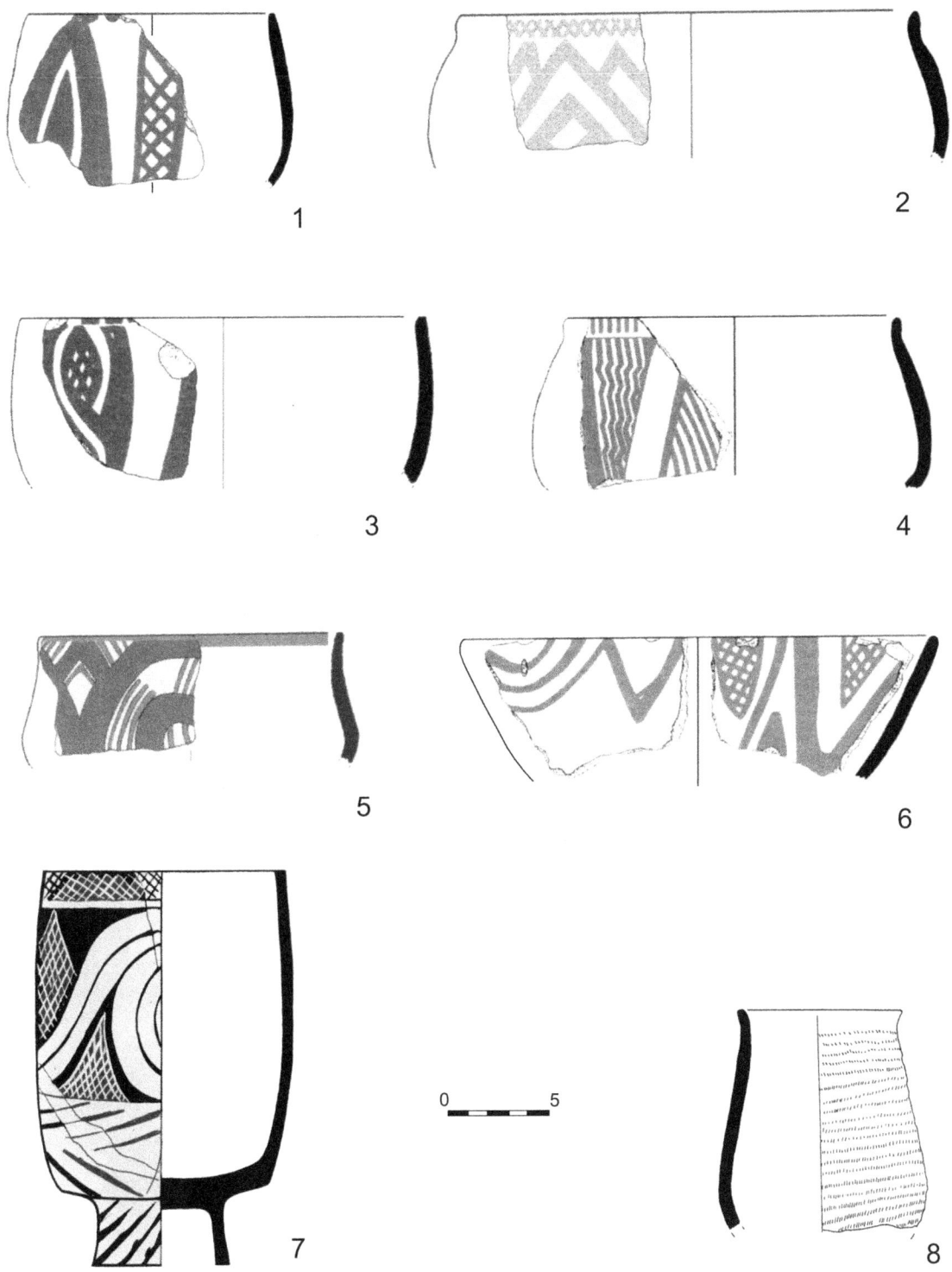

Fig. 4. EN – stage III: 1, 3 (brown painted), 2 (black painted), 4, 6 (red painted), 5 (polychrome painted) – Slatina (after Sirakova 2004, fig. 2:9; 3: 8; 2:1; 1: 2; 3: 1; 1: 7); 7 (white painted) – Chavdar (after Georgiev 1981, abb. 37b); 8 (with cannelures) - Rakitovo (after Macanova 2000, taf. IV, 1).

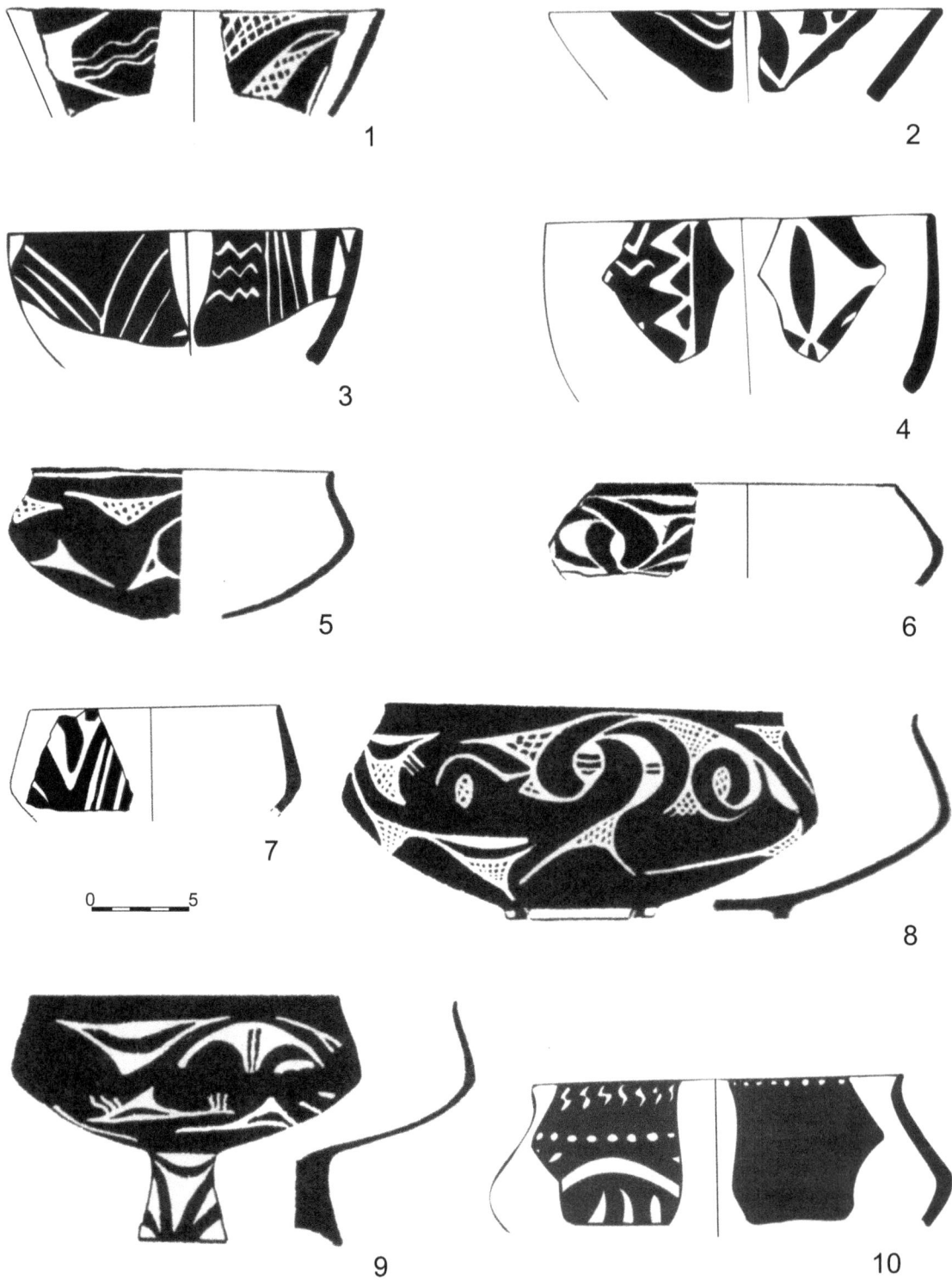

Fig. 5. WBPC, phase I (white painted): 1, 5, 6, 8 – Galabnik (after Chohadzhiev 1990, fig. 2); 2, 3, 4, 7 – Vaksevo (after Genadieva & Chohadzhiev 1994; fig. 3; 4); 9 – Pernik (after Chohadzhiev 1990, fig. 3); 10 – Drenkovo (after Grebska-Kulova 2008, fig. 4: 2).

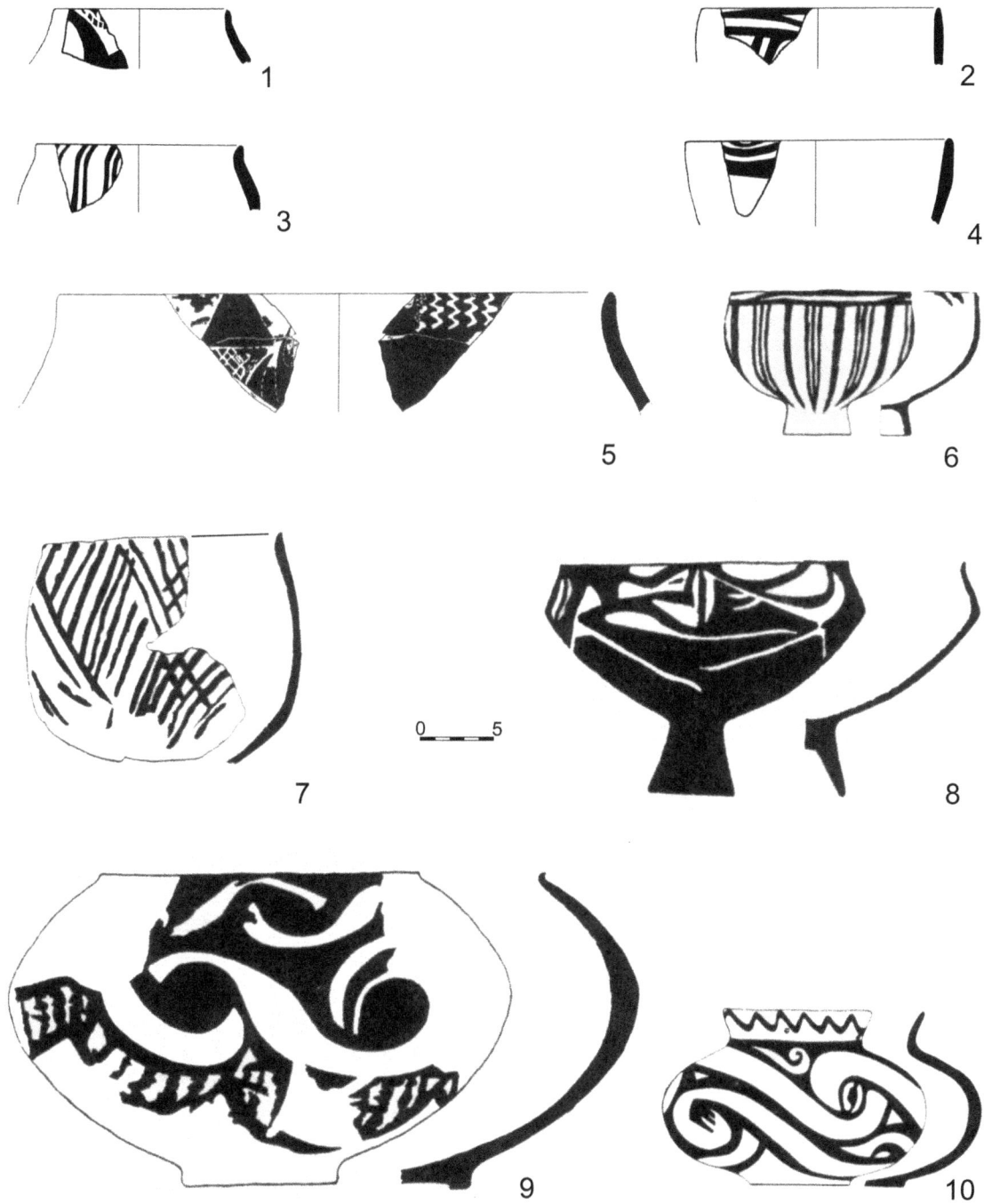

Fig. 6. WBPC, phase II (dark painted): 1 (white painted), 2 (brown painted), 3 (red painted), 4 (black painted) – Nevestino (after Chohadzhiev & Genadieva 2003, fig. 5); 5 (white painted) – Bersin (after Vandova 2007, fig. 4); 6, 7 (black painted) – Galabnik (after Chohadzhiev 1990, fig. 7; 3); 8 (white painted) – Pernik (after Chohadzhiev 1990, fig. 5); 9 (red painted) – Negovantsi (after Chohadzhiev 1990, fig. 6); 10 (black painted) – Galabnik (after Chohadzhiev 1990, fig. 8: 1).

to assume the existence of a dwelling from the late phase of the MnN which precedes the settlement of white painted pottery.

The settlements in Slatina-Gradini show clearly one of the routes for penetration of the bearers of the MnN on the territory of modern Bulgaria – along the Struma River valley[4]. The question about where its first representatives in Northeastern Bulgaria had originated from remains open. The hypothesis on a penetration from the west on the course of the River Danube (Todorova & Vaysov 1993, 61) cannot be accepted as the ^{14}C dates from the MnN in Northeastern Bulgaria are earlier than those for the same culture on the territory of Serbia (Shumadia) while the appearance of the Neolithic people in the region of Đerdap is calculated as having occurred around 6000 cal. BC. Studies in the region of Đerdap indicate that until around 6100–6000 cal. BC the Mesolithic people had been living there, and the earliest appearance of a Neolithic people had not occurred before 6300 cal. BC (Borić & Miracle 2004) but it happened most probably around 6000 cal. BC. There is a great likelihood that the answer to the above question is related to the settlement of Hoça Çeşme on the estuary of the Maritsa River (Özdoğan 1997, 23–27). Its discovery disproves the opinion that during the seventh-sixth millennia BC the valley of the river in its lower part was marshy and unsuitable for inhabiting. The imports from Hoça Çeşme discovered in EN settlements near Kardzhali and Krumovgrad, in addition to fragments of white painted pottery of the type Karanovo I found correspondingly in Hoça Çeşme indicate that the valley of Maritsa River was accessible for advancement and regular exchanges between the seashore and inner regions of Thrace had existed (and such were detected in the Rodopa Mountains region as well). The earliest settlement in Hoça Çeşme (Phase IV) is related to the MnN period. The available ^{14}C dates (which are close to those from Polyanitsa-Platoto and Dzulyunitsa-Smardesh) define its age as 6400–6100 BC (Özdoğan 1997, 27)[5]. Consequently, it is synchronous (where its beginning was probably slightly earlier) to the settlement Polyanitsa-Platoto and Dzhulyunitsa-Smardesh is located on the shortest route connecting the estuary of Marica River to Northeastern Bulgaria: Maritsa River – Tundzha River – Mochuritsa River – Varbishki Provod (Varbishki Pass) – Ticha River. Another possible connection to Maritsa River is via the upper estuary of Tundzha River, Tvardishki Prohod (Tvardishki Pass) or the Pass of the Republic and the water catching area of the Yantra River. On the usage of that route suggests the existence of the settlements of MnN on the upper course of Yantra River. A great number of analogies between the materials associated with the early phase of Fikirtepe and the settlements of Northern Bulgaria talk about contacts between Northeastern Bulgaria and the seaside of Marmara and Aegean Seas (Özdoğan 1997, 22; Elenski 2008, 98–99).

The main argument against accepting the rivers Maritsa, Tundzha and Mochuritsa as routes for migration for the bearers of the MnN is the lack of settlements on the territory of Thrace from the period in question. Nevertheless, that fact reflects the fragmentary nature of our knowledge rather than the real situation of the period. The lack of uncovered settlements does not necessarily prove they did not exist because it might be due to a number of other factors: the sparse number of people and short lifespan of those settlements; significantly higher in modern times underground water levels in Thrace than it used to be in prehistoric times and correspondingly higher modern lands than the layers where MnN settlements would have been located; thick alluvial debris covering the prehistoric surface. As a result of the late scientific discovery, differentiation and clarification of the cultural characteristics of the MnN is it very possible that artifacts from that period had remained unidentified at the times of their discoveries. There are at least two examples in support of that assumption. The first is the commented above settlement Slatina-Gradini. The second is the settlement of "Kuklen", Plovdiv Region (Detev 1976; Chohadzhiev 2002, 15–16). The discoverer of "Kuklen" P. Detev relates it to the EN period which, according to his periodisation, preceded the Karanovo I Culture that he relates to the MN period. The description of the pottery corresponds to that of the MnN – common are spherical shapes sometimes with high necks; the bottoms are thickened or ring-shaped; decoration of the "impresso" type is found. Painted pottery had not been discovered. In the announcement on the settlement there is a suggestion claiming that according to P. Detev the settlement is not the only one in Thrace for the period under investigation, "Most Early Neolithic settlements we have found so far in the catchment area of Maritsa River are single-layered and open" (Detev 1976, 36). Unfortunately, there is no other available information on those settlements.

Consequently, there is enough evidence to assume that the first bearers of Neolithic way of life had penetrated the territory of Bulgaria along three routes – along the valleys (courses) of the rivers Vardar, Struma and Maritsa[6]. Those people settled both in Southwestern Bulgaria and Thrace, and had also spread North over the Balkans. As the formerly accumulated data suggest, however, they stayed a relatively short time in Southern Bulgaria. On one side the evidence for that is the scarce number of settlements found, on another – the poor traces of existence left by them. In the three cases – Kraynitsi, Slatina-Gradini and Kuklen – the traces are just in a single, not very thick horizon. On their place in Southern Bulgaria settled the bearers of white painted pottery – Karanovo I Culture and WBPC.

In Northern Bulgaria, MnN had a longer development. Here as well the first phase of the period was short-lived – one, maximum two horizons.

---

4   Penetration by the bearers of the Early Late Neolithic period happened also along the Valley of Vardar River, but that region falls outside the range of the current research.

5   Taking into consideration the continuous development of the settlement and the series of ^{14}C dates for the subsequent horizons, most probably Phase IV, it should be dated between 6300/6200 and 6000 cal. BC.

6   It is quite possible that as a route for penetration the valley of the River Mesta had also been used, but so far the settlement unearthed there relate to a later stage of settling – after the beginning of WBPC Cultures and Karanovo I.

Table 3

Periodization of the Neolithic period in the Thracian plains

Georgiev	Todorova 1966,1981	Todorova Vaisov	V. Nikolov 1996 NE Thrace		W. Thrace	Vasil Nikolov 2004 Western Thrace, Mesta	
		BEN-Ě					
Kar. I	Kar. I	BEN-A (white painted)	Kar. I	S o u t h W e s t e r n v e r s i o n	Eleshnitsa	Period I	Eleshnitsa, Kovachevo Ia, Slatina, Kap. Dimitrievo I
					Rakitovo	Per. II	Kovachevo Ib, Kapitan Dimitrievo II
Azmak variant. Kar. I/ Karanovo II Kar. II	Kar. II	BEN-B	Kar. II			Per. III	Kapitan Dimitrievo II
							Kovachevo Ic, Dobrinishte
			Kar. II/III- Kar. I/III			Per. IV	
		BEN-C (Kar. III)	Kar. III		Dobrinishte	Per. V	Kap. Dimitrievo II – end, Kovachevo Id

Radiocarbon dates from Polyanitsa-Platoto and Dzhulyunitsa-Smardesh provide an opportunity to define also the chronological frames of the first stage of the EN period. The calibration of both dates is between 6340 and 6060 cal. BC. Considering the short duration of Phase I, and also its direct link to Phase II, synchronous to the "white painted Neolithic period" in Southern Bulgaria which appeared there around 6000 cal. BC, the beginning of MnN in Northern Bulgaria should be placed in the end of VII millennia – approximately about 6200/6100 cal. BC. There is a possibility that in Southern Bulgaria the phase had begun about 100 years earlier where the spreading of the bearers of MnN was gradual: the seaside of Marmara and Aegean seas, Southern Bulgaria, Northern Bulgaria. The lack of ^{14}C dates from Southern Bulgaria though does not allow further clarifications on the issue.

Early Neolithic period – Stage II (6000/5900 – 5750/5700 cal. BC)

The second phase of the Early Neolithic period began with the appearance of the bearers of white painted pottery. That is the "classical" Early Neolithic period represented by two similar cultures – Karanovo I and WBPC. The Karanovo Culture received its name after the eponymous site – tell-settlement Karanovo. Thanks to the publications of G. Georgiev that concept has been widely accepted both in Bulgaria and in foreign literature where it is commonly associated with the Early Neolithic period in entire Bulgaria. However, the culture was common mainly in the Thracian low-lands (Tab. 3).

In Western Bulgaria developed a single, autonomous phenomenon. Its identification and naming is not as clear as that of Karanovo I. The first researcher who differentiated the EN culture in Western Bulgaria was James Gaul. He gave it the name of West Bulgarian Painted Culture – WBPC (Gaul 1948, 10).

G. Georgiev, as far as 1944, suggested for the Early Neolithic period in Sofia plains the name "Kremikovtsi (Kremikovci) Culture" in his Ph. Thesis (Georgiev 1960, 312). He suggests that the spread of its area was on the territories of Western and Northwestern Bulgaria (Georgiev 1967a, 91; 1971, 34). He synchronized it with Culture Karanovo I and often uses both cultures on equal terms (Groups Karanovo I – Kremikovtsi I) for labeling the EN period on the territory of Bulgaria (Georgiev 1970b; 1974; 1981). After the excavations of the Chavdar settlement, he defined it as a local version of Groups Karanovo I – Kremikovtsi I (Georgiev 1974, 13) and even introduced the term "Chavdar (Čavdar) Culture" (Georgiev 1981, 109).

V. Milojčić divides culture Kremikovtsi in two phases: I – linear-geometric; II – curvy-linear (Milojčić 1950, 111–112). M. Garashanin accepted the name "Group Kremikovtsi" for the EN period in Sofia plains and divided it into three phases: Kremikovtsi A – hypothetical, would correspond to Starchevo (Starčevo) I; Kremikovtsi B – fine painted pottery where also white painted pottery with spirals appeared; Kremikovtsi C – painting with dark paint on brighter background appeared. He found traceable parallels between Kremikovtsi B and C and Starchevo (Starčevo) II-III (Garashanin 1966, 19–21; 1973, 47).

H. Todorova in 1981 divided Western Bulgaria in two parts – Northwestern and Southwestern. For the EN period of Northwestern Bulgaria she accepted the name "Culture Chavdar-Kremikovtsi (Čavdar-Kremikovci)" where she differentiated three phases. The first is represented in layers of white painted pottery and corresponds to the phase Karanovo I. The second is characterized by polychrome painting and is synchronous to Karanovo II. To the third, which corresponds to the phase Karanovo II/III, she related the black and polychrome painted vessels from Gradeshnitsa (Todorova 1981, 211).

B. Nikolov accepted the name "Culture Kremikovtsi I" for the EN period in Northwestern and Central Western Bulgaria (Kanchev & Nikolov 1981, 11–12).

V. Nikolov, after a detailed analysis of the ornamentation of the collected on Bulgarian lands EN painted pottery, differentiated four cultures – Karanovo, Kremikovtsi, Kremenik-Anzabegovo and Gradeshnitsa-Karcha (Gradešnica-Kîrča) where the last three were discovered in Western Bulgaria (Nikolov 1982a; 1982b, 1983). The author explicitly emphasizes that, "As those communities are characterized by a single, even though a very important aspect, the term "culture" for labeling them is used more or less in a conditional sense" (Nikolov 1982a, 10). Culture Kremikovtsi encompasses Sofia, Pernik, Radomir, "probably" part of the Kyustendil plains and the lands around the middle and lower course of Nishava River (Nikolov 1982a, 17). In later article publications, V. Nikolov recognises only the horizons with dark painted pottery as belonging to Culture Kremikovtsi, and those with white painted pottery – to Culture Karanovo (Nikolov 1989, 27–28). Culture Kremenik-Anzabegovo includes the EN period in Southwestern Bulgaria (south of the Radomir field) and the Group Anzabegovo-Vrashnik (Vrašnik) in Macedonia. Two phases are differentiated, mainly on the ground of stratigraphy in Anazabegovo: first – common is painting with white paint; second – ornamentation is exclusively in dark paints. Under the name of Gradeshnitsa-Cîrča Culture, the EN period is differentiated in Northwestern Bulgaria.

M. Chohadzhiev suggests for the EN period in Western Bulgaria the initial name given by J. Gaul to be restored, slightly altered in correspondence to Bulgarian language – Culture of West-Bulgarian painted pottery, arguing that the "early Neolithic phenomena in the entire region under question demonstrate, on one hand variety, but on another – a number of quite similar and identical moments which allows us to study all phenomena as an integrated cultural phenomenon with several local versions" (Chohadzhiev 1988, 66).

H. Todorova and I. Vaisov, in their summary book adopt to a great extent the viewpoints of M. Chohadzhiev with reference to cultural differentiation and the name of the EN period in Western Bulgaria (Todorova & Vaysov 1993, 97–98).

In the last couple of years there is a visible tendency for differentiation of separate stages/phases in the development of the EN period in Southwestern Bulgaria without them being in fact associated with a particular culture (Pernicheva 1995, 102–108, 135-tab. 1; Čochadžiev 2000; Chohadzhiev 2007, 98–102, tab. 7).

In the current work, I am going to adopt the name "West-Bulgarian Painted Ceramik (WBPC)" for designating the Early Neolithic phenomena with painted pottery in Western Bulgaria as I am in agreement to a great extent with the arguments of M. Chohadzhiev because, despite the presence of various local phenomena in the studied period, those phenomena gradually get integrated and demonstrate common tendencies in their development where they show characteristic features differentiating them from neighbouring regions over some of which they also managed to spread their influence.

West-Bulgarian Painted Ceramic (WBPC)

Based on the paints used for decorating the pottery, two phases in the WBPC development are differentiated: I – painting with white paint and II – painted with dark paints.

West-Bulgarian painted ceramic – Phase I

Mainly the settlements located along the Struma River valley are associated with it. Some of the settlements in the peripheral areas of the region show characteristics which related them to Culture Karanovo I: Kovachevo, Slatina.

Greatest similarities among the various settlements have been detected in the pottery technology. As a temper in the clay mould mineral mixtures of various sizes had been added, depending on the thickness of the walls of the vessel. Plant mixtures are found very rarely, only in raw pottery. The surface of fine pottery is well smoothed, often until shining. Common is the red colour, but there are also nuances of brown – from light beige to dark-brown.

Dominant are simple shapes – conical, semi-spherical, and spherical. Both among raw pottery and fine pottery widely used were open-conical and semi-spherical dishes (Fig. 5: 1–3); narrow vessels with almost vertical walls whose diameter among raw pottery is up to 1m, and their mouth is often jagged; rounded vessels with tall necks of various heights and vertical or curved upwards mouths where their height could be either less or more than the maximum diameter. Common are also big thick-walled storage pots with spherical/rounded body and funnel or straight mouth. Among fine pottery, of interest are double-carinated bowls which are typical for the culture and are not found in Karanovo I (Fig. 6: 6–8). Observed are also some shapes which a specific for different settlements. For Galabnik and Pernik such are the sharply carinated bowls on high stump (Fig. 5: 9); for Vaksevo and Nevestino – vessels on four thick stumps. The bottoms, in addition to being flat, were shaped concavely or as rings. Only during the first half of WBPC indented two or three-sectioned bottoms were common. Handles were mainly lugs.

In the decoration of fine pottery exclusively dominant is white painting (Fig. 5). Most often it was laid on a red slip but brown or cream-coloured paint is also used and the painting was made before the baking of the vessel. The most commonly used decoration motives were: groups of horizontal or slant straight lines; rows of circle or ellipse shaped dots of various sizes; lines with dots stuck to them; rainbow shaped lines; two or three parallel wavy lines; net-filled triangles; volutes – autonomously standing or interconnected. Characteristic for the culture are the so-called "ladder" filled by a variety of forms; curvilinear and spiral motives; various net-shaped motives. In the decoration as well as in the shapes, specific differences among various settlements (or groups of settlements) are observed.

Commonly spread in Vaksevo and Nevestiono are two horizontal or slant rows of white dots or "spots" – decoration which has analogies in Donya Branevitsa and Gura Bačului; "pseudo-floral motives"; rows of signs resembling the letters Σ and S. Analogies of that type of paintings are found in southwestern and western directions: Yanitsa, Anzabegovo Ia, Velushka Tumba; Vashtiomy and Podgori in Albania. Those motives are not found or are exceptions in the other settlements of Southwestern Bulgaria. At the same time, in those settlements the percentage of net-shaped motives is minimal, and they are predominant in most settlements of Southwestern Bulgaria.

In Galabnik, the motives of lines with dots stuck to them are missing. At the same time, since horizon IV are found fine vessels (most often double-carinated bowls with sharp or rounded carination) with grey-grey-black or (more rarely) brown polished surface that are decorated with narrow chanellings arranged are zig-zags in horizontal rows (fish-bone type) (Pavuk & Čohadžiev 1984, 202; Pavuk 2000, 262–264).

Specific features in decorating are demonstrated also at the settlement of Kovachevo. In addition to the motives characteristic for the Struma River valley, influences from other regions could be traced there. In its initial phase (Phase Ia) there are elements (for example, a painting with very thin slant straight lines or wavy lines and fields marked with dots) which have parallels in Southwestern and Western direction – the region along the lower course of Vardar River: in Nea Nikomedia, Yanitsa, AnzabegovoI. During phases Ib and especially Ic, the similarities with Karanovo I increase (Eleshnitsa village, Dobriniste) (Lichardus-Itten *et al.* 2002, 129–130; Lichardus-Itten *et al.* 2006, 86–88). In phase Ib is established also the use, although rare, of dark paints – dark red on red and dark brown on brown (Lichardus-Itten *et al.* 2002, 121; Nikolov *et al.* 1996, 15).

The differences in ornamentation of white painted pottery in separate settlements (or groups of settlements) pose the question what had provoked them – whether they show the differentiation of local groups or whether they are results of chronological differences. The opinions of the researchers are in great disagreement with reference to answering the question. On the ground of collected materials of white paintedpottery phase in tell Galabnik, U. Pavuk and M. Chohadzhiev differentiate Galabnik group which encompasses the region along the upper course of Struma River (Pavuk & Čohadžiev 1984, 214). They differentiated it from Anzabegovo-Vrashnik (Vrašnik) group and Slatina group. V. Nikolov initially differentiated Kremenik-Anzabegovo group and subsequently suggested a more detailed differentiation of Early Neolithic phenomena in the region.

S. Chohadzhiev, however, accepts that the differences among separate settlements are resulting from the chronological development of the culture. He differentiated three sub-phases in the white painted EN period (Phase II) in Southwestern Bulgaria (Chohadzhiev 2007, 145–147, tab. 7). To IIa, S. Chohadzhiev relates Nevestino and Vaksevo,

to IIb – Galabnik I–IV horizon, Priboy and Kraynitsi II–III horizon; to IIc – Galabnik V–VII horizon and Pernik I horizon.

Radiocarbon dating could help in clarifying the problem. ^{14}C dates collected from I–IV horizons of tell-settlement Galabnik vary between 7200 and 6800 bp. and their main concentration is between 7100 and 6950 bp. According to calibration curves, sharp and regular fluctuations of ^{14}C dates of similar estimates are registered in the interval 6000 – 5850/5800 cal. BC (Pearson & Becker 1993, 98, fig. 1B; Stuiver & Becker 1993, 56, fig. 2P). Taking into consideration that in the above mentioned interval four horizons should be included, it is clear that their existence entirely covers the time span in question where the earliest horizon should correspondingly be places in the very beginning of the period – around 6000 cal. BC, and horizon 4 – in its end. Until now this is the earliest date for a settlement of the painted Neolithic period in Bulgaria. The settling of Kovachevo could probably also be dated to the interval 6000–5850 cal. BC, but so far only the date of phase Ia corresponds to the dates for Galabnik I–IV horizons, while the dates for phase Ib appear later in time than them. Consequently, it should be dated after 5850/5800 cal. BC. Similar dating is also supported by the paleo-magnetic dating of a furnace from phase Ib/c – 5712–5571 BC. Therefore, at present there is no reason to accept that Kovachevo is the earliest Neolithic settlement in Bulgaria, as some researchers have suggested (Lichardus-Itten *et al.* 2002, 122).

For the settlements of Vaksevo and Nevestino which S. Chohadzhiev places before Galabnik (phase IIa), there are no ^{14}C dates. Nevertheless, such are available from Velushka Tumba and Anzabegovo Ib with which they have many parallels regarding their pottery (Chohadzhiev 2007, 98). The dates from both settlements are not earlier than those for Galabnik I–IV horizons (Boyadžiev 2006, 8, tab. 1). The situation is also similar to the dates from Donya Branevina which dates are the same as those from Galabnik, including those for VI–VII horizons as well. It should be noted that in Nevestino, simultaneously with the white painted pottery, related by S. Chohadzhiev to phase IIa, fragments (although relatively rarely) with dark paints – red, black, dark brown are found and they should be associated with phase IIIa–b (Fig. 5: 1–4) (Genadieva & Chohadzhiev 1994). The dark painted pottery is also found in Velushka tumba. Consequently, there are no grounds for differentiating a phase in WBPC preceding tell Galabnik.

With reference to the third phase to which horizons 5–7 from Galabnik are assigned, the author himself emphasizes that it is conditional and by now has not been filled up with realistic content (Chohadzhiev 2007, 99, 146–147).

Therefore, the available data give ground to assume that the differences among separate settlements (or groups of settlements) are due to local particularities, and not to chronological differentiation (Tab. 4).

Culture Karanovo I – Phase I

Similarly to WBPC, the first phase is characterised by painting with white paint on red slip.

Until a great extent the pottery – like technology, shape and decoration – resembles that of WBPC. Among the

Table 4

Chronological correlation of different paints used in settlements with ^{14}C dates and dark painted pottery

White Painted Pottery
Red Painted Pottery
Brown Painted Pottery
Black/Darkbrown Painted Pottery
Polychrome Painted Pottery

shapes, on a mass scale are spread upside conical and semi-spherical dishes; bowls with round bodies; vessels with spherical body and tall cylindrical neck; closed up pot-shaped vessels with comparatively low neck (Fig. 3). Characteristic for the culture though are the tall tulip-shaped vessels on a hollow stump (Fig. 3: 9) – shape that was not spread in WBPC. At the same time, in Karanovo I the double-carinated vessels are exceptions.

The monochrome fine pottery has a grey or brown colour, the decoration is mostly plastic, and in rare cases channeling, indented or pitched. The ornamental compositions painted in white paint are made of under-mouth decoration, main compositions and decoration on the stump. In mass use were vertical or slanting sheaves of lines, hanging triangles, horizontal negative interconnected spiral-meanders (horizontal Ss). Most common was the net-looking decoration – both for filling up geometric motives and as background (Fig. 3: 3, 8). Represented is also the framing of lines with dots. Characteristics for Karanovo I are also the garland-shaped motives. Rhombs are often found – decoration that is significantly rarer in WBPC.

The pottery in separate settlements of Karanovo I culture is much more homogeneous than that of WBPC – both as shapes and decoration.

A greater variety is observed in the settlements remaining in the south and western periphery of the culture. In Rakitovo, in addition to white, cream-colour paint in used on dark-brown, dark-red and wine-slip, and among decorative motives, specific are staircase shaped broken delineations, as well as Y-, X- and T-shaped elements, open angles, hanging triangles made of dots – motives that have parallels with Kremenik-Anzabegovo Group (Raduncheva *et al.* 2002, 112–132). Influences from southern direction are evidenced in Yabalkovo (Lesnakov *et al.* 2007a, b).

During that phase, a number of similarities with the pottery of Karanovo I culture, especially to the settlements on its western periphery, are traced also at the settlement of Slatina. The characteristic for the culture tulip-shaped vessels though are very scarcely presented.

A little different is the situation in two other settlements – Chavdar and Kremikovtsi located on the border zone between Karanovo I Culture and WBPC (in the Pirdop-Zlatitsa and Sofia plains). Specific for both settlements is the presence of pottery painted in dark paint. The settlement of Chavdar is better studied and published (Georgiev 1981). As shapes, the pottery bears close resemblance to that of Karanovo I. The decoration – as motives and compositions also does not show essential differences from that in Karanovo I (Fig. 4: 7). But simultaneously to the white paintings, there is a small percentage of such in dark paint as well. Dark painted pottery is found in all horizons, where all its varieties are presented: wine-red, black and dark brown, cream-coloured and light brown, poly- chrome all of which in fact had appeared and existed simultaneously (Chohadziev 1988, 54–67; Nikolov 1994; Kanchev 1995)[7]. The situation is repeated in Kremikovtsi settlement. Based on the ornament's colour, the EN layer is divided in two phases –

Ia (lower) and Ib (upper). In the lower layers of the Neolithic layer it was painted in white matter on red polished background and in exceptional cases in dark paints, while in its upper layers – predominantly in dark paints (red, wine-red, brown and others) and more rarely in white, and it is explicitly mentioned that in drill 4 all the colours are present simultaneously from the beginning to the end of the Neolithic layer (Georgiev 1975, 22).

The presence in both settlements of dark painted pottery gives reasons to most researchers to assign them to the second half of the EN period. From the Chavdar settlement, however, series of ^{14}C dates are available for five successive horizons – VI–II. Not only as estimates but also as development they are set within the interval 5900/5600 BC and the dates from the lower horizons (VI–IV) entirely correspond to the dates from other sites from the first half of Karanovo I and WBPC cultures.

Imports of dark painted pottery are found in many settlements from the first half of the Karanovo I Culture. G. Georgiev also has talked on the presence of pottery painted in black or brown colours in all EN horizons of the Azmak tell (Georgiev 1965, 7; 1967b, 151). Fragments with ornaments in brown and red colour are discovered in Kazanlak (Nikolov 1989, taf.1, 5, 6, 7). Dark painted pottery is also registered in layer I in tell Karanovo (Nikolov 1989, taf.1, 2). Especially important is the observation made by V. Nikolov that, "Fragments from imported vessels are found at various depths in about 0.80 m layer of the southwestern sector and it holds valid both at its deepest and most upper part" (Hiller & Nikolov 1997, 142). Fragments of dark painted pottery are not discovered only in the lowest horizon of the northeastern sector which V. Nikolov accepts as the earliest in the tell and preceding the three horizons of the southwestern sector. Consequently, imports of dark painted pottery were spread not only during the second half of Karanovo I Culture (the so-called Azmashki variant), but also during its first half, preceding the appearance of phase Karanovo II, and it was even from its very beginning (probably without its earliest horizon). Of special importance are the imports of polychrome painted pottery which, according to existing periodisations and the widely recognised views, is characteristic for the last phase of the EN period. Imports with polychrome ornamentation are known from four settlements in Thrace – Rakitovo, Kazanlak, Azmak Tell, Karanovo. Most important are two fragments from tell Kazanlak found in the lowest, 17 horizon, and also in horizon 7 (Nikolov 1989, taf.1, 3, 4). In the same two horizons are discovered fragments painted in brown paint (Nikolov 1989, taf.1, 5, 7). The significance of those findings lies in the great stratigraphic (and therefore also chronological) interval during which they are not found – 11 horizons with a total thickness of 3.60 m. Taking into account the thickness of the layer of white painted pottery from Kazanlak then horizon 17 should be related to the beginning of Karanovo I Culture. Therefore, in tell Kazanlak, the existence of polychrome and brown painted ornamentation since the beginning of the EN period until the beginning of Karanovo

---

7   According to V. Nikolov, only in horizon VII there are no vessels with black and cream-coloured paint on them (Nikolov 1994, 190-191).

III is clearly documented stratigraphically. The same conclusion is supported also by the imports in other sites: settlement-tell Kapitan Dimitrievo (Nikolov *et al.* 1999, 12–13), Azmak tell (Nikolov 1993, 60), Rakitovo, settlement-tell Karanovo (Nikolov 1989, taf.1, 1).

The discovery of imports of dark painted pottery in the lower horizons of most settlements in Thrace gives ground to V. Nikolov to differentiate two phases of development for the first half of Karanovo I and he reckons that the first phase to which the settlements Eleshnitsa, Kovachevo, Slatina and Kapitan Dimitrievo belong (assigned to the so-called Southwestern version of the Culture) precedes the "classical Karanovo I" (Nikolov 2004, 20). The ^{14}C dates, however, do not confirm similar synchronization. From the above mentioned four sites, there are date series for three of them (tab. 2). Neither of them though is earlier than the dates for horizon VI in Chavdar and the lower horizons in settlement-tell Karanovo. The series from Slatina and Eleshnitsa have better correspondence to the series for horizon 3 in settlement-tell Karanovo, horizon 2 and 3 in Okrazhna Bolnitsa-Stara Zagora, and horizon 4 in Chavdar. In we account also the circumstance that the dates from both settlements are related to their lowest horizons it becomes clear that the appearance of those settlements could not be considered before the beginning of Karanovo I Culture in Thrace. Only the earliest date from Kovachevo could possibly be juxtaposed to the dates from Chavdar and Karanovo.

Monochrome Neolithic period – Phase II

While in Southern Bulgaria the bearers of the white painted pottery had appeared and settled down, in Northern Bulgaria the development of MnN was still is progress. Its second phase is characterized by the appearance of white painting on a red slip (Fig. 2: 2, 4). However, it is not very common and the motives are mainly linear.

The main shapes from the preceding phase continue their development (Fig. 2). The tall hollow and compact stumps are widely spread. Big vertical handles also appeared. From a technological point of view it is important to note the more massive use of mineral tempers which gradually replace the organic ones.

Most settlements from the first phase continue their existence: Koprivets horizons 3, 4; Pomostitsa, layer II; Belyakovets-Plochite; Dzhulyunitsa-Smardesh. Some new settlements appeared as well – Cherven-Chochana, Orlovets. From the second phase on MnN are registered also settlements from Southwestern Bulgaria – Ohoden-valoga. From the last settlement there is one ^{14}C date obtained – KN5666: 6830±45 BP (Ganetsovski 2008a; b). It coincides not only with some dates from the first phase of cultures Karanovo I and WBPC, but also with such from the beginning of their second phase. Resulting from the singularity of the date, it cannot be accepted as a safe indicator on the exact chronological place of the site, but for sure the settlement did not develop before 6000 cal. BC.

Early Neolithic period – Stage III (5750/5700 – 5500/5400 cal. BC)

WBPC – Phase II

It differentiation is based on changes of the colour of the painting. Dominating is the painting in dark paints: red, black, brown (in various nuances) (Fig. 6: 6, 7, 9, 10). White paintings also continue to be spread but the colour is changed – it had become more yellowish/cream colour (Fig. 6: 5, 8). In Kovachevo settlement, until the end of the EN period, painting remained only in white paint. Generally speaking, in the region of Sandansko-Petrichka valley no site with dark painted pottery has been found which gives grounds to the researchers to suggest its relation to the area of Karanovo I instead (Pernicheva 1995, 106).

During that phase, the influence area of WBPC Culture had enlarged in northern direction and it spread also on Northwestern Bulgaria. No settlements which could be assigned to the white painted phase of WBPC have been found in that region (including in separate horizons). Clearly for the region in question, here the second phase of WBPC had developed directly after MnN. The invasion of the Culture in northern and northwestern direction had occurred by means of direct migration of people as the density of population had risen sharply. Probably the separation of the original area had led to the development of certain individual tendencies in the development of pottery, and it was exactly here that the polychrome pottery had achieved its peak (Fig. 11: 3, 4, 7).

Most researchers, based on the colour of used paint, differentiate separate sub-phases in the development of the dark painted phase of WBPC.

Sub-phase A. Pottery painted in red paint (Chohadzhiev 1988, 67; Todorova & Vaysov 1993, 104; Pavuk & Bakamska 1989, 223; Čochadžiev 2000, 254; Chohadzhiev 2007, 100). As representative of that phase, four settlements have been suggested – Pernik, Galabnik (Chohadzhiev 1988, 67; Pavuk & Bakamska 1989, 223), Kremikovtsi and Chavdar horizon IV (Todorova & Vaysov 1993, 104).

Nevertheless, so far on the territory of Bulgaria only a single site with differentiated separate phase of red painted pottery has been found. That is Slatina – horizons 3 and 4. In the other settlements that various authors relate to that phase, the red paint is found in combination with other paints: in Pernik with brown (Chohadzhiev 1978, 31); in Galabnik – with black; in Kremikovtsi – with brown and "other dark paints" (Georgiev 1975, 21, 25); in Chavdar IV horizon the red painted pottery in significantly less not only from the polychrome painted pottery, but also from that painted in light-brown and cream colour paint.

Sub-phase B. Pottery painted in black paint. As all authors have mentioned that was the dominating pottery in Western Bulgaria. In all settlements though, it was found together with other types of dark paints. Only in certain sites its predominance in the upper layers was evidenced (for example, in Galabnik horizons 8–10, Slatina 2–1). A similar tendency, however, could not be generalized for the entire Western Bulgaria, and what is more it is not reasonable to claim that in some settlements it preceded the pottery painted in red paint (for example, in Gradeshnitsa, horizon A).

Sub-phase C. Pottery painted in brown paint. It is differentiated only by M. Chohadzhiev who points that it is found in all settlements of Western Bulgaria (Chohadzhiev 1988, 67).

Sub-phase D. Polychrome painted pottery. That phase is defined by most researchers as a final phase of the EN period (Chohadzhiev 1988, 67; Nikolov 1992, 14; Todorova & Vaysov 1993, 105–107). The viewpoint is not supported solely by V. Nikolov who is the only one that has analysed in details the spreading of the polychrome decoration. According to him, "The idea for polychrome ornamenting probably emerged almost simultaneously with the appearance of dark ceramic ornamentation in the beginning of the second half of the EN period in the Central-Balkan zone." (Nikolov 1993b, 62).

Actually, there is not a single site where the successive replacement of various types of paints to have been registered. In the best cases, the replacement of two types of paint has been established (usually red and after it – black). In some settlements, there is only one type of paint used. The only settlement where all the types of used paints have been evidenced, including polychrome decoration as well (most often in combination between white and dark painted), is Chavdar. It the tell, however, there is no differentiation in horizons with reference to the colour paint used, as in every horizon all paint types have been found (tab. 4). The primary information on most sites indicates the simultaneous use of various dark paints in those sites and phases with just single paints could not possibly be differentiated.

In most miltu-layered settlements, the dark painted pottery had been used in an equal number of horizons – four: Galabnik horizons 7–10; Pernik – 1–4; Sapareva Banya – 1–4; Slatina 3–6; Tlachene 1–4 (Bojadžiev 2000, 334-abb. 3). Taking into consideration the average duration of existence of an EN horizon (of one settlement) – about 60 years, then the duration of that phase in the corresponding sites is about 250 years. Such duration entirely corresponds to the chronological frames within which the phase had developed according to the available ^{14}C dates – between 5750/5700 and 5500–5400 cal. BC[8]. Indicative is also the circumstance that in Northwestern Bulgaria settlements of more than four horizons have not been discovered – that is as mush as those corresponding to the dark painted phase of WBPC in Southwestern Bulgaria.

If four (maximum five) horizons fill up the entire time-span of the dark painted phase of WBPC then it could be suggested that for every sub-phase defined on the base of using a particular type of paint, the duration of only one corresponding horizon remains. At the same time, in the different sites each of the used paints is dominant in at least two horizons and even in some is found in all the four horizons (for example, in Sapareva Banya the brown painting is predominant in all four horizons, in Tlachene – in all four horizons the polychrome (bi-chrome) decoration is found). If the horizons from the separate settlements where predominant is only one or another paint are summed up, it will become clear that to the phase of the EN period discussed here, there are at least 11–12 horizons that could be associated with it – that is only its duration might appear longer than the entire EN period. It is obvious that the observed blurring of paints used in separate settlements is due to local and not chronological differences. It seems that in different settlements a specific "fashion" had become popular depending on local contacts, preferences, opportunities (it is not impossible the obtaining and use of various dark paints to have been "production secret")

Culture Karanovo I

The main elements characterizing the culture continue their development without alterations. That refers also to the main shapes in pottery. Regarding the decoration of the vessels though, there is an observable differentiation.

Group Karanovo I – Azmak Variant.

In the western half of the Thracian low-lands, the use of white paining continues. It does not change significantly its characteristics – with reference to ornaments and their position on the separate parts of the vessels. The main shapes had also been preserved. In some sites in the western part of the area of Culture Karanovo I, however, dark painted pottery was widely spread (Fig 4: 1–6): tell-settlement Kapitan Dimitrievo – during the second phase of the EN period simultaneously with white painted vessels were found such of dark or polychrome decoration (Nikolov 2004, 19); settlement "Manastirya" near the village of Chernichevo – the four EN horizons are characterized by white painted pottery but together with it were spread also "fragments from orange vessels painted in wine-red and dark-chocolate bands" (Detev & Yovchev 1978); settlement Dabene-Pistikova mogila – in the most upper horizon simultaneous to the white painted, dark-red paintings had existed as well (Nikolova & Madzhev 1994, 11); in Lesovo-Kaptazha – red brown painting on a light-red surface together with white painting on red (Lichardus & Iliev 2000, 76).

Group Karanovo II

In the eastern end of the culture, around 5750–5700 BC pottery with red slip, as well as ornamentation in white paint disappeared. Predominant became the grey, grey-blackish and black polished pottery decorated with channelings. It provides evidence to the researchers to differentiate the settlements having the above described pottery into a new culture – Karanovo II (Georgiev 1961; 1970a; b). In fact, all other elements of the material and spiritual culture had preserved the traditions of Karanovo I (Nikolov 1993a). The genetic link, synchronous development of both phenomena during the second half of the EN period and their great proximity, give grounds to speak about a group Karanovo II instead of about a separate culture. It is spread east of the line Stara Zagora – Haskovo and the settlements' concentration is mainly in the valleys of Tundza River (Veselinovo, Krushare, Glufishevo and others) and Sazliyka River (Mednikarovo, Okrazhna Bolnitsa-Stara Zagora, Karanovo and others). The borderline is not exactly fixed, though. Settle-

---

8   Here a certain asynchrony should be considered both in the beginning and the end of the phase among the different settlements.

ments with white painted decoration on a red slip are found also within the inner areas of group Karanovo II – for instance, Lesovo-Kaptazha. The availability of red-brown paintings on a light-red surface suggests that it could be dated to the second half of Karanovo I Culture (available are also fragments of grey and black polished pottery) (Lichardus & Iliev 2000, 84; Lichardus *et al.* 2002, 558). At the same time, dark-grey pottery decorated with channelings is also found in a number of settlements simultaneously with white painted pottery type Karanovo (Hiller & Nikolov 1997, taf. 43: 13–14, 22, 32; 44: 2; 46: 32 and others), Yabalkovo (Leshtakov 2004), Rakitovo (Fig. 4: 8) (Raduncheva *et al.* 2002, 111), Kardzhali, Chavdar (Fig. 4: 7). For most of them the lack of absolute dates, in addition to the insufficiently long stratigraphic sequence does not allow the determination of their exact place in the development of the culture and therefore it cannot be said for sure whether the spreading of grey-blackish polished and channeling having pottery in those settlements preceded its wide spreading in Karanovo II Group. However, in some settlements its emergence has been documented since the first phase of Karanovo I Culture (for example, in Karanovo). Similar looking pottery had been discovered also in the area of WBPC – settlement Galabnik in horizons IV–VI (Pavuk & Bakamska 2000, 264). The dates for horizon IV are quire early and demonstrate that in Galabnik that type of pottery had appeared autonomously and not under the influence of Karanovo II group. Consequently, pottery of the "Karanovo II type" is known since the first phase of Karanovo I, and during the second phase of the culture it becomes predominant in its eastern area. The dark-polished pottery (black, grey-blacking and dark brown) is characteristic for the classical culture of Fikirtepe which existed in Northwestern Anatolia and partially in Southeastern Thrace, and is also typical for the developed phases in the settlement of Yarýmburgaz (near Istanbul), synchronous to culture Karanovo I (Özdoğan 1989, 204–205; 1997, 21–22). It is possible that the spread of such a ceramic type in the eastern half of the Thracian low-lands was due to the close contacts with the people of Southeastern Thrace. The route along which contacts were established was mainly along Maritsa River, and from it – along Tundzha River and Sazliyka River (and correspondingly on their tributaries). There is also a great likelihood a connection through the river valleys in the Eastern Rodopa Mountains to have existed – Varbitsa, Arda (fragments of dark-polished pottery, import from southeastern Thrace have been discovered in the EN settlement near Krumovgrad).

Group Karanovo II did not spread west of the catchment area of Sazliyka River. Its influence though is clearly presented in another direction – north.

Ovcharovo (Ovčarovo) Culture.

As an autonomous EN culture which developed in Northeastern Bulgaria, the culture is differentiated by H. Todorova (Todorova 1981, 207). In Ovcharovo culture are present a number of common characteristics with Karanovo II group. Especially expressive are the similarities in pottery. During the period in question, the ceramic vessels in Northeastern Bulgaria repeat to a great extend both the shape and the decoration technique of those in the Northeastern part of Thrace. They are, however, with thicker walls and worse baked than the vessels in Thrace. Their colour is mostly brown (in different nuances) or grey. Predominant are spherical or semi-spherical shapes on a short composite stump which could be indented or jagged. Tall tulip-shaped cups and bowls are spread but here they are more often on a short composite stump. They are mainly without any decoration, but when there is such, it is channeling – horizontal, slanting, zig-zag looking. The pots are generally decorated with indented, net-looking ornaments or with slant concaves made by lifting up the clay (Todorova & Vaysov 1993, 134).

Transition phase between the Early and Late Neolithic period (5500/5450 – 5400/5350 cal. BC)

The transition from Early to Late Neolithic period was a gradual, smooth process. The Early Neolithic cultures continuatively developed into Late Neolithic cultures. During the transition, in one and the same settlements were detected characteristics (mainly in the ceramic material playing the role of major criteria when differentiating cultures) of both the early and late expressions of the culture. It gives grounds to researchers to differentiate "transition" phases between the cultures. For the region of Thrace, V. Nikolov has differentiated the phases of Karanovo II–III and Karanovo I–III for the transition to Karanovo III Culture of the two corresponding Early Neolithic phenomena in the Eastern part of Thracian plains. Each of these phases covers two horizons. The difficulty in specifically differentiating/ defining that period is demonstrated by the fact that while G. Georgiev has referred horizons 8–7 of settlement Kazanlak to that period, V. Nikolov has suggested that the transition had occurred in horizons 10–9 of the same settlement.

In settlement Samovodene (Ovcharovo Culture) two transition horizons – 8 and 7 – have also been identified (Stanev 1982, 10–11; 1997, 39; Stanev 2002).

The gradual transition has been detected in Southwestern Bulgaria as well – the area of WBPC. L. Pernicheva has commented on the simultaneous development of "the last expressions of the EN period and the dark painted pottery", as well as the presence of grey-blackish and black fine pottery of carinated and cylindrical-conic shapes, in addition to decoration of channelings "crimp" type and dotted ornament "Vinča type" (a specific example of that is the situation observed in Bulgarchevo IB) (Perničeva 2002, 106–107). In Sapareva Banya, V. Nikolov has differentiated horizon IV as transitional (Kremenik Ib – Middle Neolithic period) between the EN and LN periods (Nikolov 2003, 101). However, not in all discovered settlements the development was continuative as in some of them above the clearly differentiated EN layer follows one of clear Late Neolithic features (for example Kovachevo Id and II; Vaksevo III and IV horizons) which suggests the appearance of new people (Perničeva 2002, 107).

The transitional phase in different sites was comparatively short since it covers 1–2 horizons and its continuity barely exceeded 100 years.

Early Neolithic cultures are differentiated mainly on the bases of differences in the ceramic material. In addition to that, however, there are also other elements from the material and spiritual culture of the people which indicate the level of similarity or differentiation among archaeological cultures. The major ones among those elements will be presented/compared briefly below.

Settlements and houses (lodgings)

MnN

The settlements have an area of about 8–10000 m^2. The only data on the settlement arrangement are available in Polyanitsa-Platoto where two (or three?) rows of small square ground house measuring 3.5 × 3.5 up to 4 × 4 m have been established (Todorova 1989, 11). In the rest of the settlements, only single constructions or parts of constructions have been studied. The data from them demonstrate that predominant were constructions which were partially pit houses – up to 0.60/0.70 m below the terrain at that time – Orlovets, Dzhulyunitsa-Smardesh, Hotnitsa – "Pesterata-iztok"; Koprivets, Ohoden. The pit contructions have an oval shape. In Ohoden, remnants from massive ground double-slopped constructions have been registered (holes from columns and poles with diameter of 0.20–0.45 m; plasterings covered in bricks with imprints of chopped beams and hedge).

A heating device was built on a special platform in the ground part (Ganetsovski 2007, 157–162; 2008a, 106–107). The combination of a pit and ground part is established also in Orlovets (Stanev 1995, 61–63).

Karanovo I

The data are collected mainly from the studied settlements. That tells had been formed as a result of the continuous dwelling on a comparatively small (between 60 and 100 m in diameter) compactly built area where the constructions were regularly renewed. Greater area in its base has the tell of Karanovo but observations made during the last couple of years indicate that it was not built simultaneously but there were small settlements which during the initial phase of formation of the tell had been moving in one or another direction.

The settlements were not fortified. Data on circling the settlement with a low earth-made bank (1.50–2.00 m wide) is present in Chavdar (Georgiev 1981, 69) and tell Azmak. In Yabalkovo has been established a ditch that is up to 2.50 m wide and has a depth of digging up to 0.70 m encircles the northern periphery of the settlement (Leshtakov *et al.* 2007a, 39–40). The measures of those constructions though do not give ground to consider them defensive.

The constructions are built close to each other, but at same time separated by a reasonable distance. Among groups of several constructions narrow streets were left – about 1.5–2.00 m wide. In Karanovo tell, the buildings are located around two streets crossing each other (Nikolov 2006, 36–37). Houses that were connected to each other have been found only in the settlement of Rakitovo where the constructions were separated initially but in time extra premises were added up to the houses and eventually in horizon I a complex of four buildings had been formed. Only narrow passages among the constructions have been established in that settlement (Raduncheva *et al.* 2002, 43–46).

The houses were ground houses. So far, only in the settlement of Yabalkovo, constructions having also pit built structures resembling cellars, in some of which grain storage bins were located, have been recorded (Leshtakov 2004, 81).

The most common technique for building the constructions was a wattle-and-daub technique plastered in clay. In some cases, the foundations of the walls were fortified also with stones (for example, in four houses in Rakitovo, horizon I (Raduncheva *et al.* 2002, 49)). In Yabalkovo, the walls are *pisé* and in their fortification stones had also been used (Leshtakov 2004, 81).

The floors are rammed clay. They were plastered periodically (most probably annually) and in some cases more than 50 floor plasterings have been established – Slatina (Nikolov 1992, 33). In Yabalkovo and Chavdarova cheshma – Simeonovgrad, plastering of the floors with white clay has been found (Leshtakov 2004, 81; Radunčeva 2002). In settlements where soil humidity was greater, a wooden platform (trimmer joists) had been used for insulation. With the gradual accumulation of destructions from earlier houses and the rise of the tells the wooden platform practice had been abandoned.

On the whole, the houses were of one premise and area of between 20 and 50 m^2. They have a quadrangular shape – most often trapeze shaped resulting from inexact executions of the rectangular or square shape. Although rarer, houses of two premises and area of between 50 and 80 m^2 have been spread. In some cases, in front of the house entrance there was also a shed (the so-called houses of the megaron type) – for instance, Karanovo, Rakitovo. There are also buildings of significantly greater measures – a three-sectioned construction in tell Azmak has an area of 109 m^2. In Kapitan Dimitrievo a two-storey building is documented as well (Nikolov *et al.* 1999, 14–18).

In tell Azmak a building whose walls are decorated on the inside with relief geometric compositions has been established, and in Yabalkovo – a building "decorated with murals on the walls", interpreted as a building of representational functions (Leshtakov 2004, 80).

The entrance to the houses is most often to the south or east. The main equipments in them were the furnaces and millstone equipment. In some settlements (Yabalkovo) the hearts have been established as set outside the houses (Leshtakov *et al.* 2007a, 39).

Ovcharovo culture

In Northeastern Bulgaria and Central Northern Bulgaria are present two versions of houses building techniques. In most settlements, during the first settling of the place pit houses were used (Golyamo Delchevo – horizon I; Ovcharovo-zemnika I; Ovcharovo-gorata – horizon I) (Todorova *et al.* 1975, 15–20; Todorova *et al.* 1983, 14–15; Angelova 1988, 31–36; 1992, 42–45). Known also are ground constructions (Samovodene) which in their arrangements bear close resemblance to those in Thrace, where the development went from pit houses to ground buildings (Ovcharovo-gorata horizon II–IV).

On the west side of the settlement at tell Samovodene defensive equipment has been identified – a pitch, 2.80 m deep and 12.50 m wide, a rampart and traces of palisade (Stanev 2002, 415). A rampart made of small stones that has a length of 80 m, is 5–7 m wide and 0.90 m high had surrounded the settlement of Ovcharovo-gorata from the east and south.

WBPC

In Western Bulgaria, tells of the sizes of those in Thrace did not come into being. It is clear that the tradition of heredity in dwelling on one and the same place by many successive generations could not be followed. Even though, in the EN period such a tradition did exist but it was not as long lived as in Thrace. Only in Galabnik there is evidence of continuous existence during the entire early Neolithic period. In most settlements though, between two and four horizons have been identified. And if for Western Bulgaria the small number of early Neolithic horizons could be explained with the later assimilation of the region by the bearers of WBPC – not until its second half, such an explanation does not hold valid for Southwestern Bulgaria. It is possible that the reasons for that were the climatic and soil conditions in the region due to which the continuous, long-term (more than 200–250 years) cultivation of the land had led to its exhaustion, while the relatively narrow river valleys did not provide opportunities for sufficient expanding of cultivated lands. An indication for that is also the circumstance that much longer dwelling has been registered in the fields of Middle Western Bulgaria (Pernik, Radomir, Sofia, Pirdop-Zlatitsa regions) than along the Valley of Struma River itself. Settlements of big scales have been registered there as well: Galabnik (about 2 ha); Slatina (about 8 ha). They, just like Kovachevo as well, demonstrate horizontal-vertical stratigraphy – gradual partial replacement.

The houses in the area of WBPC to a great extent coincide to those from the area of Karanovo I Culture – both as building technique and planning, but a greater variety is observable. Here as well the most common building technique is the wattle-and-daub technique plastered in clay. Widely spread, however, is also the pisé technique. Simultaneous to its traditional version – successive pasting of horizontal clay bands, the use of sun-dried brick has also been registered – in Galabnik and Kovachevo. In Galabnik, the use of a combined technique has been identified –foundamenting of the house's wall with wooden poles placed in shallow trenches and thrust to a 1.00–1.20 m depth where only about 0.40 m of them were above the ground. Above that height, the walls were constructed in pisé technique. Such a building technique was provoked by the high levels of underground waters (Bakamska 2007, 179).

In Balgarchevo, houses of several stages of reconstruction have also been identified, and those houses were initially dug at a depth of 0.60–0.70 m in the ground (Perničeva 2002, 275–277). In the best preserved house three horizons have been established where during the first one the dwelling was a semi-pit house – approximately at a 0.60 m depth, during the second it was made of both semi-dug part (up to 0.75 m dug into the ground and with an area of 35.5 m^2) and an above-the-ground part, and during the third one – the dwelling was entirely above the ground. During the time of the second horizon when the total area was 51 m^2, the building had also a second floor (or a semi-floor) on a platform of trimmer joists plastered with 0.15–0.18 m thick clay plastering (Perničeva et al. 2000).

The shape here was also most commonly slightly trapezium-shaped close to either a rectangular or a square. The average area of the houses also corresponds to that in Karanovo I Culture. Here though, significantly larger buildings have been found. In Galabnik, in each horizon has been identified one building with an area of more than 100 m^2 among which the largest is of more than 122 m^2 (measures 14.60 x min. 8.40)[9]. The average sizes of the houses were also a bit larder than what was common – between 32 and 74 m^2 (Bakamska 2007, 175).

One large building with an area of more than 100 m^2 has been also identified in each of the other large settlements of Southwestern Bulgaria – Slatina and Kovachevo (Nikolov 1992; Lichardus-Itten et al. 2002, 108–117).

Simultaneous to the substructure of trimmer joists used for insulation against humidity, other insulation methods had been used as well – a substructure under the floor of fired ruins (Balgarchevo), of stones and rammed earth or mixing the clay for constructing the floor with ceramic fragments (Kovachevo); follows under the floors (Kovachevo).

The small areas within most settlements of the WBPC Culture which have been investigated do not provide opportunities for clarifying their planning. In it noted for Galabnik that the houses were grouped in clusters with narrow passages between them and with clearly recognizable streets between each cluster. In the area which has been examined, a yard has been identified (Bakamska 2007, 180). Five-six buildings located close to each other have been registered during phases Ia and Ib in Kovachevo as well. Ditches for leading the water away have also been discovered there (Lichardus-Itten et al. 2002, 115).

There is a great possibility that the large sizes of the houses, the presence of "yards" and the horizontal-vertical stratigraphy to have been mutually conditioned by each other and in combination to have led to the large sizes of some settlements in Southwestern Bulgaria. The ceramic material connects Kovachevo and Slatina with Karanovo I Culture, but like settlement and house arrangements the settlements bear closer resemblance to WBPC. In is not impossible during the first half of WBPC, the valley of Struma River to have played rather the role of a transit route to the fields in its upper course and there from to Thrace as during that period the permanent settlementń were quite a few.

In Northwestern Bulgaria varieties in house architecture has also been established in the settlement of Gradeshnitsa, the houses are above the ground, rectangular, built in wattle-and-daub technique (Nikolov 1975) and it Ohoden-valoga a premise dug at a depth of 0.60 m into the terrain at that time has been identified (Ganetsovski 2008b, 31–33).

---

9   It should be taken into consideration that mere 6-7 % of the entire settlement area has been studied.

Anthropomorphic plastic

Anthropomorphic plastic associated with Karanovo I and WBPC cultures demonstrate many similar traits. In both cultures only female figurine are known. Most widely spread were standing figurines (in some cases slightly bent) with more realistically shaped lower half. The legs are separated with flatly cut off feet so that the figurines could stand straight. Special attention is paid to the bottom parts which are with emphasized steatopygia (Figs 7: 3, 12; 8: 4. The sex triangle is marked with incised lines (Figs 7: 10; 12: 1). The upper body part is presented mainly in two ways. In the first it is flat and the separate body parts – torso, neck, and head had not been differentiated (or the differentiation was hardly visible/very poor) (Figs 7: 4; 12: 2). The hands are usually shown by means of conic protrusions on both sides of the torso, sometimes they are represented more realistically (Fig. 7: 10). In the second way of presenting the upper body part the torso is differentiated from the neck and the head which are made together. The torso has a rhomboid shape as a result of the overall modeling together with the hands shown as protrusions (schematical presentation of the hands bend at the elbows and placed on the belly) (Figs 7: 1, 2; 12: 1). The head and neck are cylindrical (Figs 7: 1, 2; 8: 3, 6). In both types of presenting the body, only the breast and the nose were marked – by cone shaped dots, and the eyes – by incisions.

In Karanovo I Culture, the figurines were decorated very rarely and most commonly only the lower body part was decorated – by incised straight lines or dotted contours on the upper part of the thighs (Fig. 7: 12). The upper half of a flat trapezium-shaped figurine decorated with incised ornament has been found in Rakitovo (Raduncheva *et al.* 2002, 137, fig. 77: 1). In WBPC, the upper body part is ornamented more often – by means of incised lines, nail impressions, triangle or oval-shaped dotting (Fig. 8: 1, 4). Sometimes the "hair style" was marked – by incised lines on the head-crown. During the second phase of WBPC appeared also the plastic presentation of the hair style (Fig. 8: 5) (Pavuk & Čohadžiev 1984, abb. 15: 1; Chohadzhiev 2001, fig. 91: 3). In both cultures figurines with broken or straight incised line under the nose have been discovered.

Relative cultural differentiation is visible in two other types of figurines. The first represents cylindrical or slightly conical figurines with composite body. They were made of a single clay piece. Usually only the eyes and nose were marked on them while the hands were represented most often by means of short side protrusions. They were spread in Karanovo I Culture (Fig. 7: 8, 11). The second type represents schematic human images in the shape of parallelepiped. Among them on the upper end of the wide surface, only the nose was marked – like a cone-shaped protrusion, and the two eyes – by cuts. In most cases the hair was marked by means of incisions on the upper part of the surface. There are a few short vertical cuttings in the lower part and those cuttings probably differentiate the feet. Those figurines are ornamented by circle dots or incised lines. They are well known mainly within the area of WBPC and they appeared it its second phase – in Galabnik, Pernik, Sapareva Banya (Fig. 8: 12) (Pavuk & Čohadžiev 1984, abb. 16: 2, 3, Georgiev *et al.* 1986, abb.19). In the settlement of Pernik-hokeina ploshtadka (Pernik-Hockey rink) an anthropomorphic weight for a loom decorated with an incised net-shaped ornament has been discovered (Fig. 8: 6) (Chohadzhiev 1981, 73–74). From the area of Karanovo I just single exemplars of that type have been identified – from Rakitovo (Raduncheva *et al.* 2002, 137, fig. 42: 7), Karanovo and Azmak tell.

In addition to being made of clay, anthropomorphic figurines were also made of marble. They were, however, very rare. From the Azmak tell a voluminously made statuette has been known while the figurines from Southwestern Bulgaria (Kovachevo, Galabnik) were flat and quite schematic (Figs 7: 7, 9; 8: 7) (Lichardus-Itten *et al.* 2002, pl. 22: 16, 17. Pavuk & Čohadžiev 1984, abb. 17).

In both cultures, sitting anthropomorphic figurines were rarity. Only single exemplars have been found – in Karanovo (Nikolov V. 2006, 56), Vaksevo, Piperkov chiflik. In Kovachevo a fragment of a figurine that was probably sitting on a chair has been discovered (Lichardus-Itten *et al.* 2002, pl. 22: 14).

Clear cultural differentiation is observable in another category of images – anthropomorphic vessels. During the EN period, two groups of images could be differentiated among them – vessels with anthropomorphic shape; and vessels with anthropomorphic elements on them. Vessels of anthropomorphic shape were poorly represented. Best preserved is a single vessel from Rakitovo showing the lower part of a female body where the feet are separated (Fig. 12: 5). Significantly more widely spread was the second group within which a couple of versions could be identified:

1. "Bottle shaped" vessels of spherical (or round-double carinated) lower part and tall cylindrical neck. In the upper end of the neck under the mouth, a human face was marked – in variations starting from the most schematic (a plastic nose and plastic dots on both sides to mark the eyes) (Georgiev 1981, 105-abb. 59) to realistic, both of the face itself and of the separate elements which were plastically formed (Fig. 12: 6; Georgiev 1981, 106-abb. 60). In tell Kazanlak, a fragment from such a realistically decorated vessel has been found, and on the vessel, in addition to plastic decoration, painted decoration was applied as well. In the same tell a well-preserved vessel on whose neck not only the face but also the arms, the chest and vulvae were presented has also been found (Nikolov 2006, fig. 59, fig. 57). That type of vessels is typical for Karanovo I culture and is very poorly presented in WBPC and solely in its very end in Northeastern Bulgaria – group Gradeshnitsa-Karcha which is famous for its anthropomorphic "bottles" with polychrome paintings (Fig. 11: 4; Nikolov 1974, fig. 15).

2. Spherical vessels with short necks, on whose upper part a human face is represented. A single vessel of that type has been found in both Karanovo I Culture (Fig. 9: 1) (Kalchev 2005, 38) and in WBPC (Fig. 9: 7) (Chohadzhiev 1990, fig. 4:2)

3. Vessels with plastic images of a human body. They were spread within the area of Karanovo I Culture: Azmak tell, settlement-tell Okrazhna Bolnitsa – Stara Zagora (Kalchev 2005, 20, 39), tell Chavdar (Georgiev 1981, 107-abb. 61) (Fig. 9: 2, 3, 4, 5). So far such vessels have not been found within the area of WBPC.

29

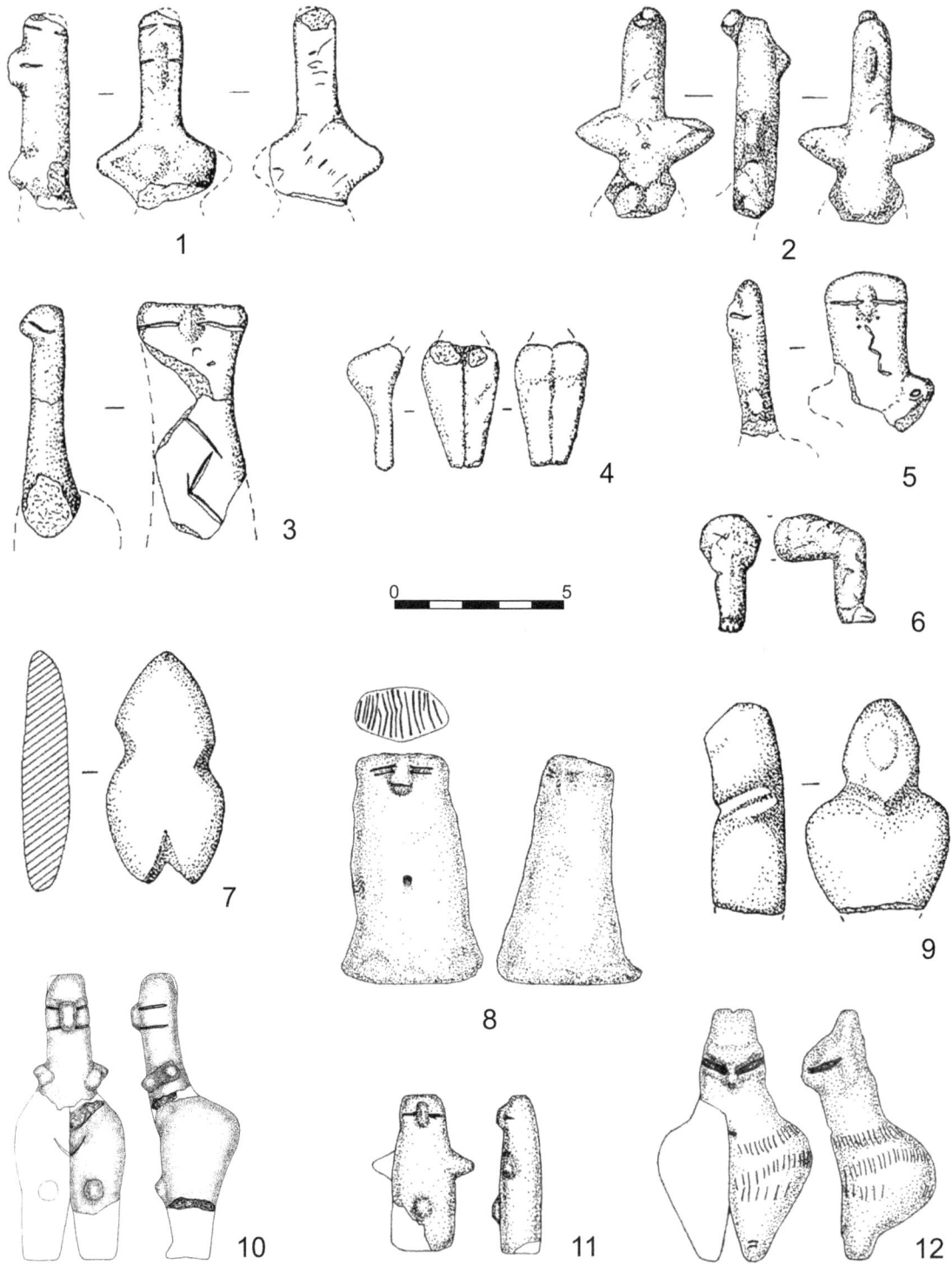

Fig. 7. Karanovo I anthropomorphic plastic: 1-6, 7 (marble), 9 (marble) – Kovachevo (after Lichardus-Itten *et al.* 2002, pl. 22: 1, 4, 10, 12, 9, 14, 16, 17); 8, 10-12 – Slatina (after Nikolov *et al.* 1991, fig. 3; 4).

Anthropomorphic plastic was poorly represented in the settlements of MnN. In Krainisti, a fragment from a sitting female figurine has been discovered (Čochadžiev & Bakamska 1990, tabl. 25: 5) and in Ohoden – a leg from a figurine (Ganetsovski 2007, tab. 17: 2). Zoomorphic figures have not been identified. Spiritual culture is presented mainly by the so-called "labreti" (Fig. 10: 1–3). They have been found in almost all settlements which have been studied. In addition to a clay one, there is also one of marble found – in Belyakovets-plochite. Those objects were spe-

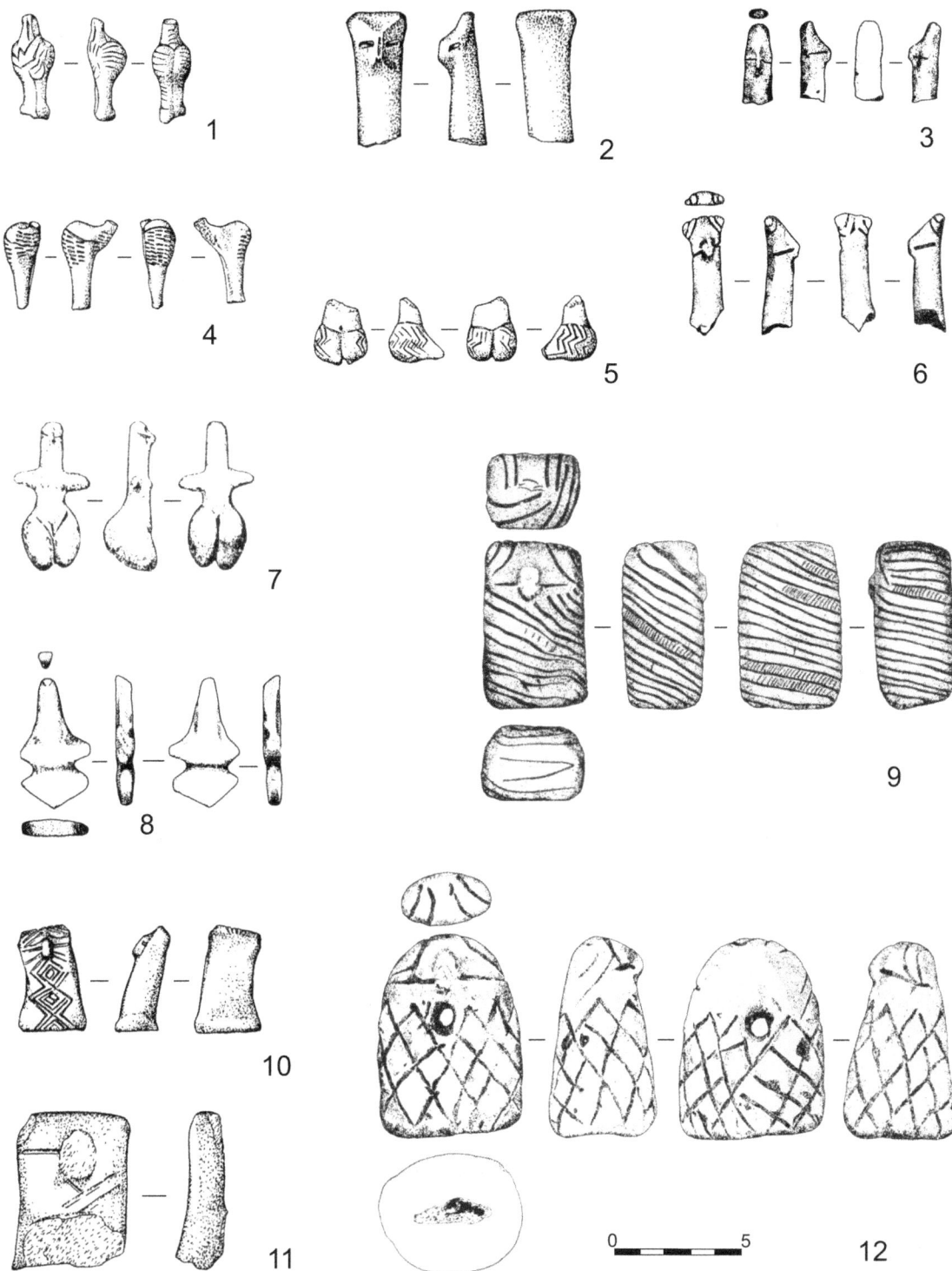

Fig. 8. WBPC anthropomorphic plastic: 1, 2, 4, 5, 10, 11 – Balgarchevo (after Pernicheva 2008, tab. 2: 4, 8, 5, 3; 1: 1, 5); 3, 7 – Galabnik (after Chohadzhiev 1981, p. 75; Chohadzhiev 1990, fig. 4: 1); 6, 12 - Pernik (after Chohadzhiev 1981, p. 74-75); 8 – Slatina (after Lichardus-Itten *et al.*, 2002, Pl. 22: 17); 9 – Kovachevo (after Nikolov *et al.*, 1991, obr. 4: i).

cific for the MnN. In Cultures Karanovo I and WBPC they have been rarely present – in Rakitovo, Vaksevo, Galabnik (Raduncheva *et al.* 2002, 142, fig. 22, 53: 2, 5 Chohadzhiev 2001, 168–169, fig. 93: 1–2; Chohadzhiev 2007, 118). In Rakitovo where their number is significant – 33, prevail the elongated labreti with straight protrusions while those from MnN have predominantly spherical-oval or cylindrical shape where the two protrusions in their upper end are slightly bent resembling a stylistic bull head. It seems that the above mentioned difference is due to incongruities in

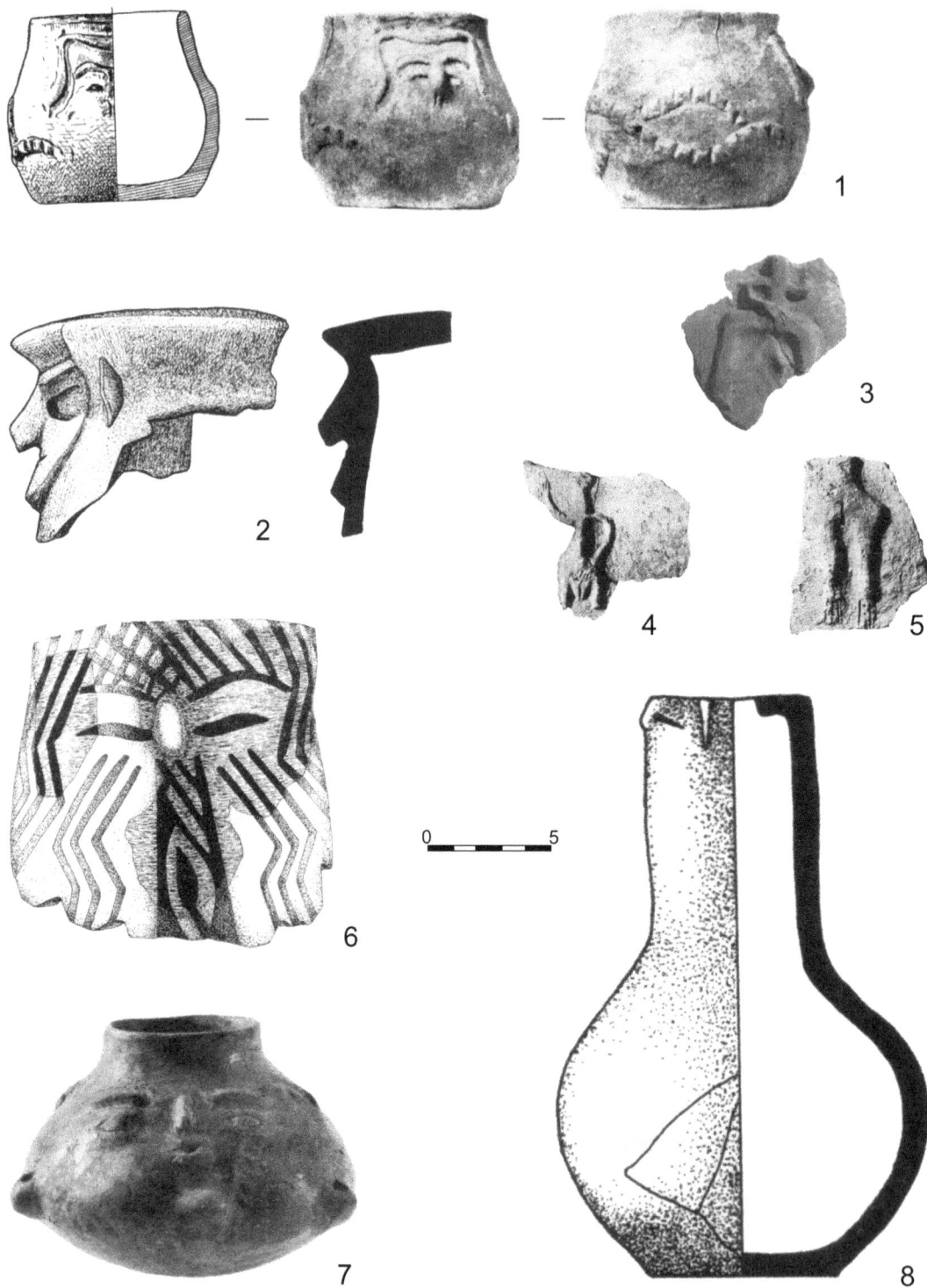

Fig. 9. Anthropomorphic vessels: 1 – Azmak (after Georgiev 1963, fig. 16); 2, 4, 5, 8 – Chavdar (after Georgiev 1981, abb. 60; 61; 59); 3 – Stara Zagora-Okrazhna bolnitsa (after Kalchev 2005, 39); 6 – Slatina (after Nikolov *et al.* 1991, fig. 3); 7 – Galabnik (after Chohadzhiev 2007, tab. 6).

their interpretation. While N. Elenski claims that they represent bucrania (Elenski 2004), V. Matsanova and S. Chohadzhiev suggest that there is a possibility of it being a phallus presentation (Raduncheva *et al.* 2002, 142; Chohadzhiev 2001, 169).

Zoomorphic plastic

In addition to labreti which probably represented a schematic bull head, there have been no zoomorphic figurines found in the settlements of MnN. They were, however, spread at a massive scale during Karanovo I and WBPC cul-

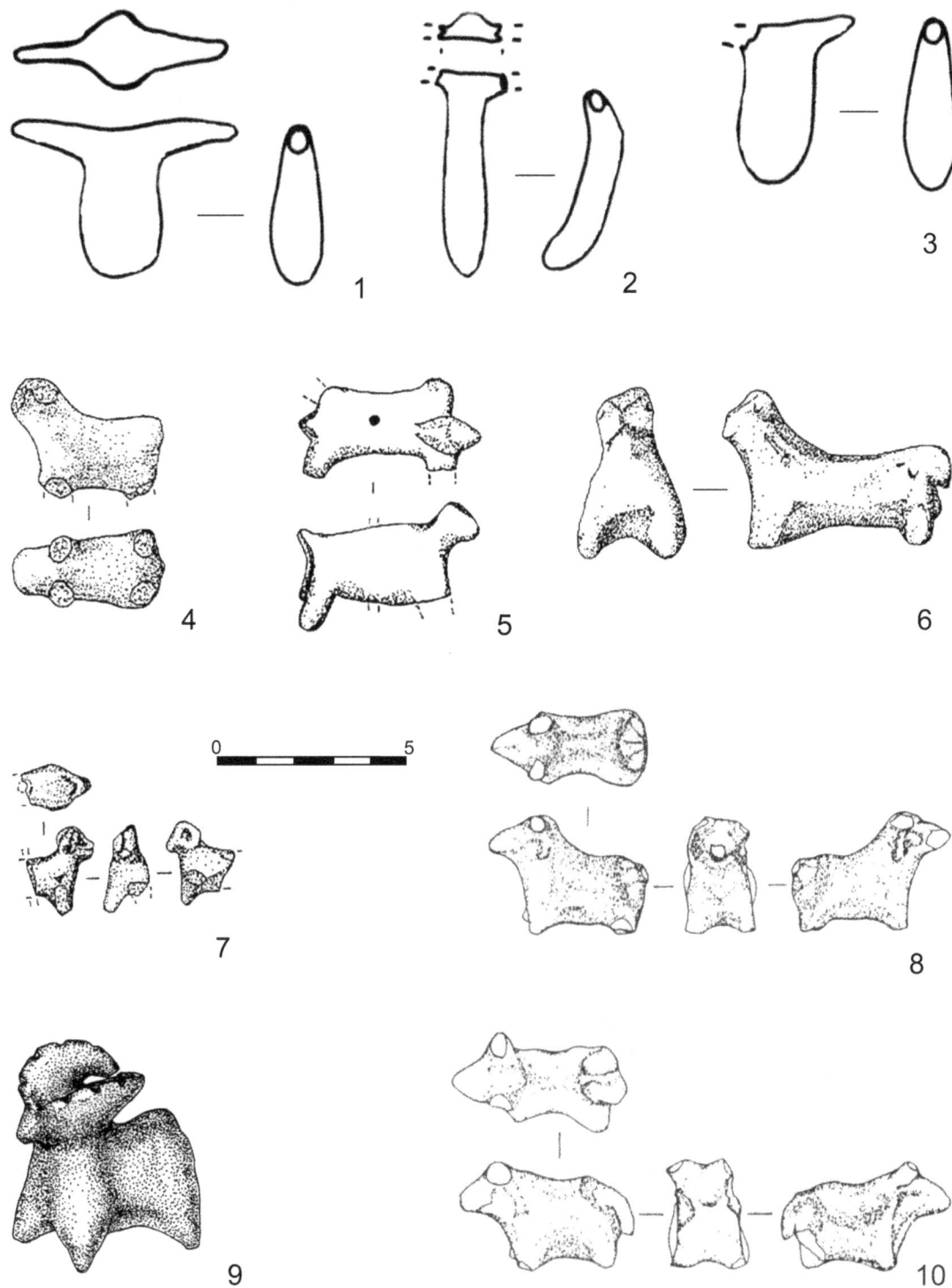

Fig. 10. Zoomorphic figurines 1-3 – Dzhulyunitsa (after Elenski 2006, fig. 13: 1, 4, 3); 4-7 – Kovachevo (after Lichardus-Itten *et al.* 2002, pl. 22: 18, 19, 21); 8, 10 – Piperkov Chiflik (after Vandova 2004, fig. 3: 3, 4); 9 – Slatina (after Nikolov *et al.* 1991, fig. 4: 3).

tures. In both cultures domestic animals were most commonly represented: bull, sheep, goat, pig. Generally speaking, they are very schematic (Fig. 10). Sometimes separate elements are presented – horns, muffles or muzzles, backbone, womb. Realistic figures are rarity – for instance, the image of a lamb from Vaksevo (Chohadzhiev 2001, 235, fig. 36: 4), a ram from Kovachevo (Fig. 10: 7) (Lichardus-Itten *et al.* 2002, pl. 22:20). From Shishkovtsi (WBPC) a fragmented zoomorphic figurine has been found and it was covered in red slip and decorated in white paint.

Fig. 11.   1, 6 – Stara Zagora-Okrazhna bolnitsa (after Kalchev 2005, 19, 18); 2- 4, 7 – Gradeshnitsa (after Nikolov 1974, fig. 6; 14; 3; 7); 5 – Azmak (after Kalchev 2005, 17).

More realistically were modeled some wild animals but such images are rarely found. From Vaksevo (WBPC) a figurine of a fox has been identified (Chohadzhiev 2001, 235, fig. 36: 2) and from Eleshnitsa – a head of a leopard (Nikolov 2006, fig. 108).

High artistry is demonstrated in the making of two zoomorphic vessels from the region of Rodopa Mountains – an image of a stag from Muldava (Detev 1968) and of a bull – from Rakitovo (Raduncheva *et al.* 2002, fig. 24) (Fig. 12: 4, 7). In Rakitovo, a fragment from a figurine with a vessel

Fig. 12. 1 – Slatina; 2, 3 – Karanovo; 4- Muldava; 5, 7 – Rakitovo; 6 - Chavdar (after Nikolov 2006, fig. 71; 68; 72; 105; 64; 57; 106).

on its back has been discovered (Raduncheva *et al.* 2002, fig. 66). A zoomorphic figure carrying a vessel on its back has also been found in Galabnik (Pavuk & Čohadžiev 1984, abb.18: 2).

During the EN period zoomorphic amulets made of nephritis have been identified. They were comparatively rare. They were spread mainly within the area of Karanovo I Cul-

ture even though predominantly in its periphery: "a frog" in Stara Zagora, Kardzhali, Kovachevo (Perničeva 1990, fig. 14: 3); "a snake" in Eleshnitsa.

Cult tables (Altars)

Another group of objects that demonstrate a particular cultural specific are the cult table. In cultures Karanovo I and WBPC they were popular in a mass scale. In accordance to their shape (horizontal section), they have been divided into three and four-angled, and the way of forming their basins has defined the various types and versions (Vandova 1995; Nikolov 2007). In Karanovo I Culture there is a clearly expressed dominance of three-sided cult tables with inscribed (that does not continue above the sides of the table) three-sided basins. Kardzhali, where three of the discovered tables were four-sided, is an exception. Tables of other types have been rarely found.

The variety of cult tables in WBPC Culture is significantly higher. Here as well the most commonly found tables are three-sided tables with inscribed basins but other varieties are also represented: three-sided with inscribed basins with sharply rounded sides or circular; three-sided with semi-inscribed circular of cylindrical basin; four-sided with circular basin where the basin was made differently – inscribed, semi-inscribed or raised; with four-sided inscribed basin (Vandova 1995; Nikolov 2007, 82–83).

In MnN, cult tables were poorly represented and solely in the second phase of the culture – from Ohoden (Ganetsovski 2007, tab. 17:1, 20: 1, 2). Most probably their appearance in that phase in the Northwestern part of Bulgaria could be associated with an influence from WBPC.

Pintaderas

So far such artifacts have not been found from the MnN period. They are well-known in association to both Karanovo I Culture and WBPC (Dzhanfezofa 2003; Chohadzhiev 2007, 131–133, fig. 103; Nikolov 2006, 73–74). The largest collection has been found in Kovachevo – 32 items (Lichardus-Itten *et al.* 2002, 126, pl. 21, 18–29). Their base could be circular, elongated-rectangular, square, oval, cross-shaped. The handle is most often conic (flattened-conic) and in some pintaderas with elongated rectangular or cylindrical base, sometimes with a hole in the upper end. In Slatina and Kapitan Dimitrievo double pintaderas have also been found (Nikolov 2006, fig. 112). On the lower end of the base, an incised ornament was made and the decoration motives were of great variety. The most common were parallel, horizontal broken or wave-looking lines; spirals, concentric circles or squares (depending on the base shape); parallel cuts or angles; meanders; cross-shaped signs. Some specific motives have also been identified.

DEVELOPMENT AND SYNCHRONISATION OF EARLY NEOLITHIC CULTURES

Comparisons of various data – archaeological materials, absolute dating, and stratigraphic situations – allows a more clear establishment of the routes and phases of Neolithisation on the territory of modern Bulgaria.

Around 6200/6100 cal. BC the bearers of MnN culture migrated along the valleys of Struma and Maritsa Rivers in the direction south-north and settled down in Southern Bulgaria (Kraynitsi, Slatina-Gradini, Kuklen)[10]. Some of them

crossed into the region through the passages of the Balkans (Stara Planina) and settled down in Central Northern and Northeastern Bulgaria.

About 6000 cal. BC, along the middle and upper course of Struma River appeared the first bearers of white painted Neolithic (Kovachevo, Galabnik). Some differences in the ceramic material give ground to suggest that the people of the two settlements had different origins. Kovachevo most probably should be associated to the region along the upper course of Vardar River (Yanitsa B). A similar point of origin has not been established yet for the settlement of Galabnik. The flow of people continued and its spreading could have happened not only directly along the valleys of Struma and Vardar rivers, but also indirectly – by means of migrating from one valley to the other along some of their tributaries whose beginnings were of immediate proximity to the valley of the neighbouring river. Most convenient in that respect are Strumeshnitsa River – right tributary to Struma River, as well as Bregalnitsa River, a left tributary to Vardar River. It is indicative that Vaksevo, Nevestino and Bersin – the three settlements with similar ceramic material relatively differentiating itself from that collected in other sites along Struma River, and having good parallels in southwestern direction, have been found very close to each other along the courses of rivers (Eleshnitsa and Bersin) running exactly to the catchment area of Bregalnitsa River. Most probably the situation concerns people who had penetrated the region exactly along the Vardar River (or at least that those people were somehow related to the people of the Vardar River region). The assumption that the differences in ceramic materials reflect only chronological changes indicates that the process of Neolithisation of the corresponding region has been accepted as a mono-centric single act after which the region's development continues in the same way. However, if it is assumed that the settling down of a region had happened in "waves" and/or from more than one centre of origin, then it is natural in synchronous settlements various "fashion tendencies" in ceramic decoration (and not only there) to be presented. The analysis of ^{14}C dating and of the stratigraphic situation demonstrates that the differences in ceramic settings of separate settlements more often reflect local and not chronological particularities.

Relatively fast, the people penetrating along the valley of Struma River migrated to the Northern or Upper Thracian plain as it settled down also the border-line territories – the Sofia (Slatina, Kremikovtsi) and Pirdop-Zlatitsa plains (Chavdar). Karanovo I Culture was formed and its beginning seems to be about 100 years later than that of WBPC. In addition to the ^{14}C dates, the gradual migration from Struma to Thrace has been confirmed also by the stratigraphic situation. So far, exactly Galabnik has been identified as the site with the greatest number of horizons from the EN period (10 in number) and the thickest layer-piling (of more than 4 m). A similar thickness of horizons has been observed on one more settlement – Slatina, but there the ^{14}C dates for the lowest horizon exclude such an early settling (correspondingly, a longer preservation of

---

10 Migration along the Vardar River valley occurred also at the same time.

the early Neolithic traditions could be suggested)[11]. The multi-layered settlements from the Sub-Balkan plains (Kremikovtsi, Chavdar, Kazanlak) and Thrace (Karanovo) have approximately the same maximum thickness – about 3.00–3.50 m with seven to nine levels, which is just slightly less than that of Galabnik (Tab. 5). An absolutely identical picture has also been identified for the valleys of Vardar River and Pelagonia: the earliest ^{14}C dates have come from the most southern site – Anzabegovo where the thickest EN layer pile-ups – about 4 m (exactly as much as in Galabnik); in Vrashnik (Vrašnik) they are about 3.70 m (Garashanin & Garashanin 1960/61) and in Velushka tumba (Simoska & Sanev 1975) – 3–3.50 m.

Karanovo I Culture gradually had spread also towards the Rodopa Mountains region and around 5800 cal. BC had reached the valley of the River Mesta as well (Eleshnitsa).

If the main regions of spreading of white painted pottery are compared – the valley of Struma River and Thrace – it could be established that there is a much greater variety among the different settlements in Struma, both with reference to varieties in ceramic decoration and to other elements of material culture. The situation is easy to explain – the valley of Struma River is on one side a very convenient route for migrating south-north (the major migration direction during the EN period) and on another, it is close to the second great route in that direction – the valley of Vardar River. The dissemination of the population could have happened both directly along the valleys of Struma and Vardar rivers, and indirectly – by means of crossing from one valley to the other along some of their tributaries whose beginnings were in immediate proximity to the valley of the other river. Opposite to the situation in the Struma River valley, the Northern or Upper Thracian plains remained aside of the "migration corridors" and their territory (together with the neighbouring regions) was vast enough to accommodate the expanding, based on natural increase, population. For that reason, Karanovo I Culture was much more homogeneous to WBPC during its initial phase. More significant differences have been observed only its southern and western periphery (Yabalkovo, Rakitovo, Kovachevo, Slatina) where influences from other neighbouring cultures have been identified.

On the borderline between Thrace and Southwestern Bulgaria (settlements of Chavdar and Kremikovtsi), simultaneous to white paintedpottery developed ornamenting of pottery in dark paints – red, black, brown and its imports had spread mainly in Thrace. Dark painted pottery had appeared also along the middle course of Struma River (Nevestino, Bersin) where most probably it should be related to a centre located in south-western direction.

In Central Northern and North-eastern Bulgaria, MnN culture continued to develop and in its ceramic painting in white paint had appeared as well. Researchers of MnN in

the region unanimously synchronize that phase to Karanovo I (Stanev 1995, 61; Popov 1996, fig.199; Nikolov 1997, 36). The bearers of MnN appeared also in Northwestern Bulgaria (Ohoden-valoga).

Significant changes had occurred around 5750/5700 cal. BC.

In Southwestern Bulgaria painting in dark paints became dominant – red, black, brown (Tabl. 4). Their use in separate settlements had been simultaneous and the dominance of one colour in those settlements was due to local preferences, and not to chronological differences.

Most researchers of the region accept that the spreading of dark painted pottery had happened under the influence of Starchevo Culture. M. Chohadzhiev and J. Pavuk include the white painted Neolithic along the valley of Struma River into the area of Protostarchevo (Protostarčevo) Culture (Groups Anazabegovo-Vrashnik (Vrašnik) II, Galabnik and Slatina) (Pavuk & Čohadžiev 1984; Pavuk 2000). The problem regarding the genesis of Starchevo (Starčevo) Culture is quite wide in order to be examined in the current work. Generally speaking though, the EN period along the Valley of Struma River shows earlier development in comparison to Protostarchevo (Protostarčevo) Culture. Not only in technology, but also as varieties and execution of painted motives, phase I of WBPC is significantly more advanced than Protostarchevo (Protostarčevo) Culture. Ceramic materials of Protostarchevo (Protostarčevo) Culture demonstrate parallels rather with MnN in Northern Bulgaria to which it was synchronous. Some common elements in the material culture of Protostarchevo (Protostarčevo) and WBPC clearly were resulting from the influence of the latter as well to the early phases of Anzabegovo-Vrashnik (Vrašnik) Culture. Without exceptions it could be suggested that the process (just like Neolithisation of the Balkan Peninsula itself) runs south-southeast and north-northwest. It seems that the bearers of painted Neolithic coming from southern direction gradually assimilated the new territories, while at the same time in the Northern parts of the Balkan Peninsula, various groups of MnN had been preserved (Tab. 6).

In Chavdar, dark painted pottery appeared about 150–200 years earlier than in Southwestern Bulgaria and Starchevo (Starčevo) Culture (Boyadžiev 2000, 328–330). It is obvious that the wide spread of dark painted pottery happened under the influence of the settlements of Chavdar and Kremikovtsi[12] – that is from eastern direction and not under the influence of Starchevo (Starčevo) Culture. After 5750 cal. BC, the influence of WBPC in western and northwestern direction increased. Bearers of the culture colonized Northwestern Bulgaria (Tlachene, Gradeshnitsa). It was here that polychrome painted reached its peak. Under the influence of WBPC – directly by migrations of people in western and northwestern direction (along the valleys of the Rivers Erma-Nishava-South Moravia) or indirectly, by

---

11 An early Neolithic layer of 6 m thickness has been reported for settlement-tell Kapitan Dimitrievo (?). That thickness, however, has not been established in one and the same sector but on the ground of summing up thicknesses of layers in different trenches with the arguments that there has been only white painted pottery in one of them and dark painted in the other as well. Until that super-position has not been identified in one and the same place with a corresponding thickness of layers, the said thickness remains questionable as characterizing the whole early Neolithic layer.

12 There are no ^{14}C dates for Kremikovtsy but taking in consideration the thickness of the Early Neolithic layer where dark painted pottery has been found – at least 3 m with 7 horizons within the layer, then most probably it is approximately synchronous with Chavdar.

Table 5

Synchronization of several main Early Neolithic Settlements on Bulgarian territory based on relative chronology and stratigraphy

MhN – I phase

MhN – II phase

Karanovo I/WBPC – horizons only with white painted pottery

Karanovo I/WBPC – horizons with dark painted pottery

Karanovo II/Ovcharovo – dark polished pottery

Karanovo II/III – transition between EN and LN

Table 6

Schematic synchronization chart of EN cultures in Bulgaria, Greece and Serbia

Greece	Serbia	Bulgaria Period	Eastern Thrace	Western Thrace	SW Bulgaria	NW Bulgaria	NE Bulgaria	Dates BC
	Star-chevo	Transition EN/LN	Karanovo II/III	Karanovo I/III	Transition EN/LN	WBPC II phase	Ovcharovo	5400
Sesklo		EN III	Karanovo II	Karanovo I	WBPC II phase			5600
Pre-Sesklo	Proto-II star chevo I	EN III	Karanovo I		WBPC I phase	MhN	MhN II phase	5800
Proto-Sesklo		EN I	MhN ?	MhN	MhN		MhNI phase	6000
								6200
ECN								6400

means of contacts between the two regions – Starchevo (Starčevo) Culture was formed. There is a possibility the spread of dark painted pottery along the Struma River Valley, and also of the formation of Starchevo (Starčevo) Culture, a number of settlements in the area of modern day Republic of Macedonia to have exercised influence. Intensified migrations of people in addition to multi-directional contacts led to differentiations of local groups – Kremikovtsi, Gradeshnitsa-Cîrča.

Disintegration processes had occurred also in the Karanovo Culture region. In the Eastern part of the Thracian plains, the monochrome grey-blackish polished pottery decorated with channeling became predominant, and on its base Karanovo II group has been differentiated.

The bearers of Karanovo II Group penetrated Northeastern Bulgaria where under their influence Ovcharovo (Ovčarovo) Culture was formed. The concentration of Ovcharovo settlements is analogical to the spread of the settlements from MnN period – middle and upper course of Yantra River and its catchment area, the catchment areas of Ticha and Golyama Kamchia Rivers. Clearly, the penetration of people in south-north direction happened on already familiar routes – Rishki, Varbishki, Tvardishki and Prohod na Republikata passages. At the same time, the influence of Western Thrace on Northern Bulgaria was insignificant. In the region between the rivers Yantra and Iskar, no permanently dwelt Early Neolithic settlements have been discovered. In Northern Bulgaria, white painted pottery did not spread on a mass scale despite the fact that in the Western half of Thrace the existence of Karanovo I continued synchronous to Group Karanovo II. The vessels or fragments white painted pottery which have been found appear exceptional among the ceramic material (Stanev 1982, 9–10).

Consequently, there are all reasons to assume that the colonization of Central Northern and Northeastern Bulgaria had occurred under the influence of the bearers of Karanovo II Group who came from the Northeastern part of Thrace.

In the end of Early and the transition to Late Neolithic, gradual settling also of the most eastern parts of Bulgaria began – the regions along the Black sea coast. The main route of penetration for the people was the Valley of Luda Kamchia River. Exactly in that valley the most eastern settlements which emerged during the EN period were located – near the village of Asparuhovo, the village of Golyamo Delchevo (horizon I of the settlement-tell), Dalgopol village – the region of Balkuzu, Boryana village (Todorova & Vaysov 1993, 142–145). Everything points that the source of that colonization wave were the most northeastern regions of the Thracian plains.

In the Western half of the Thracian plain painting in white paint was preserved. Culture Group Karanovo I – Azmak version and Culture group Karanovo II existed synchronous. Different continuity for the two phenomena has been suggested as well. V. Nikolov has differentiated three periods in the development during the second half of the Early Neolithic period in Thrace (Nikolov 2004):

– Period III. In the Northeastern areas of Thrace developed Karanovo II – represented in Glufichevo; settlement-tell Karanovo – layer II; Okrazhna Bolnitsa – Stara Zagora and others. In the remaining area, Karanovo I continued its development: Muldava; the middle layers of ohase II in Kapitan Dimitrievo; Dobriniste; phase III in Kovachevo. In borderline areas, Karanovo I was represented in its Azmak variant – the late horizons of the EN period in Kazanlak and Azmak;

– Period IV. Northeastern areas of Thrace, expanded to include Kazanlak plain as well, were included in the Middle Neolithic phenomena Protokaranovo III represented in two territorial versions – Karanovo II–III (settlement-tell Karanovo, layers II–III, Glufichevo – the most upper layer, settlement-tell Veselinovo – the lowest layer) and Karanovo I–III (tell Kazanlak, horizons X and IX). The development of Karanovo I Culture continued in the rest of Thrace;

– Period V. In the Northeastern areas of Thrace, expanded by the Kazanlak plain developed Karanovo III (settlement-tell Veselinovo – the middle Neolithic layer; tell Karanovo – layer III, tell Kazanlak – the upper horizons). In the rest of Thrace continued the reproduction of Karanovo I Culture (the final horizons of phase II in Capitam Dimitrievo, phase IV in Kovachevo and others).

According to that periodisation, Karanovo I Culture in Thrace (as during the EN in West Bulgaria – second phase of WBPC) continued its existence simultaneously with the existence of Karanovo II/II and III cultures in Northeastern Thrace. The hypothesis, however, has not been supported either by radio-carbon and archeo-magnetic dating or by the stratigraphic situation in separate sites (as the number of horizons and thickness of layer piles). The development of series of dates for sites of the Late Neolithic period (layer II in settlement-tell Karanovo, Dobriniste, Sapareva Banya, Ovcharovo-gorata) indicates that the chronological interval within which the horizons marking the end of the EN period of the corresponding regions/cultures lie, has been comparatively short – between 5450 and 5400 cal. BC. Indicative is the dating of the end of the EN period in the settlement of Kovachevo which, according to V. Nikolov, should be synchronized with Karanovo III in Northeastern Thrace (tab. 2). ^{14}C dates obtained for the two upper layers of Kovachevo – Id (EN-end) and II (LN) (Lichardus-Itten *et al.* 2006, 85), despite being identical indicate for sure that the transition between the EN period and the Late Neolithic at the site should be sought before 5400 cal. BC. That conclusion has been confirmed also by the archeo-magnetic dating of a furnace from Id phase – 5590–5410 BC (Kovacheva 1995, 220–221). Very close to that date is also the archeo-magnetic dating of a furnace in Bulgarchevo, phase Ia (which marks the end of the EN) – 5520–5450 BC (Kovacheva & Toshkov 1991; Pernicheva 1995, 107) and the transition of LN (Balgarchevo Ib) shoud begin not earlier then 5450 BC.

^{14}C dates for horizon 8 (phase Karanovo II/III after V. Nikolov) from settlement-tell Karanovo place the beginning of the transition to the Late Neolithic period around 5450 cal. BC. That was the beginning of transforming the Early Neolithic cultures. The process began in Thrace at the earliest. The dates for horizon 4 in Ovcharovo-gorata indicate that the processes ended in Northern (or probably in Northwestern) Bulgaria at the latest. The difference though is no more than 60–80 years – that is no more than one-two horizons. During that period the gradual transition to the Late Neolithic period occurred. After 5400/5350 cal. BC the Late Neolithic cultures spread on the entire territory of modern day Bulgaria.

REFFERENCES

Angelova I. 1988. Predvaritelni rezultati ot razkopkite na neolitnoto selishte "Ovcharovo-gorata". In Yordanov K. (ed.), *Terra Antiqua Balcanica* III, 31–36.

Angelova I. 1992. Predvaritelnie rezultati raskopok neoliticheskogo poselenia Ovcharovo-gorata. *Studia Praehistorica* 11/12, 41-50.

Bogdanovich M. 1996. Prilog prouchvanu apcolutne hronologie protostarchevska i starchevska kultura. *Starinar* XLVII, 187–192.

Borić D. & Miracle P. 2004. Mesolithic and Neolithic (dis)continuities in the Danube gorges: new AMS dates from Padina and Hajdučka Vodenica (Serbia). *Oxford Journal of Archeology* 23, 4, 341–371.

Boyadzhiev Ya. 1994. Datirane po radiovaglerodnia metod na rannoneolitno zhilishte ot Slatina (Sofia). *Archaeology* 2, 19–23.

Boyadžiev Y.1995. Chronology of Prehistoric Cultures in Bulgaria. In Bailey D. & Panayotov I. (eds.), *Prehistoric Bulgaria*. Monographs in World Archaeology 22. Madison Wisconsin, Prehistory Press, 149–192.

Bojadžiev Y. 2000. Entwicklung der frühneolithishen bemalten Keramik in Bulgarien. In Hiller S. & Nikolov V. (eds.), *Karanovo III. Beiträge zum Neolithikum in Südosteuropa.* Wien, 327–341.

Boyadžiev Y. 2006. The role of absolute chronology in clarifying the Neolithization of the eastern half of the Balkan Peninsula. In Gatsov I. & Schwarzberg H.(eds.), *Aegean – Marmara-Black Sea: the Present State of Research on the Early Neolithic.* Schriften des Zentrums für Archäologie und Kulturgeschichte des Schwarzmeerraumes 5. Beier & Beran, 7–14.

Chohadzhiev M. 1978. Selishta ot rannia neolit v Pernishki okrag. *Thracia Antique* 3, 29–44.

Chohadzhiev M. 1981. Neolitni antropomorfni figurki ot dolinata na Gorna Struma. *Izkustvo* 9–10, 73–77.

Chohadzhiev M. 1988. Sostoyanie isledovaniy rannego neolita Zapodnoy Bulgariy. *Studia Praehistorica* 9, 54–67.

Chohadzhiev M. 1990. Ranniat neolit v Zapadna Balgaria – poyava, razvitie, kontakti. *Izvestia na istoricheskia muzey Kyustendil* 2, 5–22.

Čochadžiev. S. 2000. Periodisierung des Neolithikums im Strumatal. In S. Hiller & V. Nikolov(eds.), *Karanovo III. Beiträge zum neolithikum in Südosteuropa.* Wien, 253–262.

Chohadzhiev S. 2001. *Vaksevo. Praistoricheski selishta.* Veliko Tarnovo.

Chohadzhiev S. 2002. Belezhki varhu neolitizatsiata na balgarskite zemi. *Godishnik na Arheologicheski Muzey - Plovdiv* IX/1, 15–21.

Chohadzhiev S. 2007. *Neolitni i halkolitni kulturi v baseina na r. Struma.* Veliko Tarnovo.

Tchohadjiev S. & Bakamska A. 1990. Etude du site neolithique ancien de Krainitsi dans le departement de Kustendil. *Studia Praehistorica* 10, 51–76.

Chohadzhiev S. & Genadieva V. 2003. Kam prouchvaniata na neolitnoto selishte v Nevestino, Kyustendilsko. Izvestia na istoricheskia muzey Kyustendil 9, 21–30.

Chohadzhiev S., Bakamska A. & Ninov L. 2007. Kraynitsi – rannokeramichno selishte ot baseyna na reka Struma. In Todorova H., Stefanovich M. & Ivanov G. (eds.), *Strymon Praehistoricus.* Sofia, 181–190.

Detev P. 1968. Praistoricheskoto selishte pri s. Muldava. *Godishnik na Narodnia arheologicheski muzey Plovdiv* V., 9–48.

Detev P. 1976. Rannoneolitno selishte pri s. Kuklen. *Rodopi* 6, 35–36.

Detev P. & Yovchev I. 1978. Razkopki na selishtnata mogila "Manastirya" pri s. Chernichevo, Plovdivski okrag. *Arheologicheski otkritia i razkopki prez 1977g.*, 23–24.

Dzhanfezofa T. 2003. Neolithic Pintaderas in Bulgaria. In Nikolova L. (ed.), Early Symbolic Systems for Communication in Southeast Europe. *BAR International Series* 1139, 97–108.

Elenski N. 2002. Sondazhni prouchvania na neolitno selishte pri s. Hotnitsa – "Peshterata-iztok", Veliko- tarnovsko prez 2001g. Arheologicheski otkritia i raz- kopki prez 2001 g., 28–29.

Elenski N. 2004. Früneolitische zoomorphe Figurinen aus dem Zentralen Nordbulgarien. In Nikolov V. & Bačvarov K. (eds.), *Von Domica bis Drama. Gedenkschrift für Jan Lichardus.* Sofia, 17–24.

Elenski N. 2008. Nai-rannite fazi na neolita v baseynite na rekite Yantra i Rusenski Lom – problemi na kulturnata identichnost. In Gurova M. (ed.) *Praistoricheski prouchvania v Bulgaria: novite predizvikatelstva.* Sofia, 96–105.

Ganetsovski G. 2007. Novi danni za rannia neolit v Severozapadna Balgaria. In Todorova H., Stefanovich M. & Ivanov G. (eds.), *Strymon Praehistoricus.* Sofia, 147–164.

Ganetsovski G. 2008a. Rannoneoliten grob ot Ohoden, Vrachansko. In M. Gurova (ed.), *Praistoricheski prouchvania v Balgaria: novite predizvikateslstva.* Sofia, 106–119.

Ganetsovski G. 2008b. Arheologicheski razkopki na rannoneolitnoto selishte v m. Valoga (Dolnite Laki) kray s. Ohoden, obshtina Vratsa. *Archeologicheski otkritia i razkopki prez 2007*, 30–35.

Garashanin M.1966. Hronologia i genezis na neolita v centralnata i yugoiztochnata chast na Balkanskia poluostrov. *Arheologia* 1, 16–30.

Garashanin M.1973. *Praistoria na tlu SR Srbiye,* I. Beograd.

Garašanin M. & Garašanin D. 1960/61. Neolitska naselba Vršnik kaj selo Tarinci. *Zbornk na Štipskiot Naroden Muzaj* 2, 7–40.

Gatsov I. 2009. Prehistoric Chipped Stone Assemblages from Eastern Thrace and the South Marmara Region 7th–5th. B. C. *BAR International Series* 1904.

Gaul J. 1948. The Neolithic Period in Bulgaria. *American School of Prehistoric Research* 16.

Genadieva V. & Chohadzhiev S. 1994. Arheologichesko prouchvane na praistoricheskoto selishte kray Nevestino. *Arheologicheski otkritia i razkopki prez 1992.*, 7–9.

Georgiev G. 1960. Glavni periodi v razvitieto na kulturata prez neolita i mednata epoha v Balgaria v svetlinata na nai-novite prouchvania. *Swiatowit* XXIII, 309–339.

Georgiev G. 1961. Kulturgruppen der Jungstein- und der Kupferzeit in der Ebene von Thrazien (Südbulgarien). *L'Europe à la fin de l'âge de la pierre.* Praha, 45–100.

Georgiev G. 1963. Glavni rezultati ot razkopkite na Azmashkata selishtna mogila prez 1961. *Izvestia na Arheologicheslia Institute* XXVI, 57–176.

Georgiev G. 1965. The Azmak Mound in Southern Bulgaria. *Antiquity* 39, 6–8.

Georgiev G. 1967a. Beiträge zur Erforschung des Neolithikums und der Bronzezeit in Südbulgarien. *Archäologie Austriaca* 42, 90–128.

Georgiev G. 1967b. Die Erforschung der neolithischen und bronze- zeitlichen Siedlungshügel in Bulgarien. *Zeitschrift fur Archaeologie* 1, 139–169.

Georgiev G. 1970a. Verbreitung und Entwicklung der neolithischen Kulturgruppen in Bulgarien. *Actes du Premier Congres International des Etudes Balkaniques et Süd-East Europeennes.* Sofia II, 209–225.

Georgiev G. 1970b. Über die Stratigraphie und Chronologie des Neolithikums, Äneolithikums und der Frühbronzezeit in Südbulgarien. *Actes des VII⁰ Congres International des Sciences Prehistoriques of Protohistoriques.* Prague, 397–400.

Georgiev G. 1971. Die Entwicklung der alteren prähistorischen Kulturen in Südbulgarien. In Georgiev V. (ed.), L'ethnogenese des peuples balkaniques. *Studia Balcanica V*, 21–35.

Georgiev G. 1974. Stratigrafia i periodizatsia na neolita i halkolita v dneshnite balgarski zemi. *Arheologia* 4, 1–18.

Georgiev G. 1975. Stratigrafiya i harakter na kulturata na praistoricheskoto selishte v s. Kremikovtsi, Sofiisko. *Arheologia* 2, 17–30.

Georgiev G. 1981. Die neolithische Siedlung bei Eavdar, Bezirk Sofia. *Cultures prehistoriques en Bulgarie.* Sofia, 63–109.

Georgiev G., Nikolov V., Nikolova V. & Čochadžiev S. 1986. Die neolithische Siedlung Kremenik bei Sapareva Banja, Bezirk Kjustendil. *Studia Praehistorica* 8, 108–151.

Grebska-Kulova M. 2008. Rannoneolitnata kultura na Sredna Struma, Yugozapadna Balgaria. In: I. Gurova (ed.), Praistoricheski prouchvania v Balgaria: novite predizvikatelstva. Natsionalen Arheologicheski Institute s Muzey, Istoricheski muzey Peshtera, 56–65.

Hiller S. & Nikolov V. (eds.) 1997. *Karanovo. Die Ausgrabungen im Südsektor 1984-1992. Österreichisch-Bulgarische Ausgrabungen und Forschungen in Karanovo.* bd. I. Salzburg.

Kalchev P. 2005. Neolitni zhilishta Stara Zagora. Katalog na ekspozitsiata. Stara Zagora.

Kanchev K. 1995. Stratigrafsko razpredelenie na risuvanata keramika v mnogosloynoto ranneneolitno selishte Chavdar, Pirdopsko. *Arheologia* 2, 1–4.

Kanchev K. & Nikolov B. 1981. Oradia na truda i stopanskia zhivot v selishtata ot staria i srednia neolit pri s. Gradeshnitsa i s. Tlachene, Vrachansko. *Izvestia na muzeyte v Severozapadna Balgaria* 5, 9–36.

Kovacheva M. & Toshkov A. 1991. Arheomagnitno datirane na niakolko neolitni selishta v Balgaria. *Arheologia*, 4, 9–13.

Kovacheva M. 1995. Bulgarian Archaeomagnetic Studies. In Bailey D. & Panayotov I. (eds.), *Prehistoric Bulgaria.* Monographs in World Archaeology 22. Madison Wisconsin, Prehistory Press, 209–224.

Leshtakov K. 2004. Keramika z vriazana i kanelirana ukrasa ot rannoneolitnoto selishte Yabalkovo na r. Maritsa. In Nikolov V., Bačvarov K. & Kalchev P. (eds.) *Prehistoric Thrace.* Sofia-Stara Zagora, 80–84.

Leshtakov K., Petrova V., Zlateva R. & Spasov N. 2007a. Spasitelni razkopki na ranneneolitnoto selishte Yavalkovo prez 2006g. *Arheologoicheski otkritia i razkopki prez 2006g.*, 39–41.

Leshtakov K., Todorova N., Petrova V., Zlateva-Uzunova R., Özbek O., Popova Tz., Spassov N. & Iliev N. 2007b. Preliminary report on the salvage archaeological excavations at the Early Neolithic site Yabalkovo in the Maritsa valley, 2000–2005 field seasons. *Anatolica* XXXIII, 185–234.

Lichardus J. & Iliev Il. 2000. Das frühe und mittlere Neolithikum an der unteren Tundža (Südostbulgarien). Ein Beitrag zu den chronologischen und kulturellen Beziehungen. In Hiller S. & Nikolov V. (eds.), *Karanovo III. Beiträge zum Neolithikum in Südosteuropa.* Wien, 75–108.

Lichardus J., Iliev Il. & Christov Ch. 2002. Die Karanovo I–IV – Perioden an der unteren Tundža und ihre chronologische Stellung zu den benachbarten Gebieten.In Lichardus-Itten M., Lichardus J. & Nikolov V. (eds.), *Beiträge zu jungsteinzeitlichen Forschungen in Bulgarien.* Bonn, Saarbücker Beiträge zur Altertumkunde 74, 325–410.

Lichardus-Itten M., Demoule J.-P., Perničeva L., Grebska-Kulov M. & Kulov Il. 2002. The Site of Kovačevo and the Beginnings of the Neolithic Period in Southwestern Bulgaria. In

Lichardus-Itten M., Lichardus J. & Nikolov V. (eds.), *Beiträge zu jungsteinzeitlichen Forschungen in Bulgarien.* Bohn, Saarbrüker Beiträge zur Alterkumskunde 74, 99–158.

Lichardus-Itten M., Demoule J.-P., Perničeva L., Grebska-Kulov M. &. Kulov Il. 2006. Kovačevo an Early Neolithic site in South-West Bulgaria and its importance for European Neolithization. In Gatsov I. & Schwarzberg H. (eds.*), Aegean-Marmara-Black Sea: the Present State of Research on the Early Neolithic.* Schriften des Zentrums für Archäologie und Kulturgeschichte des Schwarzmeerraumes 5, 83–94.

Macanova V. 2000. Neolithische Siedlung bei Rakitovo. Stratigraphie und Chronologie. In S. Hiller & Nikolov V. (eds.), *Karanovo III. Beiträge zum Neolithikum in Südosteuropa.* Wien, 59–73.

Mikov V. 1958. Kultura neolita, eneolita i bronza v Bolgarii *Sovetskaya Arheologia* 1, 47–55.

Milojčić V. 1950. Körös – Starchevo (Starčevo) – *Vinča.* In Behrens G. (ed.), *Reinecke Festschrift.* Meinz, 108–118.

Nikolov B. 1974. *Gradeshnitsa.* Sofia.

Nikolov B. 1975. Selishte ot staria neolit pri s. Gradeshnitsa, Vrachanski okrag. *Arheologia* 1, 25–40.

Nikolov B. 1992. Periodizatsia na neolitinite kulturi v Severna Balgaria – ot Yantra do Timok. *Izvestia na muzeyte v Severozapadna Balgaria* 18, 13–14.

Nikolov V. 1982a. Ornamentatsia na rannoneolitnata risuvana keramika ot balgarskite zemi: klasifikatsia, tipologia, sistematizatsia. *Avtoreferat na disertatsia.* Sofia 1982.

Nikolov V. 1982b. Prilozhenie na matematiko-statisicheskia metod za teritorialno grupirane na risuvana rannoneolitna keramika. *Interdistsiplinarni izsledvania* IO, 33–50.

Nikolov V. 1983. Ornamentatsia na rannoneolitnata risuvana keramika: sistematizatsia i harakteristika. *Arheologia* 1–2, 29–43.

Nikolov V. 1989. Zu einigen Aspekten der Kultur Karanovo I. Tell Karanovo und das Balkan Neolithikum. Salzburg, 27–41.

Nikolov V. 1990. Problemat za centralbobalkanskite migratsionni patishta prez rannia neolit. *Interdistsiplinarni izsledvania* XVII, 9–24.

Nikolov V. 1992. *Rannoneolitno zhilishte ot Slatina,* Sofia.

Nikolov V. 1993a. Die neolithischen Kulturen Karanovo I, II und III im Kontext ihrer Beziehungen zu Anatolien. *Anatolica* XIX, 167–171.

Nikolov V. 1993b. Polihromno risuvana ornamentatsia varhu rannoneolitni keramichni sadove ot Balgaria. In Nikolov V. (ed.), *Praistoricheski nahodki i izsledvania. Sbornik v pamet na prof. G. Il. Georgiev.* Sofia, 59–68.

Nikolov V. 1994. Risuvanata ornamentatsia varhu rannoneolitni keramichni sadove ot Chavdar. *Godishnik na Departament Arheologia, Nov Balgarsi Universitet* I, 185–208.

Nikolov V. 1997. Sondazhni prouchvania na praistoricheskoto selishte v m. "Izgoryalata niva" kray s. Pomoshtitsa, Popovsko prez 1995 a. *Popovo v minaloto* II, 33–37.

Nikolov V. 1998. The Circumpontic Cultural Zone during the Neolithic period. *Archaeologia Bulgarica* II, 2, 1–9.

Nikolov V. 2003. Periodization of the Neolithic Along the Struma Valley. *Thracia* XV, 99–106.

Nikolov V. 2004. Dynamics of the Cultural Processes in Neolithic Thrace. In Nikolov V., Bačvarov K. & Kalchev P. (eds.), *Prehistoric Thrace.* Sofia-Stara Zagora, 13–25.

Nikolov V. 2006. *Kultura i izkustvo na praistoricheska Trakia.* Plovdiv.

Nikolov V. 2007. *Neolitni kultovi masichki.* Sofia.

Nikolov V., Grigorova K. & Sirakova E. 1991. Rannoneolitno selishte Slatina v Sofia: parvi stroitelen horizont (perdvaritelno saobshtenie). Arheologia 3, 13-26.

Nikolov V., Matsanova V., Stefanova T., Bozhilov B, Bachvarov M.,. Gatsov I., Marinova E. & Ninov L. 1999. *Selishtnata mogila Kapitan Dimitrievo. Razkopki 1998 – 1999.* Sofia, Peshtera.

Nikolov V., Pernicheva L., Grebska-Kulova M., Lichardus M. & Demoul J.-P. 1996. Rannoneolitno selishte Kovachevo, obshtina Sandanski. *Arheologicheski otkritia i razkopki prez 1995g.*, 13–15.

Nikolova L. & Madzhev N. 1994. Sondazhno prouchvane na rannoneolitni mnogosloyni selishta pri s. Kliment i s. Dabene, Karkovsko. *Arheologicheski razkopki na praistoricheski obekti prez 1992,* 10–11.

Özdoğan M. 1989. Neolithic cultures of Northwestern Turkey. A general appraisal of the evidence and some considerations. In Bökönyi S. (ed.), Neolithic of Southeastern Europe and its Near Eastern connections. *Varia Archeologica Hungarica 2.* Budapest, 201–215.

Özdoğan M. 1997. The beginning of neolithic economies in Southeastern Europe: an Anatolian Perspective. *Journal of European Archaeology* 5 (2), 1–33.

Pavuk J. 2000. Typologie und Stratigraphie der verzierten monochromen Keramik aus der neolithischen Tellsiedlung in Galabnik. In Hiller S. & Nikolov V. (eds.), *Karanovo III. Beiträge zum Neolithikum in Südosteuropa.* Wien, 263–272.

Pavuk J. & Bakamska A. 1989. Beitrag der Ausgrabung in Galabnik zur Erforschung des Neolithikums in Südosteuropa. In Bökönyi S. (ed.), Neolithic of Southeastern Europe and its Near Eastern connections. *Varia Archaeologica Hungarica 2.* Budapest, 223–228.

Pavuk J. & Bakamska A. 2000. Typologie und Stratigraphie der verzierten monochromen Keramik aus der neolithischen Tellsiedlung in Galabnik. In Hiller S. & Nikolov V. (eds.), *Karanovo III. Beiträge zum Neolithikum in Südosteuropa.* Wien, 263–272.

Pavuk J. & Čohadžiev M. 1984. Neolithische Tellsiedlung bei Galabnik in Westbulgarien. *Slovenska Archeologia* XXXII-1, 195–228.

Pearson G. & Becker B. 1993. F. Qua. High-Precision ^{14}C-Measurement of German and Irish Oaks to Show the Natural ^{14}C Variations from 7890 to 5000 BC. *Radiocarbon* 35, 1, 93–104.

Pernitcheva L. 1990. Le site de Kovatchevo, neolithique ancien, dans le département de Blagoevgrad. *Studia Praehistorica* 10, 142–196.

Pernicheva L. 1995. Prehistoric Cultures in the Middle Struma Valley: Neolithic and Eneolithic. In Bailey D. & Panayotov I. (eds.), *Prehistoric Bulgaria.* Monographs in World Archaeology 22. Madison Wisconsin, Prehistory Press, 99–140.

Perničeva L. 2002. Die prähistorische Siedlung Balgarčevo, Kreis Blagoevgrad. In Lichardus-Itten M., Lichardus J. & Nikolov V. (eds.), *Beiträge zu jungsteinzeitlichen Forschungen in Bulgarien.* Bonn, Saarbücker Beiträge zur Altertumkunde 74, 271–324.

Pernicheva L. 2008. Antropomorfna plastika ot praistoricheskoto selishte Balgarchevo, Blagoevgradsko. In Gurova M. (ed.). *Praistoricheski prouchvania v Balgaria,* Sofia, 81.

Perničeva L., Kulov Il. & Grebska-Kulova M. 2000. Early Neolithic house from Balgarčevo. *Archaeologia Bulgarica* V, 3, 1–10.

Petkov N. 1961. Novi danni za neolitnata kultura kray Sofia. *Arheologia* 3, 64–73.

Petkov N. 1962. Risuvaniat ornament prez neolita v Sofiysko pole i blizkite mu okolnosti. Arheologia 3, 43–49.

Popov V. 1996. *Periodizatsia i hronologia na neolitnite i halkolitnite kulturi ot porechieto na reka Rusenski Lom.* Ruse.

Radunčeva A. 2002. Eine neolitische Siedlung am Ufer der Marica bei Simeonovgrad. In Lichardus-Itten M., Lichardus J. & Nikolov V. (eds.), *Beiträge zu jungsteinzeitlichen Forschungen in Bulgarie*. Bohn, Saarbrüker Beiträge zur Alterkumskunde 74, 225–243.

Raduncheva A., Matsanova V., Gatsov I., Kovachev G., Georgiev G., Chakalova E. & Bozhilova E. 2002. Neolitno selishte do grad Rakitovo. *Razkopki i Prouchvania* XXIX.

Simoska D. & Sanev V. 1975. Neolitska naselba Velulaka tumba kaj Bitola. *Macedoniae Acta Archaeologica* 1, 25–88.

Sirakova E. 2004. Rannoineolitno selishte Slatina Sofia v Sofia: vtori stroitelen horizont (predvaritelno saobshte- nie, chast II). *Arheologia*, 1–2, 15–24.

Stanev P. 1982. Stratigrafia i periodizatsia na neolitnite obekti i kulturi po baseyna na reka Yantra. *Godishnik na muzeite ot Severna Balgaria* VIII, 1–16.

Stanev P. 1995. Topografia i stratigrafia na neoliten kompleks Orlovets. *Izvestia na Istoricheski muzey-Veliko Tarnovo* O, 57–66.

Stanev P. 1997. Neolitna selishta mogila Samovodene – rezultati ot dosegashnite prouchvania. *Izvestia na Istoricheski muzey-Veliko Tarnovo* OII, 38–70.

Stanev P. 2002. Der neolitische Siedlungshügel Samovodene: Einige Ergebnisse der bisherigen Forschungen. In Lichardus-Itten M., Lichardus J. & Nikolov V. (eds.), *Beiträge zu jungsteinzeitlichen Forschungen in Bulgarien*. Bonn, Saarbücker Beiträge zur Altertumkunde 74, 411–436.

Stefanova T. 1996. A Comparative Analysis of Pottery from the 'Monochrome Early Neolithic Horizon' and 'Karanovo I Horizon' and the Problems of the Neolithization of Bulgaria. Proçilo XXIII, 15–38.

Stuiver M. & Becker B. 1993. High-precision decadal calibration of the rariocarbon time scale, AD 1950–6000 BC. *Radiocarbon* 35, 35–66.

Tao M. 2000. The Early Neo lithic Potery from Delnicite near Elešnica. In: S. Hiller, V. Nikolov (eds.), Karanovo III. Beiträge zum Neolithikum in Südosteuropa. Wien, 51–57.

Todorova H. 1981. Das Chronologiesystem von Karanovo im Licte der neuen Forschungsergebnisse in Bulgarien. *Slovenska Archeologia* XXIX, 1, 203–216.

Todorova H. 1989. Das Frühneolithikum Nordostbulgariens im Kontext des Ostbalkanischen Neolithikums. Tell Karanovo und das Balkan Neolithikum. Salzburg, 9–25.

Todorova H., Ivanov S.,Vasilev S., Hopf M., Quita H. & Kol G. 1975. Selishtna mogila pri Golyamo Delchevo. *Razkopki i Prouchvania* V.

Todorova H., Vasilev V., Yanushevich Z., Kovacheva M. & Valev P. 1983. Ovcharovo. *Razkopki i Prouchvania* IX.

Todorova H. & Vaysov I. 1993. *Novokamennata epoha v Balgaria*. Sofia.

Vajsova H. 1966. Stand der Jungsteinzeitforschung in Bulgarien. *Slovenska Archeologia* XIV 1, 15–44.

Vandova V. 1995. Tipologia na neolitnite kultovi masichki ot Yuzhna Balgaria. *Arheologia* 4, 1–7.

Vandova V. 2004. Neue Angaben über das frühe Neolithi- kum in dem Talkessel von Kjustendil (Vorläufiger Bericht) In Nikolov V. & Bačvarov K. (eds.), Von Domica bis Drama. Gedenkschrift für Jan Lichardus. Sofia, 25–32.

Vandova V. 2007. Sondazhni arheologicheski prouchvania na neolitnoto selishte v s. Bersin, obshtina Kyustendil. Arheologicheski otkritia i razkopki prez 2007g., 42–46.

LITHIC PRODUCTION OF THE EARLIEST NEOLITHIC ON THE TERRITORY OF BULGARIA

Ivan Gatsov[1,2] and Petranka Nedelcheva[1]

[1] New Bulgarian University; Department of Archaeology, 1618 Sofia, 21 Montevideo Str., Bulgaria; igatsov@yahoo.com

[2] National Institute of Archaeology and Museum, Bulgarian Academy of Sciences, 1000 Sofia, 2 Saborna Str., Bulgaria; pnedelcheva@nbu.bg

During the last decades some Monochrome Neolithic chipped assemblages in present day Bulgarian lands have been investigated and published (Tsonev 2000, 29–34; Stanev 2008). The most eminent lithic stone collection from Koprivets, NE Bulgaria is characterized by single and double platform cores as well as multidirectional ones in advanced and final stage of exploitation for flakes and irregular, relatively small size blades; flake and blade detaching was completed by hard and soft percussion. Typological tools are featured by retouched flakes, flakes and less blades with unretouched and retouched notches, flake end scrapers, single specimens of perforators, drills and burins, blades with partial irregular marginal retouches (Zlateva-Uzunova, MA Thesis, unpublished; Tsonev 2000, 29–34.)

The lithic collection from the Ohoden-Zaeshkoto workshop' located in the periphery of Ohoden-Valoga site (Zlateva-Uzunova 2008, 122) deserves special attention. The chipped stone artifacts come from 2 pits. Retouched tools are presented by flake end scrapers, notched tools, retouched flakes, perforators and drills.

The Monochrome Neolithic chipped stone assemblage from Ohoden-Valoga, Building 1 consists of flake/blade single, double and multidirectional cores; end scrapers on flakes and less on blades (Zlateva-Uzunova, in print, pl. VIII: 1, 3–5; pl. VIII: 7, 8); irregular blades with partial marginal retouches (Zlateva-Uzunova, in print, pl. XII: 9, 12, 15), notched tools (Zlateva-Uzunova, in print, pl. XIII: 6, 8, 9, 12); retouched flakes; truncations (Zlateva-Uzunova, in print, pl. XI: 15), flake and blade perforators and drills (Zlateva-Uzunova, in print, pl. X: 20, 21; pl. X: 14, 16, 17), single specimen of combine tools; splintered pieces, burins, trapezes (Zlateva-Uzunova, in print, pl. I–XV). The former are considered as an evidence of Mesolithic substratum and as an indicator for cultural transformation of the indigenous groups on the way to the Neolithisation under the impact on the first farmers (Ganetsovski 2004).

As far as the lithic artefacts from Orlovets and Plochite are concerned (Stanev 2008, 77) few blade specimens from Orlovets including 1 transversal burin, similar to the Eastern Balkan Epipaleolithic ones have been published (Stanev 2008, 78; Tsonev 2000, 33). The blades and blade typological tools from Plochite are specimens more or less irregular in shape and irregular scars on the dorsal patterns as well (Stanev 2008, obr. 66–69). The Orlovets and Koprivets lithic assemblages' display parallels with Starčevo – Criş complexes (Stanev 2008, 78, obr. 57–65; Tsonev 2000, 33) and Lepenski Vir I (Tsonev 2000, 33).

About the Monochrome lithic inventories some differences between them should be noticed. The unretouched blades and blade tools from Ohoden-Valoga, Ohoden – Zaeshkoto workshop (Zlateva-Uzunova, in print, pl. III: 7–9) Orlovets and Plocite settlements are different from the Koprivets ones. On the other hand all Monochrome assemblages mentioned above are different from Karanovo I phase in Northern or Eastern Thrace and from the Western Bulgarian ones (Stanev 2008, 78, obr. 57–65; Tsonev 2000, 33). The last suggestion is based on the lack of blades with high semi steep and steep retouches among the Monochrome lithic inventories and totally different technological features.

In the same time the presence of several trapezes among the lithic artefacts in the assemblage of Ochoden wouldn't be taken automatically into consideration as an undoubted evidence for existing of local Mesolithic substratum. It's not enough to see them as a certain evidence for existing indigenous Mesolithic bands. Still more to lead to these conclusions that these groups, for which there isn't clear evidence for their existing to be under the influence of the Earliest Neolithic comers. Up to now no evidences supporting the existence of some human groups from 9 mill. BC till the end of 8mill BC have been recorded. The appearance of microlithes is rather due to the functional variability, different range of activities of the given group, and even different level of excavation then some obligatory compulsory cultural division.

The other problem arises with the occurrence of single specimens of burins. Single items of burin on the snap have been found among the Karanovo I inventory from the eponymy tell.

Burins have been recorded in Orlovets and Plochite

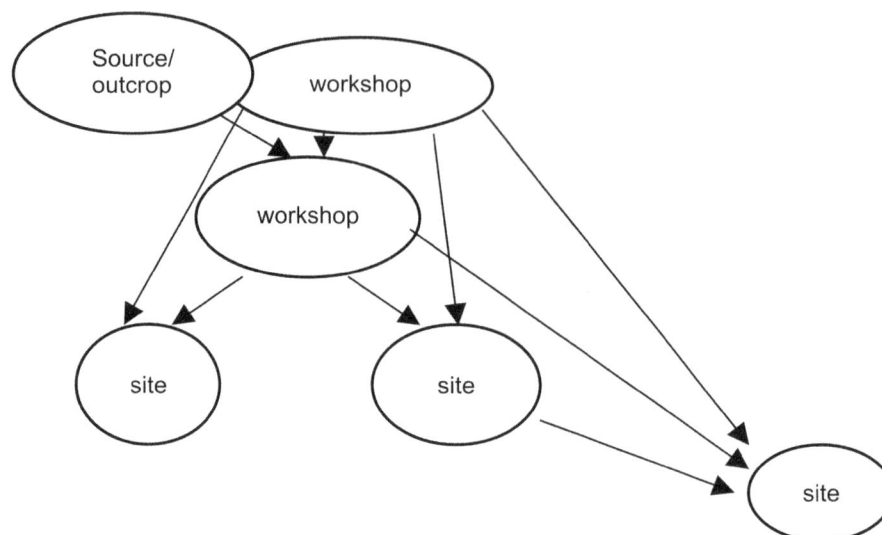

Fig. 1. Early Neolithic system of raw material procurement and supply.

sites lithic collections (Stanev 2008, obr. 59, obr. 65). Single items of burins have been noticed among the lithic artifacts from the Early Neolithic tell Samovodene, Northern Central Bulgaria (Stanev 2002, obr. 78).

The question is whether or not this is an evidence of some local traditions and/or functional requirement. Burins come from the Aegean EN settlement such as Ulucak Höyük (Altan Çilingiroğlu & Çiler Çilingiroğlu 2009, unpublished; we would like to express my gratitude to A. Çilingiroğlu and Ç. Çilingiroğlu for their help).

The appearance of burins related to the Bulgarian Monochrome and Early Neolithic-phase Karanovo I has to be explained but in this stage of research it's realistic to wait for more evidence.

The other question is linked with the appearance of blades, which morphometrical characteristics closer to the Chalcolithic ones (Zlateva-Uzunova, in print, pl. XI: 4, 19; XII:15, 17). But we don't know much about the Monochrome technology and this assumption should be confirmed or rejected after acquiring more material from different sites.

The other phenomenon is the appearance of very characteristic macroblade technology. The former is connected with the white painted, dark painted and dark polished pottery Early Neolithic assemblages dated to end of 7 mill. BC till the middle of 6mill. BC in Southern Bulgaria, Sofia and Pernik fields (Gatsov 2009).

The lithic inventories reflected well developed system of supply, blade production, labor division, distribution and exchange. The high level of the craft specialization and the functioning of long distance exchange or supply (e.g. of blades with high retouches in Hoça Çeşme II) supposed that diversity of activities is to be expected. It's all suppose of appearance of define level of production and social dynamics in respect of settlements within the tell space and those which existed beyond those limits. The stone production was based on exploitation of high quality yellow, yellow brown to reddish flint acquired of some distance to the settlements (Fig. 1).

The earliest Neolithic Karanovo I and II phases of Northern/Upper Thrace are characterized mostly by the third type of Chapman's pioneer communities long term (multilayer) limited earth mounds (Chapman 2008, 68–80). The macroblade production consisted of several episodes which took places off the sites. The core preparation and reduction has been completed in the workshops probably closed to the extraction places or points and a clear distinguishing between tell space lithic activities and those from the external area can be detected. This was one well organized and long lasting process, which included a raw material acquisition, functioning of workshops for blade manufacturing and transportation of ready made products to the settlements during the Early Neolithic period, phases Karanovo I and II existed. The settlements connected with this macroblade technology were the last point where blades have been transported and used. As a rule the discard of debitage products is more or less closed to zero. The lithic assemblages display the same attributes connected with the same taphonomic process. The former produced assemblages similar from the standpoints of their contents: raw material used, technological features, tool morphology, social meaning.

In this model the place for specimens different from blade retouched tools and an unretouched blade is very small. The assemblages investigated are characterized by very high frequency of modified blades by high semi steep and steep retouches and unmodified ones, lack of cores, cortical and crested specimens, debris and flakes. The operation chain approach doesn't give an overall picture of divergences and likenesses among the groups during the Early Neolithic painted horizon. This approach is orientated rather to particular elements than to the whole operation sequence (Fig. 2).

The fact that standardized blades with or without retouch done on the same raw material varieties were found at all settlements investigated proves this assertion. This type of macroblade production was organized and passed to the regional level – e.g. at the level of inter settlements organi-

Fine-grained material-flint

↓

Concretions, nodules

↓

Full decortication

↓

Preparation techniques – g.e. cresting

↓

Mostly indirect/soft percussion

↓

Blades

end-scrapers   retouched blades   truncations   perforators and drills

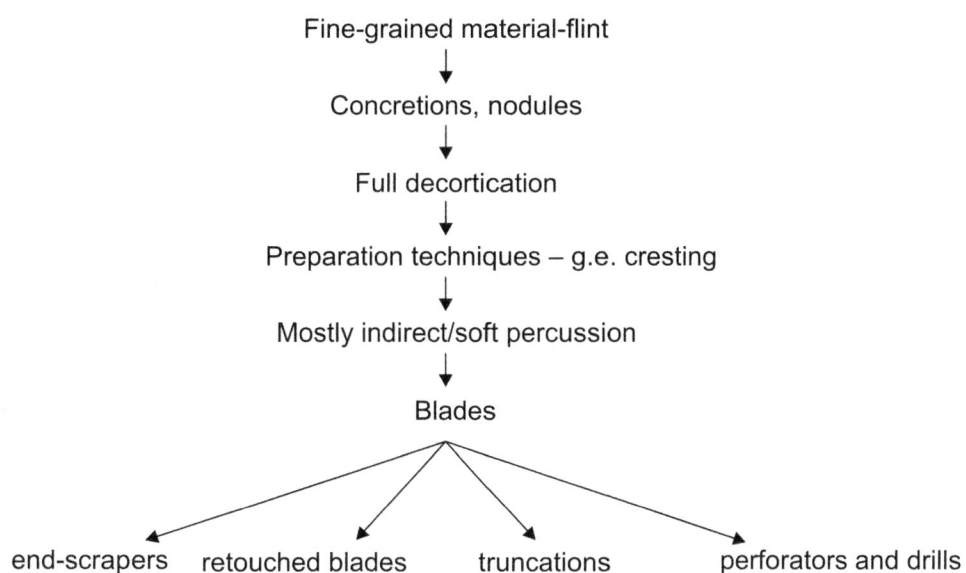

Fig. 2.   Main features of the Early Neolithic stone assemblages.

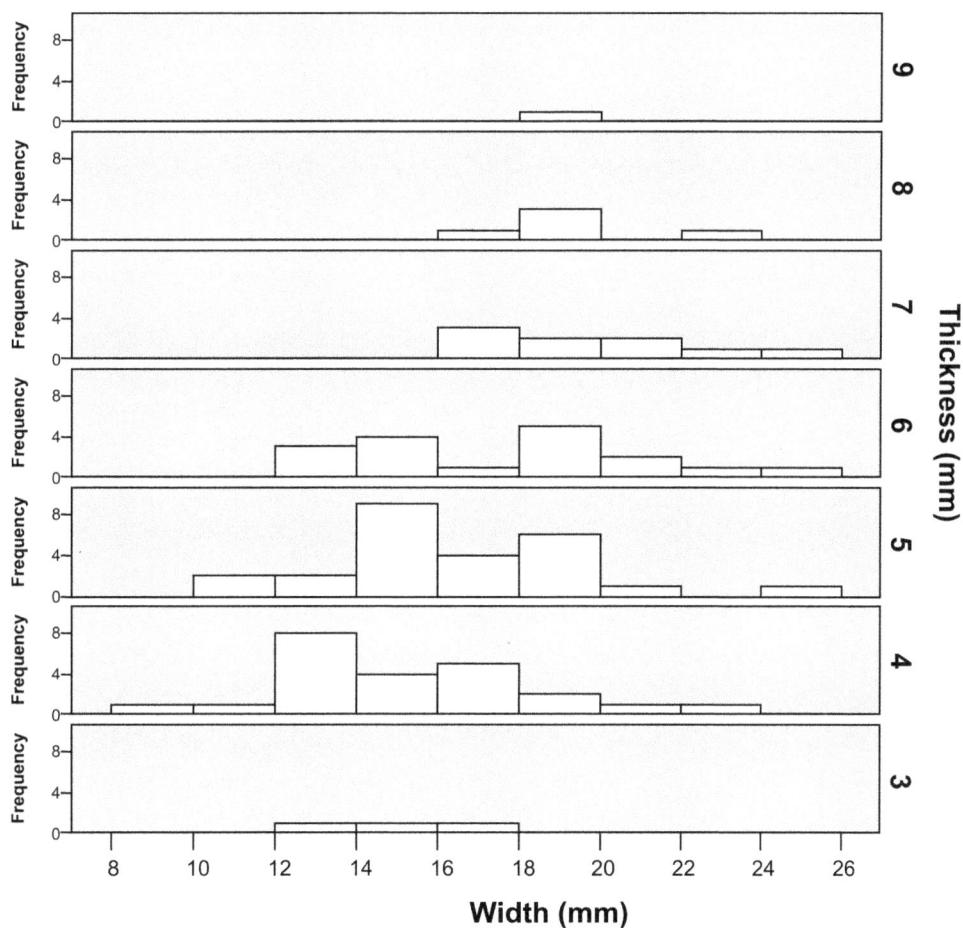

Fig. 3.   Azmak – Early Neolithic Layer. Building levels I–V. Correlation of thickness and width of highly retouched blades.

47

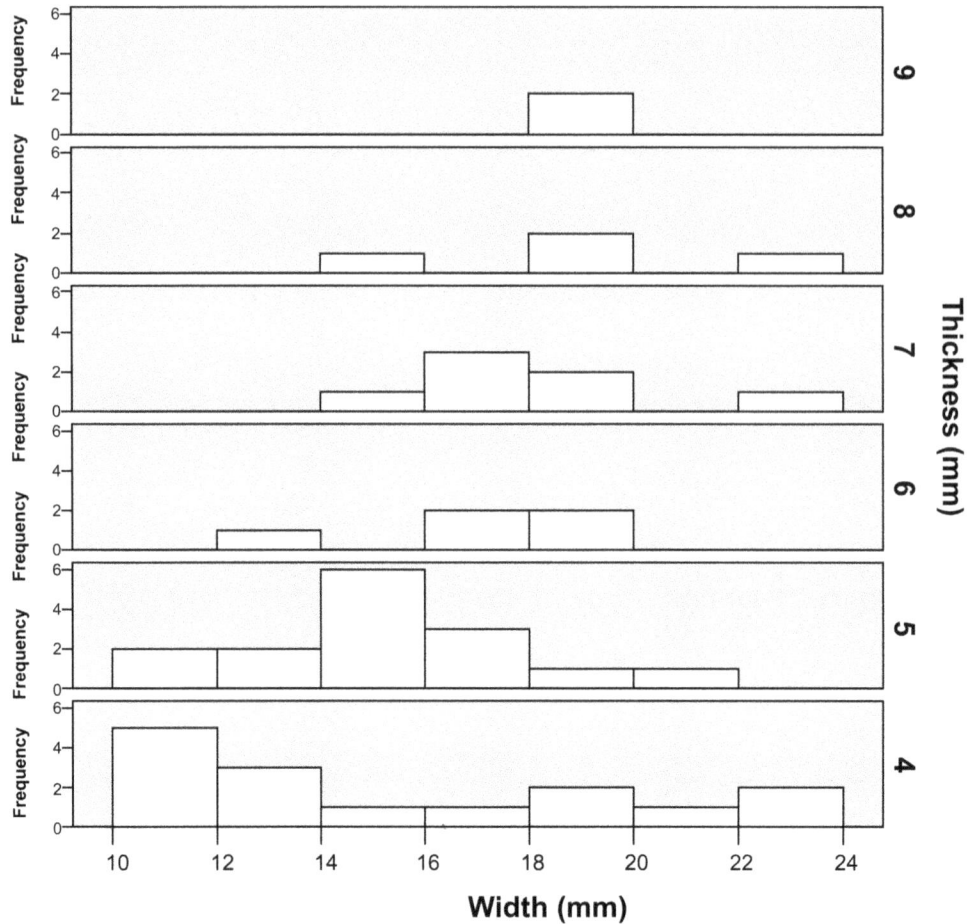

Fig. 4.   Karanovo – phases I and II. The correlation of thickness and width of highly retouched blades.

zation and communication. A priori this model excludes individual household activities linked with blade core knapping process. The production conception and corresponding logistic and the needed skills for that high level standardized blade production were too high to be according to the possibilities of household lithic production. The high level of correlation between thickness and width of high retouched blades and unretouched ones from Azmak and Karanovo phases I and II supports this assertion (Figs 7–10).

About the presented graphs a clear similarity can be recorded among them. The width mean values of blades with high semi steep and steep retouches are lower in respect to the unretouched ones. The lowest value of thickness of blades with high semi steep and steep retouches is 4 mm This way the already made observation done by G. Goşkunsu that the high steep and semi steep retouches were used in order to narrawing the blank in some extent and they can be considered "a kind of e-sharpening".

From the above presented graphs a firm established connection between the blade's mean value of width and thickness could be noticed. The thickness lower value corresponds to lower mean values of width. As far as the unretouched blade specimens of Azmak – Early Neolithic layer is concerned the mean values of thickness fall between 2–3 mm.

It is not by chance that any differences in raw material

base, lithic technology and tool morphology between both phases are observable. The technological and typological pattern exchange analysis does not express any differences among the assemblages from the settlements investigated. Unfortunately the spatial analysis is impossible to be applied in most of the cases because of lack of patterns.

On the other hand the importance and influence of the Monochrome lithic assemblages to the formation of the white painted pottery, dark painted pottery and dark polished ones lithic assemblages are zero. The Monochrome lithic assemblages are totally different in respect of those inventories. The differences could be detected in the raw material base, stone technology and tool morphology.

Due to fact that the Early Neolithic main source areas are still not exactly defined, there should be at least two options. The first one is connected with the possible model of long distance high quality flint import from the NE Bulgarian territory to the settlements investigated. As an absolute distance the long system of supply is considered as itinerary exceeding 180–200 km straight line; following the modern roads this distance is more than 250 km.

The other option is linked with shorter system distance of supply which took place in the area of Northern Thrace. In this case the nearest flint sources in other potential zones: the region of Eastern Rodophes, St. Ilia hills or Sredna Gora Mountains is inside the range of ca 100–150 km.

local low quality raw material

↓

small concretion

↓

partial decortication

↓

partial preparation

↓

direct – soft and hard percussion

small irregularar blades   Flakes

↓

end scraper, retouched flakes

retouched blades

perforators and drills

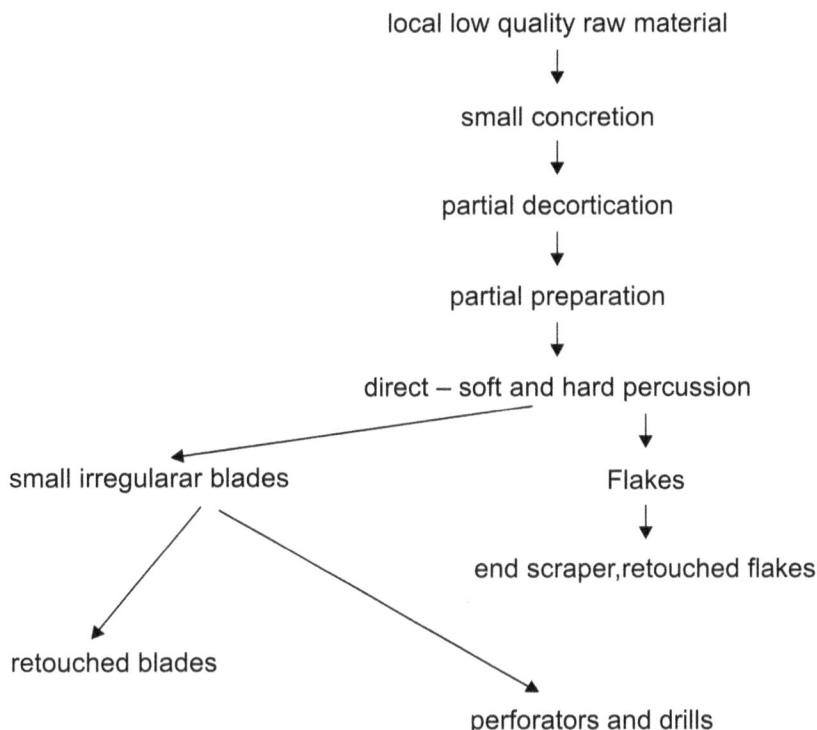

Fig. 5. Main features of the Middle and Late Neolithic assemblages.

Concerning the raw material supply one thing is sure – specialized physics-chemical analysis on the geological samples from the relevant areas and outcrops haven't been undertaken. Any of the potential zones such as the Eastern Rhodope Mountains, the area the Sredna Gora Mountains and Dobrudzha region in NE Bulgaria as well couldn't be excluded. In this situation to accept or reject one of these hypothesizes one should wait for the final results and without these results the question is still open.

Here, one other phenomenon arises between Early (phases Karanovo I and II) and Middle and Late Neolithic periods connected with abrupt alterations in the lithic assemblages after 5550–5500 BC in Northern/Upper Thrace and SW Bulgarian territory. These changes are clearly expressed in the choice of raw material, technological features, type distribution, and artefact dimensions in the assemblages processed (Fig. 11). The changes can be detected in intra-site distribution of lithics in term of raw material provenance and typological composition. All net of activities connected with stone technology took place on spot, in the settlement area.

The lithic assemblages from the Middle and Late Neolithic periods are featured by flake based industry – irregular multidirectional or cores with change orientation, most of them core remnant only, flake and fewer blades retouched tools with smaller dimensions (Fig. 5).

The Early Neolithic off site system of procurement was substituted with routine works for gathering local raw material and the entire production chain/cycle was carried out in frame of the family groups in the given settlements. This

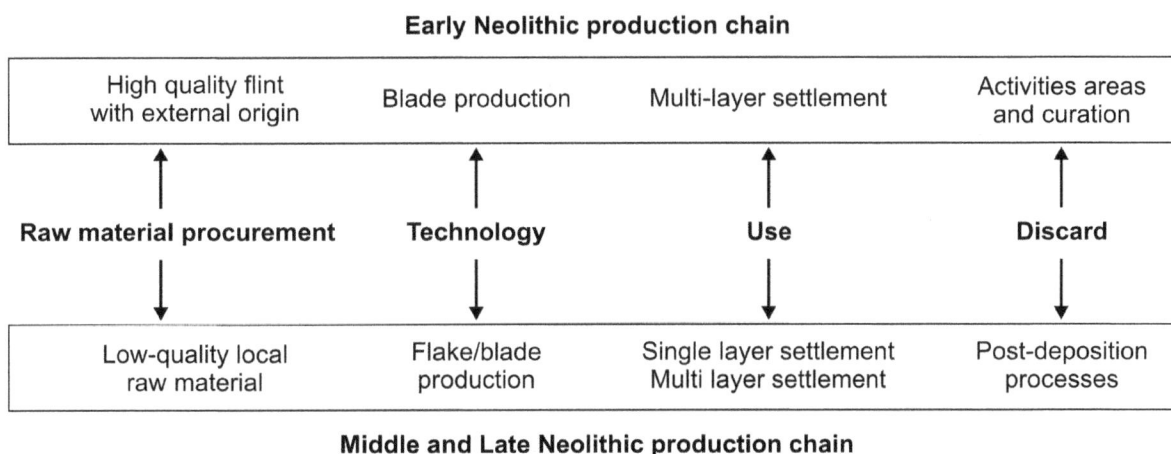

Early Neolithic production chain

High quality flint with external origin	Blade production	Multi-layer settlement	Activities areas and curation
Raw material procurement	**Technology**	**Use**	**Discard**
Low-quality local raw material	Flake/blade production	Single layer settlement Multi layer settlement	Post-deposition processes

Middle and Late Neolithic production chain

Fig. 6. Early, Middle and Late Neolithic production chain.

49

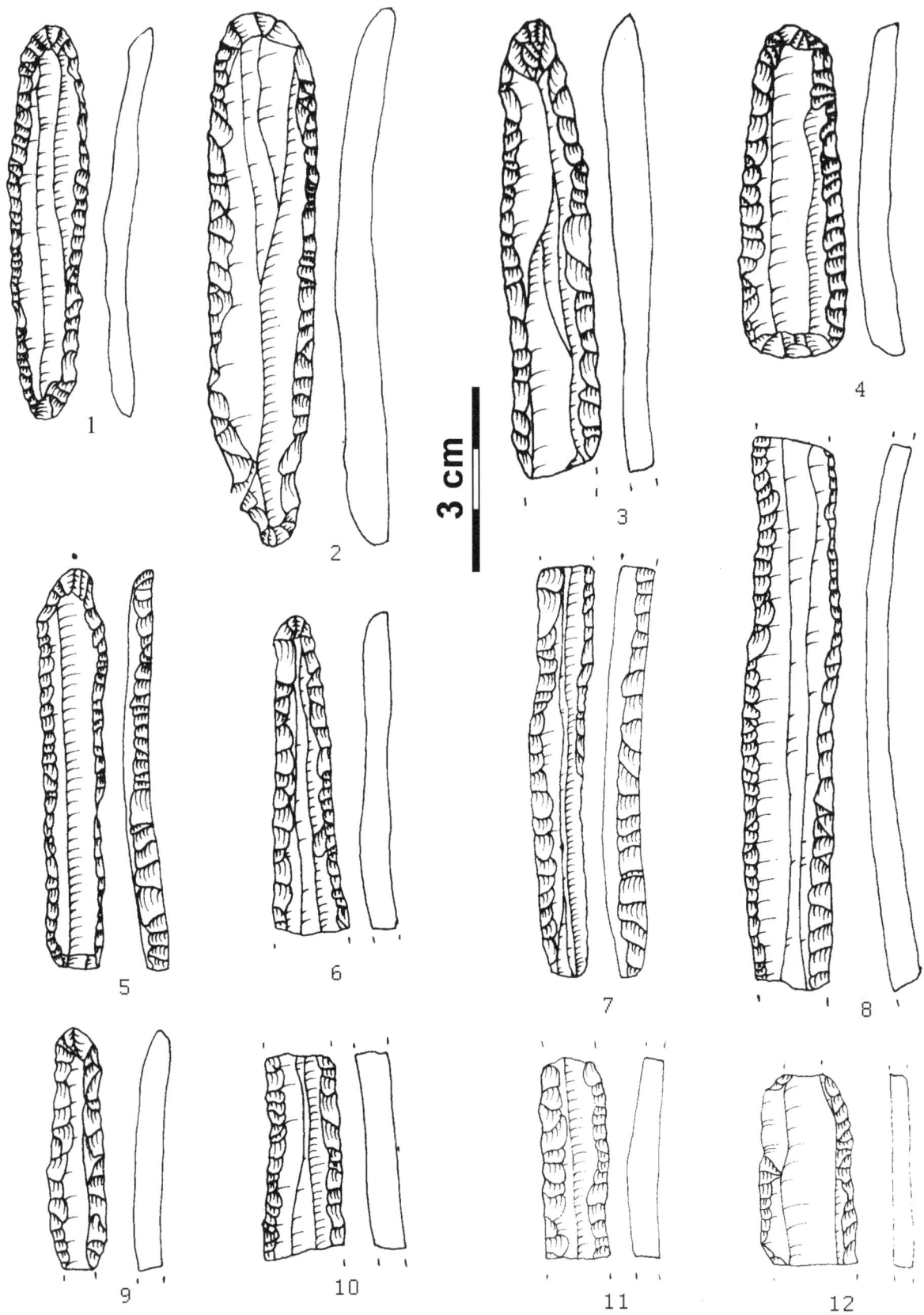

Fig. 7. Blades with high retouch. Early Neolithic. Azmak.

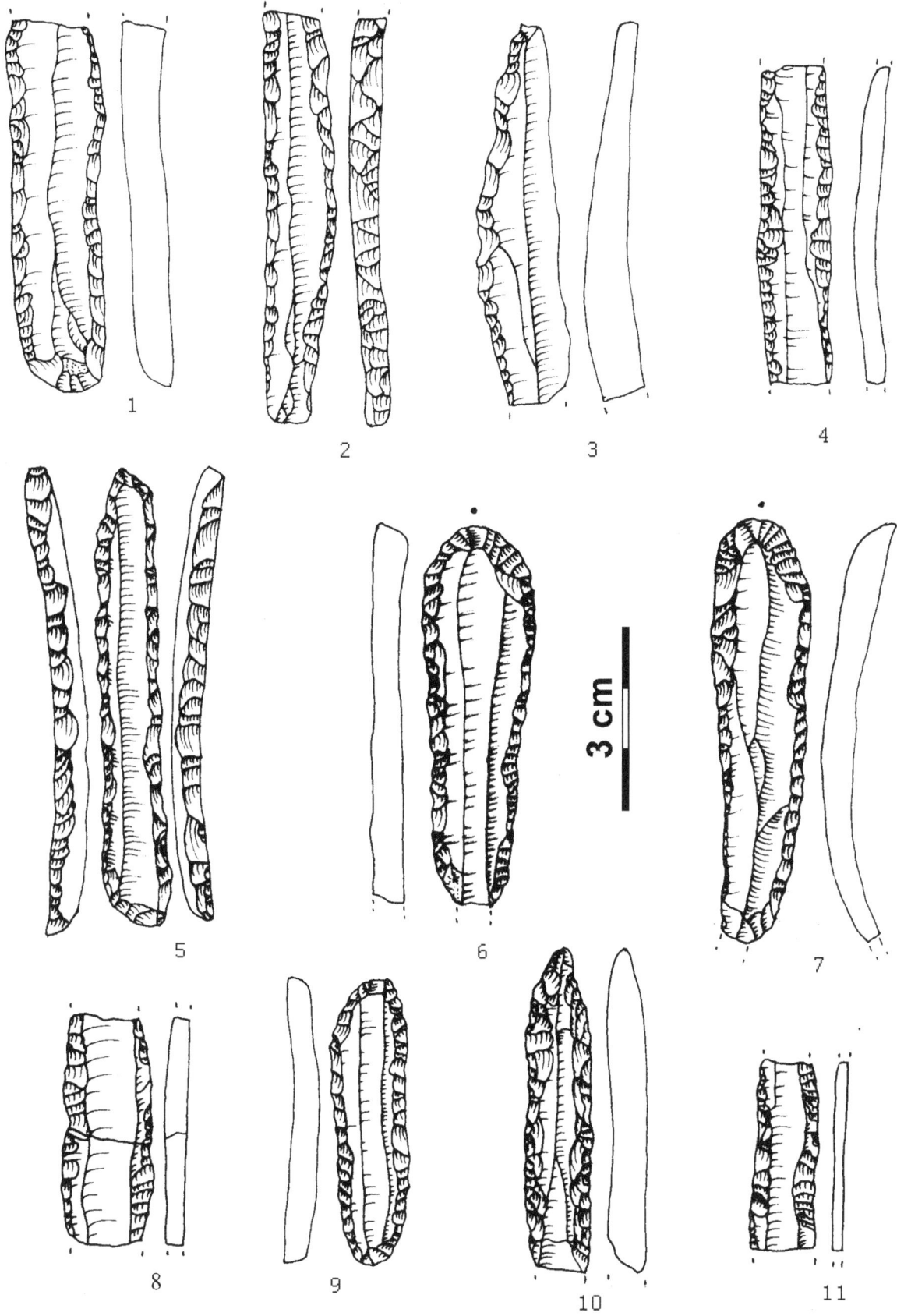

Fig. 8. Blades with high retouch. Early Neolithic. Karanovo 1–4; Hoça Çeşme 5–11.

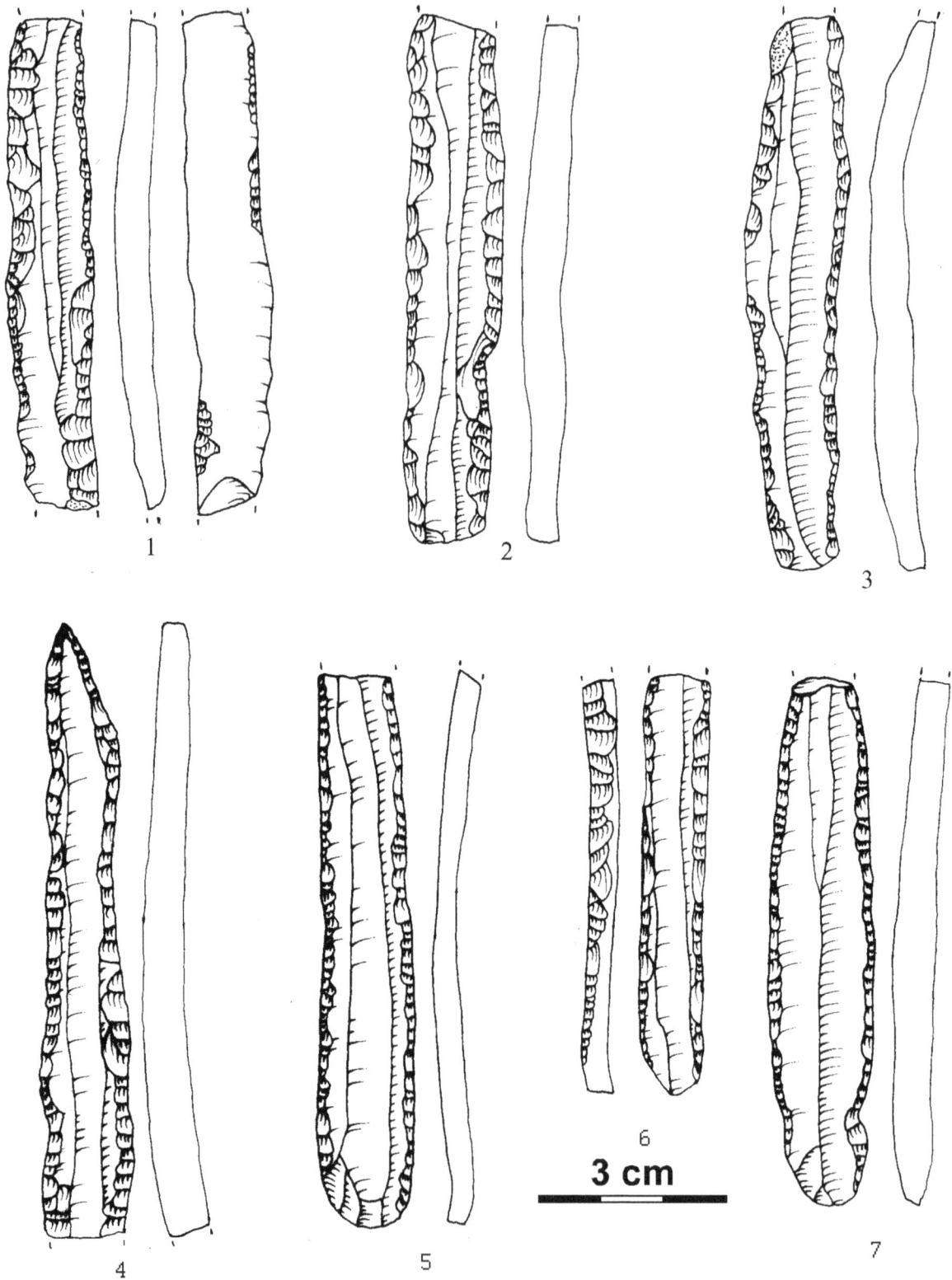

Fig. 9.   Blades with high retouch. Early Neolithic. Karanovo 1–3; Galabnik 4–7.

model reflected a sophisticated system connected with workshops functioning for blade and macroblade production indented for one broad demand (Fig. 6).

During the Middle and Late Neolithic periods the production chain or cycle is characterized by household production base on low and medium quality local raw material varieties. Raw material varieties with external origin are

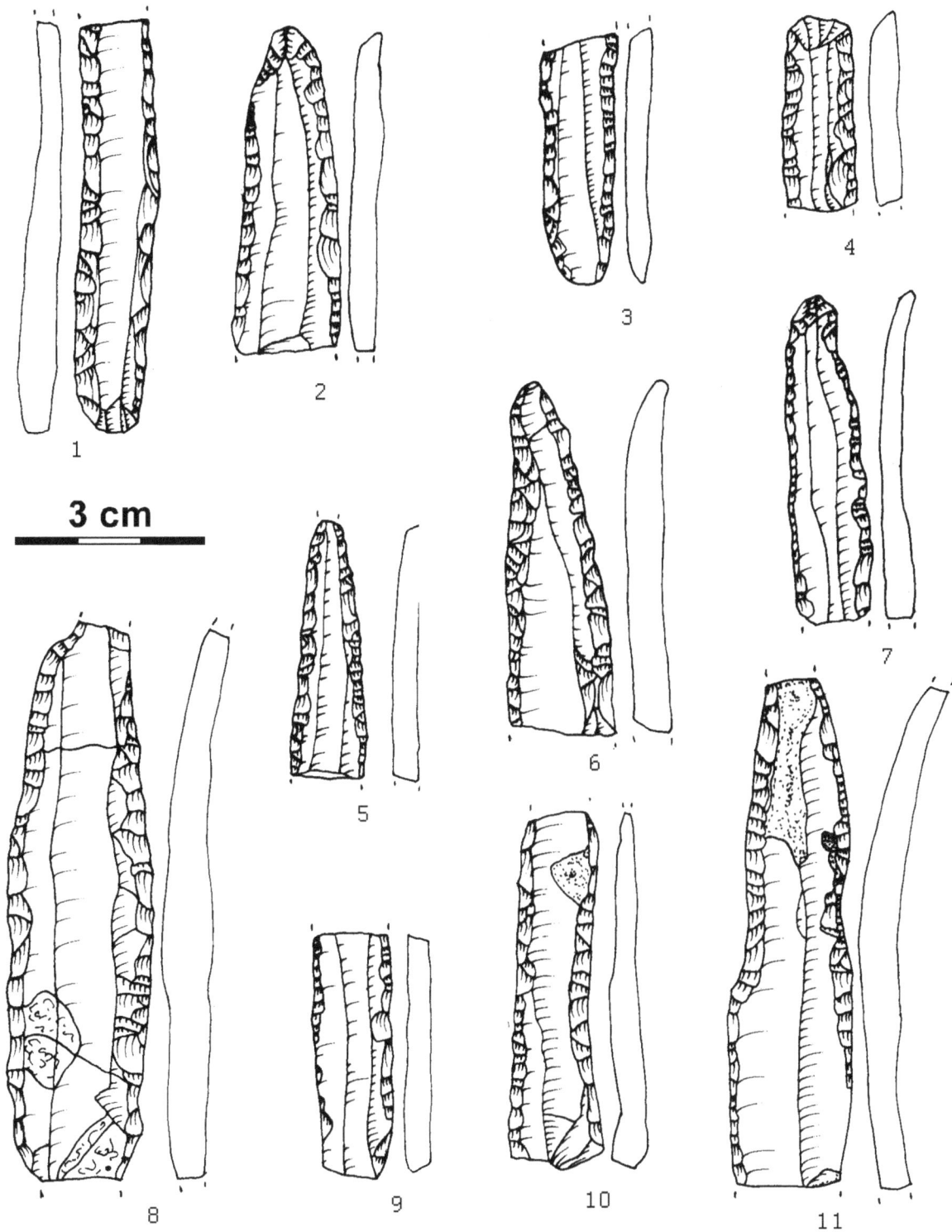

3 cm

Fig. 10. Blades with high retouch. Early Neolithic. Galabnik 1–3; Chavdar 4–11.

practically missing and they were replaced by local ones with low and medium level of knapping features. The alteration in the lithic technology reflects detectable changes of the traditional Early Neolithic framework.

Conclusion

As a whole the main problem concerning the Monochrome Neolithic chipped stone assemblages in present day Bulgarian lands is linked with the weak comparative base. Most of the the settlements related to the Monochrome Neolithic are featured by small sizes of the excavated parts. Lithic finds from different type and different level of archaeological research have been compared and some corresponding conclusions were formulated. On the base of single lithic artifacts appearance evidences for common traits or parallels have been distinguished. This approach makes

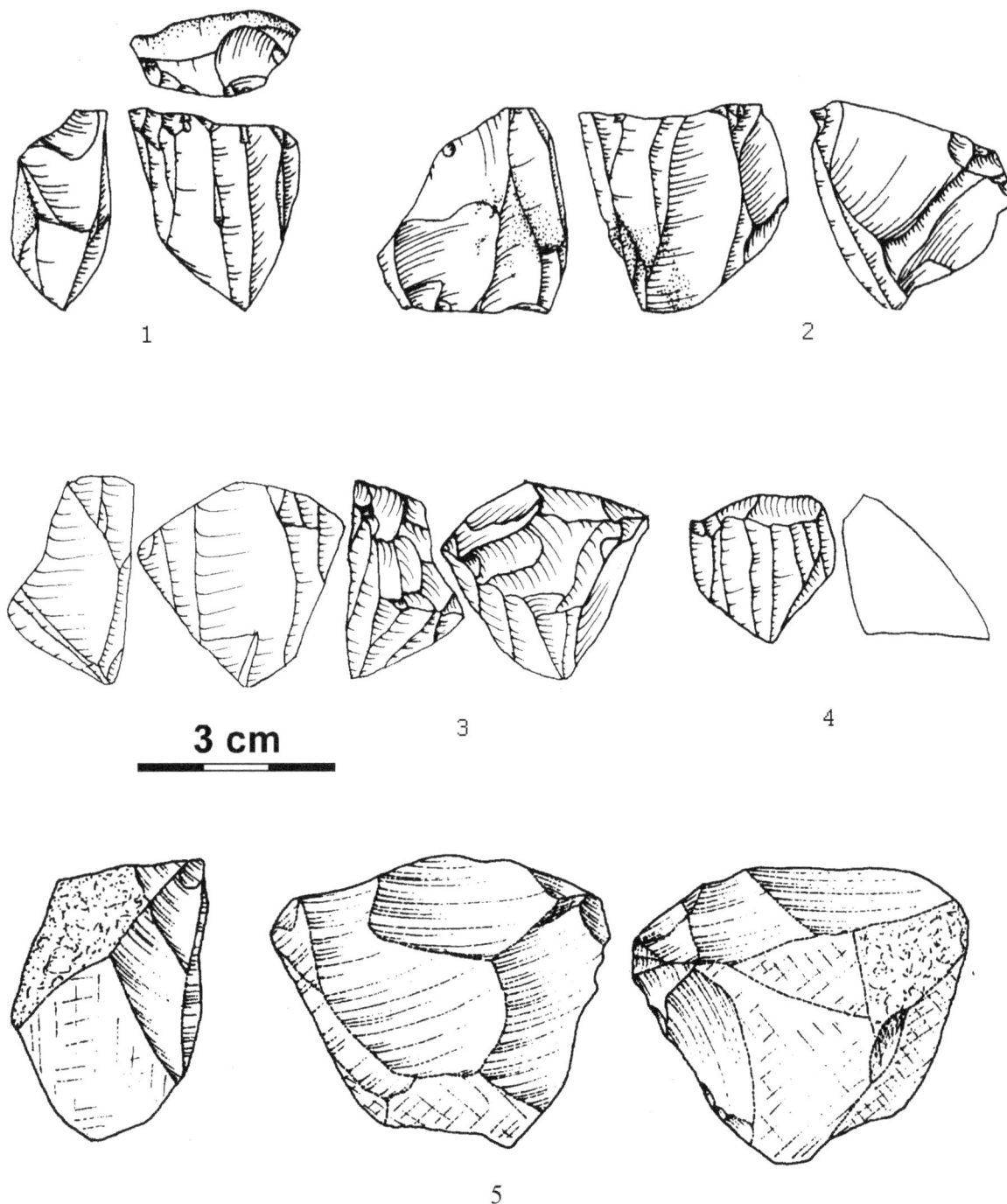

Fig. 11. Flake cores. Late Neolithic. Karanovo 1, 2; Topolnitsa 3, 4; Balgarchevo 5

the picture additionally unclear. In some cases it is not very clear what kind of basic distinguishing criteria by the different scholars have been taken into consideration. It should be pointed out the lack of absolute dates from the key site such as Koprivets. At this stage of research it should be supposed that the differences between the Monochrome and first phase of Karanovo I culture lithic inventories in highest degree are due to the lack of continuity among them. These differences reflect different social structures and subsistence modes employed. As a consequence the different

modes reflect differences in the chosen means of exploiting similar environments, rather than being adjustments to different environmental resources. The cultural changes were more important than the subsistence model in setting features determining the Neolithic cultures in the territory under study.

The cultural differences which appeared around 5500/5450 BC can be sought among the Early Neolithic versus Middle and Late periods comparing all possible elements of the lithic assemblages operation chain. The changes in the lithic technology are seen as the consequence of some new cultural and social events. It's very likely that put together these changes had more weight in the cultural development than the alteration in the environmental conditions. The paleobotanical research doesn't reveal any important differences in the paleo surrounding and the resource exploitation among the Early Neolithic period and the Middle and Late ones (see E. Marinova'part).

If one assumes a larger concentration of population in some Early Neolithic villages especially in Northern Thrace then a pattern emerges of larger base sites. It's very likely that from these sites small groups go out in order to secure for raw material supply from defined area or areas, as opposed to the family groups functioning in and around the tell. These groups were able to complete different tasks organizing the whole net of activities covering one broad spectrum and especially to provide for the settlements the standardized blades.

From lithic perspective the appearance of this technology was a result of combination of common cultural characteristics such as social organization, technological tradition, raw material system of procurement, rituals. It's very likely the roots of this technology were with Anatolian origin. But probably lithic assemblages with the same technological and typological traits shouldn't be found there. It should be supposed the bearers of this technology brought from Anatolia the idea and the necessarily and relevant skills. Here, on spot, using the high quality flint outcrops they materialized their mental and physical abilities, whose final product is this characteristic technology which we are revealing today. Hence, it should be considered this macro technology as a chronological and cultural marker for the area and period mentioned above.

Contrary to the Early Neolithic lithic production schema the Middle and Late Neolithic chipped stone assemblages reflect number of tell activities which took place in the topographic limits of the settlements'. In the Middle and Late Neolithic settlements it's impossible to make difference between activities from the tell space and those from the external area. The shifting from macro blade technology towards flake/blade production goes with number of changes in lithic production, raw material use and labor organization detectible in the research periods. In this connection it is impossible to link the appearance of the macro technology to the bearers of the Monochrome Neolithic.

Concerning the Monochrome lithic collection from Koprivets, Northeastern Bulgaria (Popov 1996) and the material from Hoça Çeşme – phases IV the existence of some kind of contacts between the delta of the Maritsa (Meriç) River and NE Bulgarian lands should be supposed (Gatsov 2006, 153–156).

The base for this assumption is some similarities in stone technology between both Monochrome sites. Thus an additional and possible road beside Struma and Vardar valleys for the first spreading of Neolithic comers from the South to the North might have been realized via the valleys of the Maritsa, Tundzha, Sazliyka, through Stara Planina Mountain and Russenski Lom at the end of 7th mill. BC (Gatsov 2009).

The Maritsa/Meriç River delta' might be one of the points from where the first Neolithic groups arriving from Central Anatolia could have been entered in the Balkan Peninsula. These groups might come from Anatolia – from Konya plain via Plato? (if they mixed the road – Dr. J. Roodenberg), or via Aegean Sea and Aegean coast. (Çilingiroğlu & Abay 2005). Thus, one additional route of movement of the first Neolithic comers should be taken into consideration.

REFERENCES

Chapman J. 2008. Meet the ancestors: settlement histories in the Neolithic. In Bailey D., Whittle A. & Hofmann D. (eds.), *Living Well Together*. Oxbow books. Oxford, 68–80.

Çilingiroğlu A. & Abay E. 2005. Ulucak Höyük excavations: new results. *Mediterranean Archaeology and Archaeometry* 5, No 3 Special Issue, 5–21.

Çilingiroğlu A. & Çilingiroğlu C. (unpublished). Towards Understanding the Early Farming Communities of Central Western Anatolia: Contribution of Ulucak. In Özdoğan M. & Başgelen N.(eds.), *The Neolithic in Turkey: new excavations and new developments*. Istanbul, Arkeoloji ve Sanat Yayýnlarý.

Gatsov I. 2006. The state of research into the problem of Pleistocene – Holocene transition in the present area of Bulgaria. In Gatsov I. & Schwarzberg H.(eds.) *Marmara-Black sea: present stage of the research of the Early Neolithic*. Schriften des Zentrums für Archäologie und Kulturgeschichte des Schwarzmeerraumes 5. Beier & Beran, 153–156.

Gatsov I. 2009. Prehistoric Chipped Stone Assemblages from Eastern Thrace and the South Marmara Region 7th–5th mill. B.C., *BAR International Series* 1904.

Leshtakov K., Todorova N., Petrova V., Zlateva-Uzunova R., Özbek O., Popova Ts., Spassov N. & Iliev N. 2007. Preliminary report on the salvage archaeological excavations at the Early Neolithic site Yabalkovo in the Maritsa valley, 2000–2005 field seasons. *Anatolica* XXXIII, 185–234.

Popov V. 1996. Periodizatsia i hronologia na neolitnite i halkolitnite kulturi ot porechieto na r. Rusenski Lom. Ruse.

Tsonev Ts. 2000. Knapping technology vs. pattern of raw material supply. In Nikolova L. (ed.), Technology, style and society. Contributions to innovations between the Alps and the Black Sea in Prehistory. *BAR, International Series* 854, 29–34.

Ganetsovski G. 2004. Novi svedenia za rannia neolit v Severozapadba Balgaria. *Godishnik na Departament Arheologia, Nov Balgarski Universitet* 6, 22–34.

Stanev P. 2002. *Samovodene. Neolitna selishta mogila*. Veliko Tarnovo.

Stanev P. 2008. *Orlovets. Neoliten kompleks*.Veliko Tarnovo.

Zlateva-Uzunova R. (MA thesis, unpublished). Rannoholocenski kremachni amsambli ot porechieto na Risenski Lom.

Zlateva-Uzunova R. 2008. Neolitni artefakti ot kremachno nahodishte i rabotilnitsa Ohoden-Zaeshkoto, Vrachansko. In Gurova M. (ed.), *Praistoricheski Prouchvania v Balgaria: novite predizvikatelstva*. Natsionalen Arheologicheski Institut s Muzey, Istoricheski muzey-Peshtera, 120–125.

Zlateva-Uzunova R. (in print). Early Neolithic Stone Assemblages from Ohoden-Valoga Site, Building No 1, pl. I–XV.

FLINT RAW MATERIALS IN BULGARIA

Chavdar Nachev

Musem for Earth and People, 1421 Sofia, Bulgaria; chnachev@hotmail.com

The flint has a widely spread in Bulgaria in different geographic and tectonic zones. The significant deposits are located in the Moesian Platform and adjustment parts of Balkan Alpine Orogen (Fig. 1). In the Phanerozoic in Bulgaria, siliceous concretions are found in 16 stratigraphic levels. According to geological data the following main stratigraphic levels important for Prehistory are distinguished: Upper Jurassic (Oxfordian); Low Cretaceous (Aptian); Upper Cretaceous (Campanian and Maastrichtian). Geographic and stratigraphic distribution of the three main type's flint in Bulgaria is as follow.

Siliceous concretions in Upper Jurassic limestones from NW Bulgaria – Stara Planina flint

The silica concretions are hosted in grey micrite limestones. The flint-rich level have stratigraphic range from Oxfordian to Early Kimmeridgian. The shape of concretions is approximately ellipsoidal, with pale grey color. The size of concretions varied from 1 to 15 cm, mainly 8–10 cm. Crust is pale yellowish from 0.2 to 1 cm thickness. The grey flint formed characteristic yellow patina in water (alluvial and karst) conditions. The fracture is smooth (in grey varieties) – conchoidal in separate parts of specimens. This flint has a many tectonic cracks in two or three directions. The mineral composition is chalcedony, quartzine, quartz, and calcite. Biodetritus is from Foraminifera and Spongia (Porifera). The all biocomponents are silicified.

The Upper Jurassic limestones are widespread and characteristic topography element in the West Stara Planina mountain. This fact caused abundance of small flint deposits in the whole region. In this area primary deposits and secondary (placer) deposits are described – result from their weathering. The secondary deposits are divided to the following genetic types – eluvial, colluvial (slope embankments), proluvial, alluvial (river) fnd karsts deposits. The Upper Jurassic flint-rich limestones formed two stripes of outcrops one from Granitovo to Yanovets village and second from Salash to Dolni Lom village. Due to the small size and tectonic cracks in concretions artifacts have small dimensions. The Stara Planina flint is used as source during Paleolithe.

Siliceous concretions in Low Cretaceous limestones from NE Bulgaria – Luda Gora flint (Dobrogea flint, Razgrad flint)

The silica concretions are hosted in Early Cretaceous (Aptian) micrite limestones with pale grey color. The color of concretions is predominantly pale brawn or beige, very rare grey. Very often shows concentric-zonal structure (pale brawn, reddish and grey stripes). The size is from 1 to 50 cm, mainly 5–15 cm, very rarely (30–50 cm). The shape is approximately ellipsoidal, rarely rod-like. Distinctive feature is white silica-carbonate crust, irregular (6–12 mm) thick, in separate specimens with onion weathering. The intercalations are small with little size (1–5 mm), round, pale cream color. The fracture is smooth (in brawn and beige varieties) – conchoidal or cone in separate parts of specimens. The grey varieties show rough fracture. Mineral composition is micro and crypto grain chalcedony, moganite, quartz. Biocomponents are many spiculae and little biodetritus from Foraminifera and Radiolaria. The all biocomponents are silicified. On the Aptian flint-rich limestones different types of flint placer deposits are formed. The main type of them is eluvium-proluvium deposits, where angular flint pieces are hosted in soft sandy-carbonated masses. Such examples are Kriva Reka, Tetovo, Chukata locality etc. Another placer deposits in this region are paleoalluvial type like Drianovets locality etc. The Aptian flint has geographic distribution only in North East Bulgaria between Rouse, Doulovo, Dobrich, Novy Pazar and Razgrad. Distribution of outcrops well coincided with Luda Gora Region, but don't touch Dobrogea Region. Diagnostic features are thick crust (6–12 mm), approximately ellipsoidal shape, even outer surface and concentric-zonal structures. The highest quality of Luda Gora flint (Dobrogea flint, Razgrad flint) is a result from coinciding of many factors: suitable primary sedimentary and early diagenetic conditions; none folded hosted rocks; permanent uplifting of NE Bulgaria (from Upper Cretaceous till now) and as a result good exposures of flint-bearing rocks; origin of big secondary (placer) deposits predominantly eluvial and proluvial type. Such coinciding of factors is not realized during geological history in other parts of this area. For this reason the Luda Gora flint is

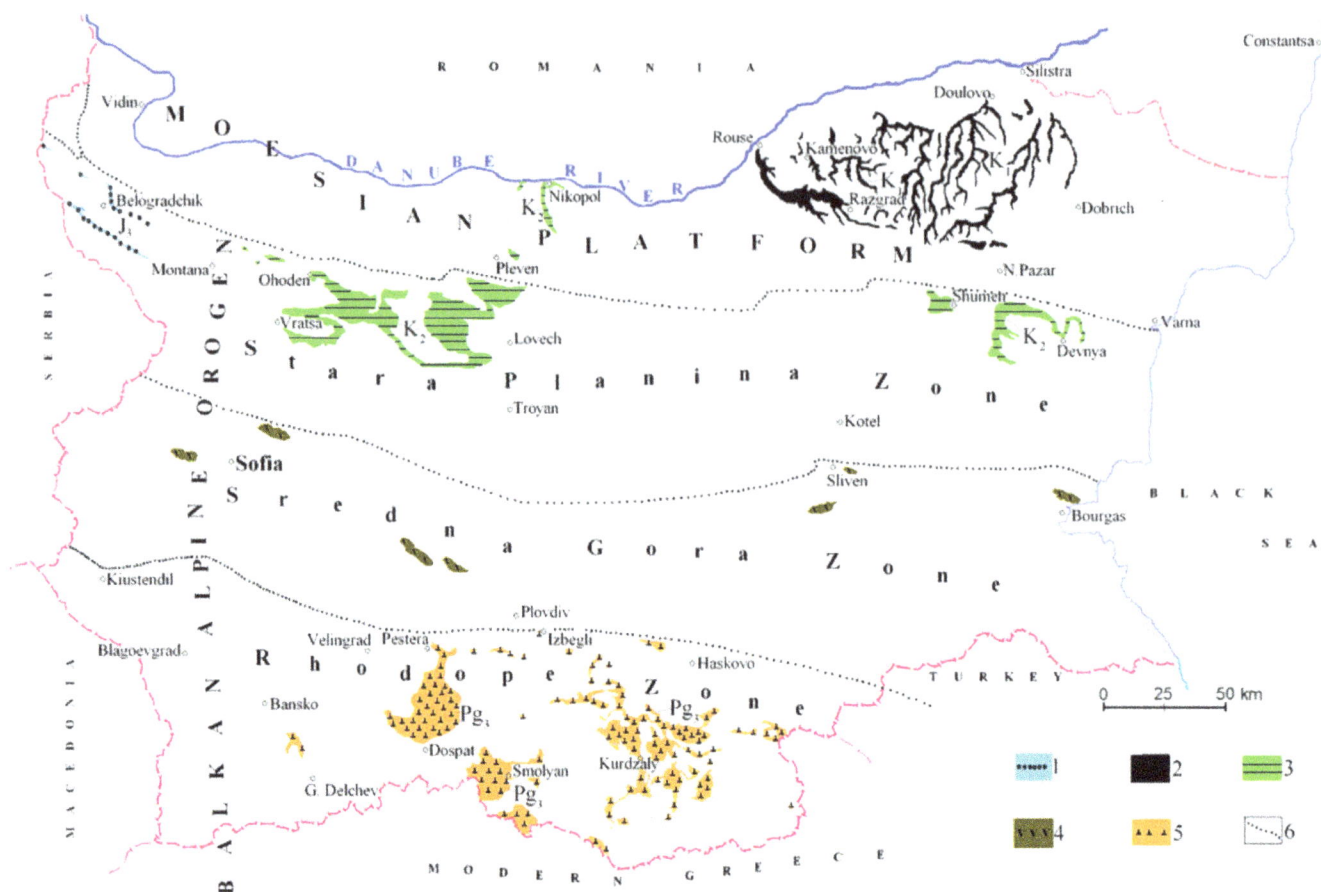

Fig. 1. Geological map of the main types flint-contain rocks in Bulgaria (Nachev, 2009): 1 – Upper Jurassic limestones (Oxfordian age) with siliceous concretions (J_3^{ox}) – Hemus flint; 2 – Low Cretaceous limestones (Aptian age) with siliceous concretions (K_1^a) – Luda Gora flint (Dobrogea flint); 3 – Upper Cretaceous chalk and chalk-like limestones (Campanian and Maastrichtian ages) with siliceous concretions (K_2^{cp-m}) – Moesia flint; 4 – Chalcedony veins in Upper Cretaceous volcanogenous rocks (Coniacian, Santonian and Campanian ages) in Sredna Gora Zone (K_2^{Cn-Cp}) – Sredna Gora atypical flint; 5 – Chalcedony veins in Oligocene volcanogenous rocks in Rhodope Zone (Pg_3) – Rhodope atypical flint; 6 – boundary between tectonic zones and structures.

the only one source for high quality flint in Ukraine, Balkans and West Asia Minor. Other parts of these territories are in permanent insufficiency of high quality flint raw materials. Only the Luda Gora flint concretions are suitable. for obtaining of long flint blades. This fact is very useful for provenance of flint artifacts.

Siliceous concretions in Upper Cretaceous limestones from Moesian Platform and adjustment parts of Balkan Alpine Orogen Moesian flint

The silica concretions are hosted in Upper Cretaceous (Santonian, Campanian) chalk, chalk-like limestones and fine grained biomorphic limestones (Maastrichtian). By such way they formed a few stratigraphic levels, but very rich of flint is Upper Campanian, where the concretions are condensed in layer with 1 m thickness. The color of concretions is brawn, pale brawn and grey, massive or spotted structure. Concentric-zonal structure is very rare. The size varied from 5 to 100 cm, mainly 15–35 cm, rarely up to 100 cm. The shape is extremely irregular, with many branches (ameba-like). Distinctive feature is very often big relics from host rocks, sometime dissolved, with dimensions up to 10 cm. The crust is thin (1–2 mm), white, chalk contain, with silica-carbonate composition. The fracture is rough to smooth. The natural polish and yellow patina are typical for recent alluvial depositions. Mineral composition – the main component is micro and crypto chalcedony, moganite (up to 25%), opal, quartz (2–3%), framboidal pyrite. The Upper Cretaceous flint-rich rocks formed three big areas of outcrops in North Bulgaria as follow: Montana – Lovech; Pleven – Nikopol; Shumen – Devnya. Diagnostic features are thin crust (1–2 mm), irregular shape, none even outer surface, absence of concentric-zonal structures. Very often are relics from silicified macro fauna. Moesia flint has lowest quality than Luda Gora flint.

In South Bulgaria chalcedony veins and geodes (atypical flint) hosted as rule in limestones or volcanic tuffs are described. Their origin is connected with Upper Cretaceous volcanism in Sredna Gora tectonic zone or Oligocene volcanism in The Rhodope tectonic zone. Atypical flint has very low quality and is used as local and semi local source during the Prehistory.

REFERENCES

Nachev Ch. 2009. `Osnovnite tipove flint v Bulgaria, kato surovini za naprava na artefakti. Interdisciplinarni Izsledvania, XX, 1–20. in print.

PLANT ECONOMY AND VEGETATION DURING THE EARLY NEOLITHIC OF BULGARIA

Elena Marinova

Katholieke Universiteit Leuven, Center for Archaeological Sciences, GEO-Instituut, Celestijnenlaan 200E, bus 2408, 3001-Leuven, Belgium; draka@gmx.de

INTRODUCTION

The territory of modern Bulgaria is situated on one of the routes of distribution of early Neolithic agriculture from the Near East to Europe. One of the sources of information about the dispersal processes is the archaeobotanical studies carried out on Neolithic sites in the area. Although there are numerous archaeobotanical studies on the Bulgarian Neolithic, these from its earliest stages are still scarce. The reasons for this are of different nature, but probably the most important is the lower density of such sites compared with the later stages of the Neolithic.

In this contribution an overview of the early Neolithic plant economy of Bulgaria will be presented in relation to the later stages of the Neolithic and in comparison with the information from the neighboring regions.

The first farmers of Bulgaria settled in the foothills around the Thracian plain and in those of south-western Bulgaria. Possibly the Struma valley played an important role during the introduction of Neolithic subsistence from Thessaly to Bulgaria (Perles 2001; Nikolov 2004). It is still a matter of dispute whether the new subsistence arrived from Greece exclusively or from Anatolia via Turkish Thrace or from both regions (Özdoğan 2008).

THE ARCHAEOBOTANICAL INFORMATION BY REGIONS

The different geographical conditions in the study area suppose also the division of the study area in different regions with certain differences in the cultural developments of the study area. In the following the four sub-regions widely accepted also in the archaeological literature will be used: Struma valley (Southwest Bulgaria), Thrace and Southeast Bulgaria, Nordwest Bulgaria, Nordeast Bulgaria.

For the area of the Struma valley until now archaeobotanical information on the Early Neolithic from ca. 8 sites exists [Kovachevo (Kovačevo) (Marinova 2006), Eleshnitsa (Elešnica) (Dotcheva not published), Slatina (Dotcheva 1990, Marinova 2006), Galabnik (Gâlâbnik) (Marinova *et al.* 2002), Chavdar (Čavdar) (Dennel 1978),

Balgarchevo (Bâlgarčevo) (Marinova in print, a), Kremenik-Sapareva Banja (Čakalova, Sârbinska, 1986) Vaksevo (Popova 2001)].

The main cultivated crops were the hulled wheats einkorn and emmer. Usually they were cultivated together and it depends on the growing condition if the more resistable to unfavorable conditions einkorn or more productive emmer will prevail. In the sites Kovachevo, Slatina and Eleshnitsa seems that the einkorn is more important in the first stages of their occupation. For the later stages of the Early Neolithic in the Struma valley it seems that also emmer starts to prevail and this is especially good visible in the archaeobotanical record of the second half of the Early Neolithic in Kovachevo, Slatina, Balgarchevo, Galabnik and Chavdar. In this evidence could be connected with climatic factors, but also with local conditions and adaptation on the surrounding environment. For example at the site Kremenik-Sapareva Banja, situated in mountainous environment, the dominating cereal crop through all of its occupation is einkorn. Modern observations of einkorn fields have shown thet in difference to other cereal crops (like emmer), the einkorn is very resistant against beating down from heavy rains (Kreuz 2007). This ability was most probably the deciding factor for prevailing of einkorn during the earliest stages of the Neolithic, especially if the paleoclimatological reconstructions for this period speak for more temperate and wet summers than today (Davis *et al.* 2003). Further the einkorn is quite good adapted to cold conditions and frost so has some advantages over emmer in mountainous regions. Most probably the combination of complex factors have let to prevailing of the not so productive, but resistant to unfavorable conditions einkorn.

Except of wheats also barley was grown, in the Early Neolithic this mostly is hulled barley (storage find from Vaksevo), but naked occurred too (storage find from Galabnik).

The leguminous crops or pulses are the next of importance group of cultivated plants grown in the area, most abundant and numerous of them were lentils, pea and grass pea. The finds from chick pea during the final stages of the

Early Neolithic from Kovachevo, Galabnik and Balgarchevo are particularly interesting. It was spread from the Near East to southeastern Europe during the Neolithic, but until recently it was not thought to have reached further north than the territory of modern Greece. Its appearance is most probably connected with the cultural processes during the second part of the Bulgarian Early Neolithic (5700–5500 B.C.) in which repeated contacts with Anatolia have been observed in the archaeological record. The chick pea finds from the Bulgarian final early Neolithic are more or less synchronous with those from western Anatolia. They come from the early Chalcolithic of Ilıpınar, and are dated from 6700–6545 B.P. to 6605–6580 B.P., or about 5630–5407 cal B.C. (Cappers 2001). Therefore, a probable option is that the finds from the Bulgarian early Neolithic correspond to direct contacts with Anatolia, which took place through the eastern part of the study area and not necessarily through Thessaly, from which such finds are lacking until mow. One hint for this could be that the earliest radiocarbon date for the Bulgarian chick pea finds comes from the site, Kapitan Dimitrievo. Also, the evidence based on pottery of contacts with Anatolia and Thrace established at Kovachevo Ic and Id (Lichardus-Itten et al. 2006) could argue for this hypothesis. Given the scarce evidence available, further studies are needed to confirm this suggestion.

One of the earliest of considered sites seems to be the site Kovachevo. The site gives the opportunity for investigating the earliest stages of the Neolithic agriculture and associated anthropogenic vegetation change at the territory of modern Bulgaria. Thanks to the excellent support of the interdisciplinary works at the site by the team of the excavators extensive archaeobotanical information was collected. Comparable with only few other sites in the region the botanical material was collected through flotation sampling, during several excavation seasons and great variety of plants were recorded: more than 60 species, genera or others were identified. In comparison for the most of the other Early Neolithic sites studied in the Struma valley usually not more than 10–15 plant species or genera were identified. The general picture provided information on the plant subsistence of the site and can be used as example to get idea on it for the other sites in the region.

For example thanks to the flotation sampling wide variety of collected wild growing plants is available from the site. The fruits of cornel, wild grapes, plum, raspberry, blackberry, strawberry, physalis/winter or bladder cherry, hazel, elder, mountain ash and apple/ pear were collected and consumed either immediately or later, in dry state.

No pollen-bearing sediments have so far been found near the Early Neolithic sites in the South Western Bulgaria and information about past vegetation could only be gained through studying plant macrofossils recovered from the archaeological settlement layers, especially useful for this are the wood charcoals. They usually are the most abundant plant macroremains found in the settlement layer and have the advantage to belong to the vegetation used from the immediate surrounding of the sites. Information of the wood charcoal analysis or anthracology for the Struma valley is available from the sites Kovachevo and to more limited extent from Balgarchevo and Galabnik.

The most abundant and frequently used wood was deciduous oak. The deciduous oaks prevailing in the vegetation of the area were obviously used for fuel and building materials. In Kovachevo wood charcoal of species from outside oak forests was present in very low quantities. This probably indicates that the oak forests were well developed and extensive enough to cater for most wood needs, making it unnecessary to enlarge the area exploited to supply wood. According to the analysis of burnt posts oak was one of the main woods used for building material.

Results of anthracological studies showed that during the Early Neolithic (6159–5630 cal B.C.) the vegetation in the area of Kovachevo was dominated by open deciduous oak forests. This forest was the most widely used vegetation, although riverine forests and pine stands, probably in close proximity to the site, were also reachable by the Neolithic population (Marinova & Thiebault 2008). Land use and management by early Neolithic communities in the region favoured the opening of forested areas and lead to an increase in area of forest edge zones and secondary forests. Such changed habitats were useful for grazing animals, collecting fruits, fodder, firewood and the protection of arable fields. Hence the subsistence practices adopted by Neolithic farmers subtly shaped the wooded landscape with only slight and gradual changes in forest composition and transition to secondary forest and managed hedges of variable extent. So this shows that the anthropogenic modification of the vegetation was gradual and this fits well also with the results of comparable studies of Neolithic wood charcoal assemblages from northern Greece (Ntinou & Badal 2000) and Turkey (Asouti & Hather 2001).

The region of the Thracian plain and the adjacent areas is the best studied in Bulgaria from archaeobotanical point of view. Nether less the information about the Early Neolithic comes from six sites and give information mainly on the second half of the Early Neolithic: Rakitovo (Bozilova & Tchakalova & Bozilova 2002), Kapitan Dimitrievo (Marinova 2006, Marinova in print, b), Azmak (Hopf 1978), Karanovo (Thanheiser 1997), Okrazhna Bolnitsa (Lisitzyna & Filipovich 1980), Yabalkovo (Leshtakov et al. 2007). In is of importance to mention that in 3 of the sites – Karanovo, Kapitan Dimitrievo and Yabalkovo extensive flotation sampling was applied, so representative and broad information is available.

In the most of the sites the dominating cereal crops is the emmer especially for the later stages of the Early Neolithic. Similar to the Southwestern Bulgaria here also the main leguminous crops found are pea, grass pea and lentil, the first two found also as storages. Special interest deserves the site Kapitan Dimitrievo. Its geographical position supposes connections as with the Struma valley as well as with the Thracian plain. Also of importance is the excellent preservation of the botanical materiel at the site, what allow to gather very detailed information. One of the earliest evidences for food cooking from the region of Southeastern Europe comes from this site, as detailed analyses of bulgur-like cereal remains have shown (Valamoti et al. 2008). The most common for the site cultivated leguminous plant during all of the Neolithic is the grass pea – the same most common for southwestern Bulgarian Early Neolithic.

In Kapitan Dimitrievo also the only find of chick pea for the Thracian plain is present. Until now all other such finds appear in southwestern Bulgaria (Marinova & Popova 2008). Like in southwestern Bulgaria, also in the Early Neolithic of the Thracian plain numerous wild growing plants could be found in the after applying flotation sampling. In Kapitan Dimitrievo beside of the common for the study are collected plants also fruits of terebinth were used. This is a sub-Mediterranean plant rich in etheric oils found in many Neolithic sites in Greece and Turkey; it could be considered as indication also for at least similar environmental conditions with this areas. Another interesting plant found in the archaeobotanical record is the woolly distaff thistle an indicator for forest free habitats in the surrounding of the site. This means that the first farmers in the are found an still not completely covered by forest landscape with sub-Mediterranean vegetation. In the earliest Neolithic of Tell Karanovo also remains of fig fruits were found (Thanheiser 1997). As the fig plant with subtropical origins, but can grow spontaneously on the territory of Bulgaria, most probably this early finds mean that it was brought by the humans with or without intention from the Mediterranean region.

From the Early Neolithic of Northeastern Bulgaria archaeobotanical information is available from five sites: Polyanitsa Platoto (Hopf 1988), Dzhulyunitsa (Marinova, not published), Orlovets (Marinova 2007), Koprivets (Marinova 2007), Malak Preslavets (Panayotov *et al.* 1992). In the most of the sites only few samples are analyzed so the available until now dataset on the region is not completely representative. In general it seems that the dominating cereal crop was again the resistant to not so favorable conditions einkorn. The most common leguminous crops are similar to those from southern Bulgaria: lentil and pea. In only one of the studied until now sites – Dzhulyunitsa also grass pea occurs. Except of southern Bulgaria the grass pea occurs in some Neolithic sites inn Greece, but is lacking from Serbia and Romania (Fischer & Rösch 2004). For Anatolia this crop plant gain more importance during the late Chalcolithic about 6700 BC, although is also available in small quantities during the earlier periods (Nesbitt 1996).

In the region of Northwestern Bulgaria almost no significant archaeobotanical information on the Early Neolithic exists. Until now only the information from one site – Ohoden (Marinova, not published) can give us brief insight in the plant economy of the region. The agriculture of the site, like in the other sites in the region, was based on hulled wheats (einkorn and emmer), barley and leguminous crops (lentil and pea). The other known from the Southern Bulgaria crop plants are lacking until now from the Neolithic archaeobotanical materials from Ohoden. Further studies are needed to proof if this is due to real absence of these crops or to bad preservation condition characteristic for the site and restricted study area.

The wood charcoal analysis at the site showed that together with the oak forests the wet areas around the rivers were used as additional source of plant resources for the Neolithic inhabitants of Ohoden. At the site, as in the situated in Northeast Bulgaria Djuluynica also evidence of collection of the water chestnut was found. The plant produces a nut-like fruit that can be cooked, eaten out of hand, or used in other foods. It is known from other prehistoric sites in Romania (Fischer & Rösch 2004) and Hungary (Bogaart *et al.* 2005). Its presence indicates presence of shallow, nutrient-rich water basins in the surrounding of the sites.

At the site also feather grass was found. This steppe plant arouses the question of existence of open grassland areas in the supposed to be covered with woods landscape and as the evidence from southern Bulgaria indicates that probably it had more mosaic structure combining light forests with more or less open areas.

CONCLUSIONS

Considering the plan spectrum found at the Early Neolithic sites of Bulgaria and the found storages of cultivated plants, it could be concluded that almost all of the typical for the Neolithic and Chacolithic cultivated plants were present already during the earliest stages of the Neolithic. Hence the cultivated plant inventory arrived as the defined by Zohary and Hopf (2000) Near eastern crop assemblage.

The plant economy of the sites situated south of the Balkan mountain shows basically homogeneity in terms of crop plant composition, used wild resources and weeds accompanying the fields. Some regional variations are noticeable between the Struma valley region and the Thracian plane, mainly in the second part of the Early Neolithic. During this period in Thrace start to dominate emmer and in many sites from the Struma valley a new crop plant – chick pea – appears. Basically the same plant economy, but a smaller spectrum of used crops, compared to southern Bulgaria, is visible in the northern part of the considered study area. This should be related more to the not enough large data basis collected from there, than as real absence. A hint for this is for example the grass pea quite wide spread in southwestern Bulgaria, found also in Dzhulyunitsa. To proof reliable this hypothesis the future efforts of the studies of Early Neolithic agriculture and land use of Bulgaria should cover also the northern parts of the region.

The found wild growing plants, especially from the sites in southern Bulgaria allow reconstruction of a variety of natural habitats used by the Neolithic inhabitants of the sites. In general the wide spectrum of wild collected plants also shows a good knowledge and optimal exploitation of the wild plant resources during the considered period.

The wood charcoal analyses of several sites show domination of light oak forests, in southern Bulgaria rich in sub-Mediterranean elements too. Beside of them also not forested or not dense forested area were present. This evidence shows that the Neolithic population had quite riche and favorable environment available and this offered good conditions for plant economy from the type known from the modern Greece and Anatolia.

REFFERENCES

Asouti E. & Hather J. 2001. Charcoal analysis and the reconstruction of ancient woodland vegetation in the Konya Basin, south-central Anatolia, Turkey: results from the Neolithic site Catalhöyük East. *Vegetation History and Archaeobotany* 10, 23–32.

Bogaart E., Bending J. & Jones G. 2005. Archaeobotanical evidence for plant husbandry and use. In Whittle A. (ed.), The Early Neolithic on the Great Hungarian Plain. Investigations of the Körös culture site of Ecsegfalva 23, County Békés. *Varia Archaeologica Hungarica* 21 (2), 421–446.

Cappers R. 2001. Plant remains from phase VB. A preliminary report. In J. Roodenberg & L. Thissen (eds.), *The Ilýpýnar excavations II*. Nederland Instituut voor Nabije Oosten. Leiden, 236–237.

Čakalova E. & Sârbinska E. 1986. Pflanzenreste aus der Neolithischen Siedlung Kremenik bei Sapareva Banja. *Studia Praehistorica* 8, 156–160.

Davis B., Brewer S., Stevenson A. & Guiot J. 2003. Data Contributors. The temperature of Europe during the Holocene reconstructed from pollen data. *Quaternary Science Reviews* 22, 1701–1716.

Dennell R. 1978. Early farming in South Bulgaria from the VIth to the IIIth Millenia b.c. *BAR International Series*, 45. Oxford University Press.

Dotcheva E. 1990. Plant macrorest research of Early Neolithic dwelling in Slatina. *Studia Praehistorica* 10, 86–90.

Fischer E. & Rösch M. 2004. Archäobotanische Untersuchungen. In: Schier W. & Drasovean F. (eds.), Vorbericht über die rumänishdeutschen Prospektionen und Ausgrabungen in der befestigten Tellsiedlung von Uivar, jud. Timis, Rumäniens, *Prähistorische Zeitschrift* 79 (2), 209–220.

Hopf M. 1973. Frühe Kulturpflanzen aus Bulgarien. *Jahrbuch des Römisch-Germanischen Zentralmuseums Mainz* 20, 1–47.

Hopf M. 2000. Frühneolithische Kulturpflanzen aus Polajnica-Palteau bei Targoviste (Bulgarien). *Studia Praehistorica* 8, 34–36.

Kreuz A. 2007. Archaeobotanical perspectives on the beginning of agriculture north of the Alps. In Colledge S. & Conolly J. (eds.), *Archaeobotanical perspectives on the origin and spread of agriculture in southwest Asia and Europe*. UCL Press, London, 137–151.

Leshtakov K., Todorova N., Petrova V., Zlateva-Uzunova R., Özbek O., Popova T., Spassov N. &. Iliev N., 2007. Preliminary report on the salvage archaeological excavations at the early Neolithic site Yabalkovo in the Maritsa valley. 2000–2005 field seasons. *Anatolica* 33, 185–234.

Lichardus-Itten M., Demoule J-P., Perničeva L. & Grebska-Kulova M. 2006. Kovačevo, an early Neolithic site in South-West Bulgaria and its importance for the European Neolithization. In Gatsov I. & Schwarzberg H. (eds.), *Aegean-Marmara-Black Sea: the present state of research on the Early Neolithic*. Schriften des Zentrums für Archäologie und Kulturgeschichte des Schwarzmeerraumes 5. Beier & Beran, 83–94.

Lisitzyna G. & Filipovich L. 1980. Palaeoethnobotanical Findings in the Balkan Peninsula. *Studia Praehistorica* 4, 5–90.

Marinova E. 2006. Vergleichende paläoethnobotanische Untersuchung zur Vegetationsgeschichte und zur Entwicklung der prähistorischen Landnutzung in Bulgarien. *Dissertationes Botanicae 401*. Stuttgart. Gebr. Borntraeger Science Publishers.

Marinova E. 2007. Archaeobotanical data from the Early Neolithic of Bulgaria. In Colledge S. & Conolly J. (eds.), *Archaeobotanical perspectives on the origin and spread of agriculture in southwest Asia and Europe*. London. UCL Press., 85–98.

Marinova, E., Popova, Tz. 2008. Cicer arietinum (chick pea) in the Neolithic and Chalcolithic of Bulgaria: implications for cultural contacts with the neighbouring regions? Vegetation History and Archaeobotany 17, Supplement 1: 73–80.

Marinova E. & Thiebault S. 2008. Anthracological analysis from Kovacevo, southwest Bulgaria: woodland vegetation and its use during the earliest stages of the European Neolithic. *Vegetation History and Archaeobotany* 17, 223–231.

Marinova E., Tchakalova E., Stoyanova D., Grozeva S. & Dočeva E. 2002. Ergebnisse archeobotanischer Untersuchungen aus dem Neolithikum und Chalcolithikum in Südwestbulgarien. *Archaeologia Bulgarica* VI, 3, 1–11.

Marinova E. (in print) a. Archaeoboanical analysis of Neolithic plant macrofossils from Bâlgarčevo (SW Bulgaria). In Pernicheva L., Grembska-Kulova M. & Kulov Il. (eds.), The praehistoric settlement Balgarchevo.

Marinova, E. (in print) b. Archaeobotanical studies. In Nikolov V. (ed.), Kapitan Dimitrievo the excavation seasons 2002–2005.

Nesbitt M. 1996. Plants and People in Ancient Anatolia. *Biblical Archaeologist* 58, 68–81.

Nikolov V. 2004. Dynamics of the cultural processes in Neolithic Thrace. In Nikolov V., Bačvarov K. & Kalchev P. (eds.), *Prehistoric Thrace*. Sofia-Stara Zagora, 18–25.

Ntinou M. & Badal E. 2000. Local vegetation and charcoal analysis: an example from two late neolithic sites in Northern Greece. In Halstead P. & Frederick C. (eds.), *Landscape and land use in postglacial Greece*. Sheffield. Sheffield Academic Press, 38–51.

Özdoğan M. 2008. An alternative Approach in Tracing Changes in Demographic Composition. In Bocquet-Appel J.- P. & Bar-Yosef O. (eds.), *Neolithic Demographic Transition and its Consequences*. Springer Verlag, 139–178.

Panayotov I., Gatsov I. & Popova Tz. 1992. Pompena stantsia" bliz s. Malak Preslavets-rannoneolithicheskoe poselenie s intramuralnymi pogrbeniyami. *Studia Praehistorica* 11/12, 51–61.

Perles C. 2001. The Early Neolithic in Greece. The first farming communities in Europe. *World Archaeology*. Cambridge University Press.

Popova Tz. 2001. Study of archaeobotanical material. In Cohadzhiev S. (ed.), *Vaksevo – prehistorical settlement*. Veliko Tarnovo, 21–23.

Thanheiser U. 1997. Botanische Funde. In Hiller S. & Nikolov V. (eds), *Karanovo I. Österreichisch-Bulgarische Ausgrabungen und Forschungen in Karanovo. Die Ausgrabungen im Südsektor 1984–1992*. Salzburg-Sofia. Berger & Söhne, 429–480.

Tschakalova E. & Božilova, E. 2002. Palaeoecological and paleoethnobotanical materials from the tell near town Rakitovo. In Raduncheva A. (ed.), Neolithic settlement near Rakitovo. *Razkopki i Prouchvania* XXIX, 192–201.

Valamoti S. M,. Samuel D., Bayram M. & Marinova E. 2008. Prehistoric cereal foods from Greece and Bulgaria: investigation of starch microstructure in experimental and archaeological charred remains. *Vegetation History and Archaeobotany* 17, Supplement 1, 265–276.

Zohary D. & Hopf M. 2000. Domestication of plants in the Old World: the origin and spread of cultivated plants in West Asia, Europe, and the Nile Valley, 3rd edn. Oxford University Press.

Catalogue of the Early Neolithic settlements on the Territory of Bulgaria

Ekaterina Stamboliyska and Zhivko Uzunov

New Bulgarian Univerity, Department of Archaeology, 1618 Sofia, 21 Montevideo Str., Bulgaria;
estambioliyska@gmail.com, jivko_uzunov@abv.bg

Identification and location of sites
Name of a site (and number on the map)
1. Administrative unit appropriate to a given site
2. River basin
3. Geographical coordinates
4. Geomorphological situation (river basin, location in relation to the land relief)

A. Information on excavated sites
1. Name(s) of researcher(s) responsible for the excavation
2. Date of excavation (years)
3. Bounded research area: excavated and surveyed

4. Type and number of features
5. Relative chronology based on archaeological seriation and absolute chronology; number of settlement phases

B. Information on sites recognized on the basis of surface finds
1. Area of occurrence of portable finds
2. Taxonomic attribution and – when possible – chronological framework of sites
C. The most important references

Location of archaeological sites on the map.

SOUTH BULGARIA

1. Azmak
1. Stara Zagora district
2. Maritsa River
3. 42°27'55"N, 25°42'37"E
4. The settlement is situated in the Thrace valley, nearby the contemporaneous city of Stara Zagora

A
1. G. Il. Georgiev
2. 1960–1961, 1963
3. 6000 m²
4. Houses are arranged into a row. They are orientated in east-west direction and are rectangular in plan. There are no streets between them.
5. Layer I: chronologically corresponds to the Early Neolithic. Within this layer were revealed five building horizons of Karanovo I culture, Azmak variant.
   Layer II: chronologically corresponds to the transition of the Early Neolithic to the Late Neolithic period. One building horizon of Karanovo I/III culture was distinguished within the second layer.
   Layer III: chronologically refers to the Early Chalcolithic period. This layer consists of four building horizons. They correspond to Mariča culture (Karanovo V).
   Layer IV: is assigned to the Late Chalcolithic period. It is comprised of four building horizons of Karanovo VI culture.
   Layer V: corresponds to the Early Bronze Age. Two building horizons of Ezero culture are presented within this layer.

Absolute dates see Table 1
B
1. 6000 m²
2. Karanovo I culture, phase II – Azmak variant, chronologically synchronous to Karanovo II
C
Georgiev 1961a, b, 1963, 1965, 1969
¹⁴C dates: Görsdorf & Bojadžiev 1996, 133–136

2. Balgarchevo (Balgarčevo)
1. Blagoevgrad district
2. Struma River
3. 42°01'15"N, 23°02'44"E
4. The settlement is situated on the second river terrace, on the right bank of Struma River

A
1. L. Pernicheva
2. 1977–1978
3. 1200 m²
4. As a result of the excavations of 1983, the remains of a dwelling were discovered. It measures 8.60×6.00 m. The remains of two other dwelling were revealed too. The buildings used to have wooden construction, plastered by clay. Dwellings are assigned to the first building horizon. In 1985 the remains of another dwelling were discovered. It measures 8.5×5 m. In 1986 were revealed the remains of dwelling 1 and dwelling 4.
5. The Early Neolithic is presented by one horizon of 0.40 m thickness.
   The Late Neolithic is comprised by two horizons with a thickness of 0.70 m.

Table 1

Sample material	BP Data [years]	Cal BC [years]	Level	Provenance	Lab No
Charcoal	7303±150	6360-6020	I- 1	qu. W85	Bln-293
Charcoal	7158±150	6220-5890	I- 1	qu. B84 or B99	Bln-291
Triticum diococcum triticum monococcum	6878±100	5880-5660	I -1	qu. A84	Bln-292
Charcoal	6768±100	5750-5560	I-1	qu. W85	Bln-294
Charcoal	6779±100	5770-5560	I-2	qu. 99	Bln-296
Triticum dicoccum	6720±100	5720-5550	I-2	qu. W83	Bln-295
Charcoal	6870±100	5880-5660	I-3	burned layer at eastern side of the central profile	Bln-203
Charcoal	6812±100	5800-5620	I-3	qu. B99	Bln-299
Charcoal	6758±100	5750-5560	I-3	burned layer at eastern side of the central profile	Bln-267
Charcoal	6650±150	5720-5470	I-3	central profile	Bln-224
Triticum dicoccum	6675±100	5670-5510	I-3	qu. A100	Bln-297
Charcoal	6540±100	5620-5380	I-3	qu. A100	Bln-298
Charcoal	6426±150	5530-5220	I-4	qu. B132	Bln-300
Charcoal	6483±100 (1,3)	5530-5340 5620-5370	I-4	qu. G70	Bln-301
Seeds	6279±120	5380-5060	I-5		Bln-430
Grain	6476±100	5520-5330	II (I-6)	Nd	Bln-140A
Carbonized wood	5840±100	4810-4550	III-2		Bln-136
Seeds	5729±150	4770-4450 4420-4390	III-2	qu. W70	Bln-143
Seeds	5632±150	4690-4640 4620-4330	III-2	qu. G83	Bln-150
Seeds	5807±100	4790-4540	III-3	qu. G69	Bln-151
Charcoal	5697±100	4690-4450 4420-4400	III-4	qu. W115	Bln-137
Seeds	5214±150	4250-3910 3880-3800	III-4	qu. W97	Bln-147
Seeds	5793±150	4820-4460	III-4	qu. A84	Bln-142
Seeds	5888±100	4940-4680 4660-4590	IV-1	qu. W84	Bln-149
Seeds	5006±150	3970-3650	IV-1	qu. W84	Bln-146
Seeds	5387±100	4340-4080	IV-1	qu. B116	Bln-145
Charcoal	5683±100	4680-4640 4620-4450 4420-4370	IV-2	qu. B99	Bln-131
Seeds	5698±100	4690-4450 4420-4410	IV-2	qu. G83	Bln-139
Seeds	5592±120	4450-4320 4290-4250	IV-2	qu. G83	Bln-144
Charcoal	5689±100	4690-4450 4420-4390	IV-3	qu. B113	Bln-135
Charcoal	5546±200	4700-4100	IV-3	qu. B98	Bln-134
Seeds	5642±100	4680-4660 4590-4340	IV-3	qu. B84	Bln-141
Charcoal	5618±200	4720-4250	IV-3	qu. A115	Bln-138

Table 2

Sample material	BP Data [years]	Cal BC [years]	Layer	Provenance	Lab No
Charcoal	6100±50	5070-4940	IV	qu. VII E	Bln-2614
Charcoal	5960±70	4930-4780	IV	qu. VII D	Bln-2613

The Early Chalcolithic period is marked by two building horizons of 0.50 m. thickness.

Absolute dates see Table 2

B
1. 10000 m²
2. Second phase of WBPC-West Bulgarian painted pottery culture

C
Pernicheva 1995, 2002; Perničeva *et al.* 2000, 2002
¹⁴C dates: Görsdorf & Bojadžiev 1996, 129

3. Bersin
1. Kyustendil district
2. Bersin River, feeder of Struma River
3. 42°15'11"N, 22°46'31"E
4. The settlement was extended on a small terrace in the middle part of Pirin Mountain.
The Neolithic site of Bersin is in the centre of nowadays territories of the village of Bersin. It lies on a river terrace on the right bank of Bersin River.

A
1. V. Vandova
2. The settlement was discovered in 2006. Excavations were undertaken in 2007.
3. 26 m²
4. –
5. The thickness of the Early Neolithic layer varies between 0.70–1.00 m
Cultural deposits of the Late Neolithic, Late Antiquity and Early Medieval Age are also presented
2. West Bulgarian painted pottery culture
The pottery of Bersin shows similarities with the pottery assemblage of Vaksevo, horizon I and II. Some of the ceramics has common features with this of the Galabnik group.
The pottery assemblage is characterized by red or brown slipped surface. Decoration consists of white painted motifs. However dark and wine-red painted decoration is also attested. Among the presented pottery shapes are bowls and dishes. The biconical vessels are predominant as well as inverted conical dishes. The decoration pattern is comprised by bands and triangle motifs. As far as bowl's decoration it consists of horizontal rows of dots, zig-zag lines, hanging triangle motifs, Σ-motifs and S-motifs. Apart of the white and dark painted pottery, in all trenches grey-black or black burnished ceramic sherds were attested.

C
Vandova 2007a, b; 2008

4. Brezhani (Brežani)
1. Blagoevgrad district
2. Struma River
3. 41°51'50"N, 23°11'13"E
4. The settlement was extended on a small terrace in the middle part of Pirin Mountain

A
Surveys were based on filed walking
1. M. Grebska-Kulova

5. Early Neolithic

B
1. 10000 m²
2. West Bulgarian painted pottery culture. There are common features between pottery assemblages of Brezhani, Kovachevo Ic.

C
Grebska-Kulova 2008

5. Chavdar (Čavdar)
1. Sofia district
2. Topolnitsa River
3. 42°39'43"N, 24°03'24" E
4. The prehistoric settlement of Chavdar is situated on the right bank of Topolnitsa River

A
1. G. Georgiev
2. 1968–1974
3. 1200 m²
4. Dwellings are rectangular or slightly trapezium in plan. They measure 5.70x5.40 m and 8x6 m. Buildings used to have wooden construction plastered by clay.
The remains of four dwellings were revealed. Three of them are assigned to the sixth building horizon. The other one corresponds to the fifth horizon. The dwelling of the fifth horizon is rectangular in plan. It is 6.30×4.60 m. It is orientated in north-south direction. The building of the sixth horizon has square plan. It measures 7.60×7.50 m. It is orientated in northeast-southwest direction. Within the houses were found the bases of ovens, mile stones.
5. There are 6 settlement phases of Karanovo 2 culture – Kremikovtsi group. The life of the settlement continues also during the Karanovo II–III.

Absolute dates see Table 3

B
1. 40000 m²
2. Karanovo I–II phase
Concerning the Early Neolithic pottery assemblage of Chavdar, it reveals common features of Karanovo I culture – phase I and II. White painted vessels are presented. However dark painted pottery of red, black and brown colors also appears. It marks the earliest documented phase of dark painted pottery which put the bases of Kremikovtsi group. A particular feature of pottery decoration of Chavdar is the polychrome ornamentation.
Most abundant pottery shapes are: jar shaped vessels of spherical body, tulip-shaped vessels, bowls, cups, shallow bowls and dishes.

C
Georgiev 1981; Kanchev 1995; Nikolov 1997
¹⁴C dates: Görsdorf & Bojadžiev 1996, 124–126

6. Chavdarova Cheshma (Čavdarova češma)
1. Haskovo district
2. Maritsa River
3. 42°02'37" N, 25°49'53"E

Table 3

Sample material	BP Data [years]	Cal BC [years]	Level	Provenance	Lab No
Charcoal	6994±55	6210-6010 6220-6000	VI	qu. F16	Bln-1583
Charcoal	7003±45	6210-6000 6210-5990	VI	qu. G14	Bln-1580
Charcoal	7195±65	6210-5590	VI	qu. C15/C 16	Bln-2108
Charcoal	7070±50	6010-5900 6050-5840	VI	qu. G15	Bln-1663
Charcoal	7020±45	5990-5840	VI	qu. G15	Bln-1582
Charcoal	7000±60	5990-5810	VI	qu. G15	Bln-1581
Charcoal	6994±55	5980-5810 5990-5780	VI	qu. G16, house	Bln-1578
Charcoal	6400±100	5740-5655	VI	qu. A15	Bln-2662
Charcoal grain	6550±50	5550-5475	VI	qu. B13	Bln-2107
Charcoal	7120±80	6070-5900	V	qu. P14	Bln-4261
Charcoal	6840±50	5760-5660	V	qu. O14 house	Bln-4106
Charcoal	6852±100	5850-5670	IV	qu. J14	Bln-1241
Charcoal	6830±100				Bln-1241 A
Charcoal	6400±100	5480-5300 5980-5760	IV	qu. G16 house	Bln-1162
Charcoal	6985±100	5980-5700	IV	qu. G16 house	Bln-1162A
Charcoal	6997±100	5990-5780	IV	qu. G16	Bln-1251
Charcoal	6680±100	5680-5510	IV	qu. H15	Bln-1160
Charcoal	7040±100	6020-5810	IV	qu. H15	Bln-1160 A
Charcoal	6990±150	6000-5730 5990-5770	III	qu. I 10	Bln-908
Charcoal	6870±120	5880-5650 5880-5660	III	qu. K13, house	Bln-911
Charcoal	6815±100	5810-5620	III	qu. J11	Bln-909
Charcoal	6665±100	5620-5480	III	qu. J11	Bln-910
Charcoal	6555±100				Bln-910A
Pea	6320±100	5470-5210	III	qu. F15	Bln-907
Pea	6760±100	5750-5560	III	qu. F15	Bln-1030
Charcoal	6720±100	5720-5550	II	qu. G11	Bln-906

4. The settlement lies on 600 m of the contemporaneous town of Maritsa, Haskovo district

A

1. Excavations were supervised by A. Raduncheva
2. 1979
3. 1100 m²
4. The remains of several dwellings were reveled. Well preserved are the dwellings of horizon I. In the dwellings remains of ovens were found as well as grains store bins and other household installations.
5. Cultural deposits of Karanovo I culture are presents as well as of Karanovo III

B

1. –
2. Three horizons of the Early Neolithic were revealed

C

Raduncheva 2002

7. Chernichevo – "Manastirya"[7]
1. Plovdiv district
2. Selska reka

3. 42°26'41N, 24°42'37"E
4. The settlement extends on a river terrace

A

1. P. Detev
2. 1977
3. 450 m²
4. Foundations of a square house were reveled, another two floors of a dwelling were revealed. The remains of an oven were excavated too.
5. Four building horizons of the Early Neolithic were revealed and one building horizon of the Late Neolithic period

B

1. 7500 m²
2. Karanovo I – phase II
The Early Neolithic horizons are characterized by slipped were and white painted decoration. Sherds of brown and wine-red motifs are presented also within the Early Neolithic deposits.

C

Detev & Yovchev 1978

8. Dabene-Pishtikova mogila (Dabene-Pištikova mogila)
1. Plovdiv district
2. Stryama River, tributary of Maritsa River
3. 42°35'58"N, 24°45'45"E
4. The settlement lies on a river terrace, on the left bank of Striama River

A

1. L. Nikolova, N. Madzhev
2. 1992
3. 15 m^2 (trench 3×5 m)
4. –
5. The Early Neolithic is presented by four building horizons. Their thickness varies between 1.90–2.10 m.
The cultural deposits of the Chalcolithic period are disturbed.

B

1. 12000 m^2
2. Based on analysis of pottery assemblage the first two horizons are characterized by white painted pottery – Karanovo I culture. Within the upper horizon dark painted pottery is presented.

C

Nikolova & Madzhev 1994; Nikolova 1998

9. Dobrinishte (Doibrinište)
1. Blagoevgrad district
2. Mesta River
3. 41°49'15"N, 23°33'45" E

A

1. V. Nikolov
2. 1987
3. 130 m^2
4. The remains of two dwellings were discovered.
5. The Early Neolithic layer is comprised of one horizon with thickness of 0.75 m. Chronologically the settlement marks the third phase of the Early Neolithic, Karanovo I–II culture
Absolute dates:
Bln-3785: 6650±60 BP – dates of dwelling 1
Bln-3786: 6610±50 BP – dates of dwelling 2

C

Nikolov & Radeva 1992
^{14}C dates: Görsdorf & Bojadžiev 1996, 127

10. Drenkovo
1. Blagoevgrad district
2. Drenkovska River, tributary of Struma River
3. 42°00'30"N, 22°56'19"E
4. The site of Drenkovo is situated in Vlahina Mountain. The settlement expands on the left bank of the Drenkovska River.

A

1. M. Grebska-Kulova, Il. Kulov
2. 2004
3. 37 m^2 (trenches with restricted area were done)
4. In trench No. 2 several structures of the early Neolith have been recorded – floor level of light clay concentration of pottery and gravel stones; deep dug filled with greenish clay and sand.
5. PH – The Early Neolithic layer is very thin and almost disturbed. The thickness of the Late Neolithic is 0.40–0.60 m.

B

1. There is a contradiction concerning the surface of the site. Resent researches show that the site covered a surface of 50000 m^2. While according to D.Dimitrov the site used to spread out on a surface of 5000 m^2.
2. The settlement of Drenkovo corresponds to the first phase of the West Bulgarian painted pottery culture.
Concerning the pottery assemblage, the site of Drenkovo shows similarities with Kovachevo Ib. The Early Neolithic pottery is characterized by red slipped wfre. Shapes are presented by: bowls with a base, dishes, biconical vessels. The painted decoration is on the external site of the vessels. The decoration pattern consists of crossing or vault lines. Triangle hanging motifs are rarely presented.

C

Dimitrov 1996; Grebska-Kulova 2008

11. Eleshnitsa (Elešnitsa, Elešnica) [11]
1. Blagoevgrad district
2. Zlatfritsa River, tributary of Maritsa River
3. 41°52'50"N, 23°37'21"E
4. The site is situated in a kettle formed by the slopes of Rodopa Mountain. The settlement extends on a terrace close to the river.

A

1. V. Nikolov, A. Raduncheva
2. 1983–1985
3. 900 m^2 (surface of the site 3000 m^2)
4. As a result of the excavations were revealed the remains of 8–10 houses. Only several parts of them were preserved (part of floors and bases of furnace). There are two burned houses of Eleshnitsa which were studied in details:
Dwelling 1. Dwelling one measures 13.30×6.50 m. It was rectangular in plan and covered a surface of 86 m^2. The entrance of the building was on the South-West side.
Dwelling 2. Dwelling two measures 9.90×5.40 m. Its surface is of 53 m^2 and is also rectangular in plan. The orientation of the dwelling is approximately West-East (Nikolov & Maslarov 1987).
5. Two Early Neolithic horizons of total thickness of 0.80 m. were revealed.
Absolute dates see Table 4.

Table 4

Sample material	BP Data [years]	Cal BC [years]	Horizon	Provenance	Lab No
Charcoal	7010±60	5990-5840	2	Quadrant P8, house 2	Bln-3238
Charcoal	6960±60	5990-5750	2	Quadrant P14, house 1	Bln-3241
Charcoal	6940±50	5880-5750	2	Quadrant P13, house 1(?)	Bln-3242
Charcoal	6920±60	5880-5730	2	Quadrant P8, house 2	Bln-3239
charcoal	6850±50	5780-5660	2	Quadrant P13, house 1	Bln-3940
Charcoal	6730±90	5730-5560	2	Quadrant K3	Bln-3245
Charcoal	6790±50	5720-5640	2	Quadrant P8, house 2	Bln-3237
Charcoal	6720±70	5710-5560	2	Quadrant K1, pit 4	Bln-3244

B

1. 2000 m²
2. Chronologicaly the site of Eleshnitsa is assigned to the first phase of the Early Neolithic, Karanovo I culture, Southwestern variant

C

Nikolov 1996; Nikolov & Maslarov 1987, 1996; Tao 2000
¹⁴C dates: Görsdorf & Bojadžiev 1996, 126–127

12.Galabnik (Galabnik)

1. Pernik district
2. Blato River, tributary of Struma River
3. 42°25'10"N, 23°04'41"E
4. The settlement is situated on a low river terrace on the left bank of Blato River. The lowest building horizons get under the present-day subterranean waters.

A

1. M. Chohadzhiev, A. Bakamska, J. Pavuk
2. The settlement was discovered in 1977; 1979–1989
3. 1200 m²
4. Dwellings vary in plan. They are rectangular, square or trapezium in plan. The surface of the houses is between 35 and 55 m² There is a building of over 100 m². In every horizon dwellings are built in wooden construction plastered by yellowish clay on internal and the external side.
   As a result of the excavations of 1983, remains of a house were revealed. It measures 7.20x6.60 m. The dwelling is orientated in northeast-southwest direction. The entrance is on the long side. During the 1986, near by the south profile was discovered part of a burnt house. In the central part of the trench was localized another burnt premises. There is a grain store close to one of the walls. Many tools were discovered too.
5. The thickness of the Early Neolithic layer is 4 m. It is comprised of ten building horizons. The Early Bronze Age is marked by four building horizons. A necropolis of the antiquity and the medieval age was discovered too.
   The thickness of the layer characterized by white painted pottery is more than 1 m. It is synchronous to Karanovo I in Thrace.

Absolute dates see Table 5.

B

1. According to S. Chohadzhiev the settlement expanded on a surface of 20000 m²
2. The settlement refers to the West Bulgarian painted pottery culture
   Horizons from 1 to 7 correspond to the first phase of the Early Neolithic. The first six horizons are characterized by white painted pottery. Within the seventh horizon, for the first time appears the red painted pottery.
   Horizons from 8 to 10 comprises the second phase of the Early Neolithic. Dark painted pottery is presented within these horizons. Decoration consists of black painted ornaments. Red painted ones are rarely presented.

C

Bakamska 2007; Pavuk & Čohadžiev 1984; Pavuk & Bakamska 1989
¹⁴C dates: Görsdorf & Bojadžiev 1996, 122–123

13. Ginova mogila

1. Sofia district
2. Iskar River
3. 42°41'44"N, 24°06'32"E

A

1. N. Petkov
5. The thickness of the Early Neolithic layer is 0.40 m. The Late Neolithic layer is 2.60 m thick.
   The settlement refers to the second phase of the East Bulgarian pottery culture-group of Kremikovtsi.

C

Petkov 1948

14. Ilindentsi (Ilindenci)

1. Sandanski district
2. Struma River
3. 41°38'56"N, 23°14'31"E
4. The site of Ilindetsi lies at the foot of Pirin Mountain, on a high unflooded terrace in Struma River's valley

A

1. M. Grebska-Kulova
2. 2004–2005
3. 20 m² (trench surveys)
4. In trench 1 the remains of a house have been identified.

Table 5

Sample material	BP Data [years]	Cal BC [years]	Level	Provenance	Lab No
Charcoal	7120±70	6070-5910	I-1	qu. 73, D 4.3 m, house (1)	Bln-3580
Charcoal	7030±70	5990-5840	I-1	qu. 73, D 4.5 m (1)	Bln-3579
Humic acid	7220±80	6210-6010	I-1	qu. 73, D 4.5 m (1)	Bln-3579 H
Charcoal	6950±70	5900-5740	I-1	qu. 71, D 4. 5-5 m(1)	Bln-3582
Charcoal	6790±80	5750-5620	I-1	nd. D 4.4 m (1)	Bln-3581
Charcoal	7070±180	6090-5730	I.4	qu. 105, house 275, floor (2,3)	GrN-19786
Charred seeds	7020±60	5900-5840	I.5	qu. 33, house 273, grain storage (2,3)	GrN-19785
Charcoal	7070±60	6010-5890	I-6	qu. 45 (2,3)	GrN-19784
Charred wood	7020±150	6020-5740	I-7	qu. 104, D 2.8 m, house 253 (1)	Bln-4095
Charred wood	7140±80	6080-5900	I-7	qu. 104, D 2.8 m, house 253 (1)	Bln-4096
Charred wood	6760±80	5730-5570	I-7	qu. 104, D 2.8 m, house 253 (1)	Bln-4094
Charred wheat	7100±80	6050-5890	II.8	qu. 32, D. 2.2-2.4 m, house 238 (1)	Bln-4093
Charred seeds	6970±50	5970-5780	II.8	House 194, grain storage (2,3)	GrN-19783
Charred wheat	6760±60	5715-5625	II.8	qu. 32, D 2.3-2.4 m, house 238 (1)	Bln-4091
Charred wheat	6710±60	5710-5560-	II.8	qu. 32, D 2.3-2.4 m, house 238 (1)	Bln-4092
Charred grain	6670±70	5650-5530	II.8	qu.32, D 2.00 m, house floor (1)	Bln-3576

Several floor levels of yellow and white clay have been recorded. In South direction the house was marked by a row of postholes on the East-West direction. The house was orientated to the four cardinal points.
5. An Early Neolithic layer was revealed

B

1. The settlement used to extend on a surface of 10000 m²
2. There are common features of the pottery decoration between Ilindentsi and Kovachevo Ic

C

Grebska-Kulova 2007, 2008

15. Kamenik
1. Kyustendil district
2. Kamenishkata River, tributary of Struma River
3. 42°12'59"N, 23°01'01"E
4. The settlement is situated on an elevated terrace between the two branches of Kameničkata River

A

1. D. Dimitrov
3. 18 m²
4. There are no evidence
5. The Early Neolithic is presented by one horizon 0.10–0.20 m thickness. Deposits of the Early Bronze Age and Late Iron Age are also presented. The site is assigned to the West Bulgarian painted pottery culture.

C

Dimitrov 1996

16. Kapitan Dimitrievo
1. Peshtera district
2. Stara reka River tributary of Maritsa River
3. 42°06'17"N, 24°19'43"E
4. –

A

1. P. Detev, V. Nikolov
2. 1947–1948; 1998–2005
3. As a result of the excavations of 1947–1948 the surveyed surface of the settlement was 348 m². In 1998–1999 four trenches were excavated by V. Nikolov: trench 1: measures 20 m²; trench 2: measures 7.5 m² (2.5×3); trench 3: measures 7.5 m² (2.5×3); trench 4: measures 7 m².
4. The remains of three dwellings were revealed. Houses used to have wooden construction plastered by clay. One of the buildings is two-storied. On the second floor there used to be an oven. An oven was also reveled on the first floor together with mile stone installation and four grain stores. Hearths were situated outside the building.
5. The Early Neolithic layer has a thickness 3.80 m. The Late Neolithic is marked by a layer of 0.80 m. thickness. Cultural layers of the Early Chalcolithic period were registered as well as of the Late Chalcolithic. Deposits of the Bronze Age and Late Antiquity are also presented. Karanovo I, phase I and II.

C

Detev 1950; Nikolov 1999 *et al.*

17. Karanovo [17]
1. Sliven district
2. Maritsa River
3. 42°30'44"N, 25°54'55"E
4. Tell Karanovo is situated in the Northern Thracian valley in close proximity of south mountain side of Sredna Gora, at the foot of Sarnena Gora Mountain

A

1. V. Mikov, G. Georgiev, V. Nikolov and S. Hiller

2. 1936, 1946–1957, 1984–2005
   The first excavations were carried out during 1947–1957. In 1984–1992 surveys were conducted by a Bulgarian-Austrian archaeological expedition. One year later, in 1993 excavations were continued and brought to an end in 1999.
3. –
4. The remains of above 25 houses of the early Neolith were revealed at the settlement of Karanovo. Dwellings are square or rectangular in plan.
5. The Early Neolithic layer of Karanovo I culture has a thickness of 0.80–1.00 m. Within this layer were distinguished three building horizons. On the ground of the pottery assemblage analysis, V.Nikolov considers that the lowest horizon of the north-east sector chronologically precedes the three horizons in the south sector (Hiller, Nikolov 1997, 142). If the stratigraphic dates confirm this view/opinion so in this case Karanovo I culture would be presented by four horizons:
   Karanovo II layer: 1/?/–1.80 m thickness. Four building horizons were revealed in this layer.
   Karanovo II/III layer: 0.40–0.60 m thickness. This layer is characterized by two horizons.
   Karanovo III layer: 0.80–1.15 m thickness. It is comprised by three building horizons
   Karanovo IV layer: the thickness of this layer varied from 0.7–1.0 to 1.20 m. At least two horizons were reveled within this layer.
   Karanovo I and Karanovo II cover the period of the Early Neolithic. In the profil were revealed also cultural deposits of the Early Chalcolithic, Late Chalcolithic and Early Bronze Age.

Absolute dates see Table 6.

B

1. It measures around 250x150 m
2. Karanovo I – phase I; Karanovo I – phase II (group of Karanovo II)
   In terms of typology of the vessels, Karanovo I culture is characterized by the red slipped, often white painted pottery. Single dark painted vessels are presented too. Vessels are round shaped. Among the widespread shapes are: tulip-shape cups/vessels on a hollow base, vessels with spherical bodies and approximately cylindrical tell neck, cups with slightly conical bodies, sometimes with a strip handle, high-mouthed jars, high-mouthed semispherical bowls, bowls with rounded bodies. As far as the decoration, it covers different parts of vessel's body. There can be distinguished under rim decoration, basic composition and decoration of the base. Certain motifs/pattern was used in depicting the decoration. In the table below are shown some of the basic motifs.

C

Georgiev 1961; Hiller 1990, 2004; Hiller & Nikolov 1997, 2002; Nikolov 2004a
Radiocarbona dates: Kohl & Quitta, 1966; Quitta & Kohl 1969; Görsdorf & Weninger 1993
[14]C dates: Quitta & Kohl 1969, 37; Görsdorf & Weninger 1993; Görsdorf & Bojadžiev 1996, 133–136

18. Kardzhali [18]
1. Kardzhali district
2. Varbitsa River, tributary of Arda River
3. 41°38'34"N, 25°23'10"E
4. –

A

1. A. Popov
2. Rescue excavations were undertaken in 1972

Table 6

Sample material	BP Data [years]	Cal BC [years]	Level	Provenance	Lab No
Charcoal	7090±90	6060-5840	I-1	qu. Q19/III-IV	Bln-4339
Charcoal	7110±50	6050-5910	I-1	qu. P19/III	Bln-4336
Charcoal	6955±45	5890-5770	I-1	qu. P18/IV	Bln-4338
Charcoal	6810±65	5740-5635	I-1	qu. Q19/II	Bln-4337
Charcoal	6710±55	5670-5560	I-1	qu. Q19/II	Bln-4335
Charcoal	6820±50	5750-5640	I-1/2	qu. Q 17/IV	Bln-3942
Charcoal	7110±50	6050-5910	I-2	qu. P18/III	Bln-4177
Charcoal	7130±70	6080-5900	I-3	qu. Q19/II	Bln-4179
Charcoal	6730±80	5720-5560	I-3	qu. P19/III	Bln-4178
Charcoal	6760±50	5710-5630	II-4	qu. P19/III house IV.2 oven	Bln-3943
Charcoal	6750±50	5710-5625	II-4	qu. P19/IV	Bln-3941
Charcoal	6785±60	5720-5635	II-5	qu. P19/III house V.2 oven	Bln-3944
*Charcoal	6910±60	5880-5720	II-6	qu. Q17/II posthole	Bln-3716
*Charcoal	6850±60	5810-5660	II-6	qu. Q17/II posthole	Bln-3716 H
*Charcoal	6780±60	5725-5625	II-6	qu. Q17/II posthole	Bln-3586
Charcoal	6807±100	5810-5620	II	Sector III/SW side of the tell	Bln-152
Charcoal	6540±100	5620-5380 5630-5460	II	Sector III North section burned building horizon	Bln-201
Charcoal	6490±150	5610-5310 5620-5320	II	Sector III east section burned building horizon	Bln-234
Charcoal	6130±60	5200-5170 5140-5120 5080-4950	III	qu. Q18/I	Bln-3585
Charcoal	6375±70	5430-5400 5380-5250	III	qu. Q18/I	Bln-3904
Charcoal	6440±60	5440-5320	III	qu. P18/I	Bln-3458
Charcoal	6420±60	5430-5290	III	qu. P18/II	Bln-3459
Charcoal	6440±60	5440-5320	III	qu. P18/II	Bln-3460
Carbonized wood	6480±60	5440-5330	III	qu. P18/II	Bln-3461
Seeds/ probably lentils	6500-50	5520-5330	III	qu. P18/II	Bln-3464
Seeds/probably lentils	6350±60	5430-5360 5340-5260	III	qu. P18/II	Bln-3463
Seeds/probably lentils	6410±60	5430-5280	III	no data	Bln-3465
Carbonized seeds	6380±60	5430-5360 5340-5270	III	qu. P18/II	Bln-3587
Carbonized seeds	6450±60	5440-5280	III	qu. Q17/II	Bln-3717
humic acid	6510±60	no data	III	qu. Q17/II	Bln-3717 H
Carbonized grain	6395±100	5440-5260	V	Sector IV/ North-East part of the tell	Bln-158
Carbonized grain	5625±100	4550-4340	V	Sector V	Bln-153
Carbonized grain	5520±100	4460-4250	V	no data, depth 5.50 m	Bln-1182
Carbonized grain	5830±250	5000-4350	VI	Sector VI	Bln-154

*From the same sample

3. 1050 m[2]
4. Dwellings were excavated and surveyed. They are rectangular in shape and measure 8×6 m. The exact number of the dwellings was not given by the excavator.
5. Five building horizons of the Early Neolithic were revealed of 2.00–2.20 m thickness. The settlement of Kardzhali corresponds to Karanovo I culture in Thrace.

C

Peykov 1973, 1978

19. Kazanlak

1. Stara Zagora district
2. Abayata River, tributary of Tundzha River
3. 42°38'13"N, 25°23'40"E
4. The prehistoric settlement of Kazanlak is situated in the Southwest part of the modern town of Kazanlak. The tell lies on a ledge on the right bank Abayata River.

A

1. G. Georgiev
2. 1967–1971
3. The settlement is entirely investigated

Table 7

Sample material	BP Data [years]	Cal BC [years]	Layer	Provenance	Lab No
Charcoal	6335±160	5440-5200 5180-5070	Hor-6	qu. O11	Bln-730
Charcoal	6330±100	5430-5400 5380-5210 5170-5140 5110-5090	Hor-3	qu. O9	Bln-729

4. Several dwellings were revealed. But the exact number was not recorded. The dwellings are rectangular in plan, they are almost square. They measure around 7×6m.
5. Nine building horizons of the Early Neolithic were revealed. They have a thickness of 3 m. The Late Neolithic is comprised by eight horizons with thickness of 2.40 m. Karanovo I – phase I and II, Azmak variant; Transition Karanovo I–III.

Absolute dates see Table 7.

C

Georgiev 1974; Nikolov & Karastoyanova 2003

20. Kovachevo (Kovačevo)
1. Sandanski district
2. Pirinska Bistritsa River, feeder of Struma River
3. 41°30'18"N, 23°28'13"E
4. The site was discovered in 1980. It is situated on the left bank of Pirinska Bistritsa River in the locality of Podini. The settlement lies out on a vast plateau. It extends up to the border of the plateau. In South-Southwest direction the plateau descends, transforming into gentle slope, which goes down to the river basin. The first inhabitants of this area have settled down in the east periphery of terrace nearby the river basin. The dimensions of the earliest Neolithic settlement were limited/ confined.

A
1. L. Pernicheva, V. Nikolov, M. Lichardus-Itten, J.-P. Demoule, M.Grebska-Kulova, Il. Kulov
2. 1980–1981; 1986–2007
3. 1500 m²
4. During the existence of the earliest settlement dwellings were built up directly upon the ancient terrain Buildings are built up in wooden construction plastered by clay. They are quadrangular in plan, in some cases with square shape. Walls have a length of around 5 or 6 m. In the next horizons house used to have a ditch under the floor. Usually this space is filled in by stones, house destructions. Houses have a surface of 20–30 m² However a dwelling of a surface of 100 m² was discovered.
5. Early Neolithic deposits were revealed as well as deposits of the Late Neolithic

Absolute dates see Table 8.

B
1. The site covers a surface of 60000 m²
2. There are four phases of development of the Early Neolithic at the site of Kovachevo Ia, Ib, Ic and Id. These phases are mainly characterized by different features of the pottery style:

Ia – shapes and decoration: The decoration of the vessels during this stage is comprises simple motifs of parallel lines marked by points and triangle motifs, which cover the surface of biconical bowls with slightly pointed bottoms. The surface is slipped. The surface color varies from red to wine red while the color of the paint is white and grey.

Ib – shapes and decoration: Lattice pattern, triangle motifs as well as wavy motifs appear within stage Ib. The decoration covers considerable part of vessels' surface. The color of the paint is white or creamed-colored but however dark color is also used in the decoration.

Ic – shapes and decoration: Shifts appear in vessels' decoration. The variety of motifs is enriched. It is presented by: parallel bands/lines, spiral motifs, meander, semi oval motifs, narrow bands marked by points. In regard to the pottery shapes, biconical vessels disappear. They are replaced by three-pieced ceramic shaped/vessels which shapely neck, body and ring-shaped bottom. Very often are decorated the two parts of the vessel – the infernal and the external.

Id – shapes and decoration: Standardization of the pottery decoration could be observed during Id stage. The main motifs consist of lattice pattern and pints. The decoration of the internal side of the vessels is not as widespread as it is in the previous stages. However shapes of the vessels continue to be the same, do not suffer any changes.

The pottery assemblage is influenced by the Early Neolithic were of Thrace (Karanovo I) as well as by Southwest Bulgaria (West Bulgarian painted pottery culture) and Macedonia (Anzabegovo culture).

C

Grebska-Kulova 2008; Lichardus-Itten *et al.* 2000, 2002, 2006; Kovacheva 1995; Pernitcheva 1990

Table 8

Sample material	BP Data [years]	Cal BC [years]	Neolithic phase	Lab No
Charcoal	7180±45	6075-6005	Ia	Ly-1437 (OxA)
Charcoal	7090±70	6030-5890	Ia-Ib	Ly-1654 (OxA)
Charcoal	6975±50	5970-5790	Ib	Ly-1439 (OxA)
Charcoal	6990±45	5980-5810	Ib	Ly-1438 (OxA)
Charcoal	6980±65	5980-5790	Ib	Ly-1620 (OxA)
Charcoal	6760±160	5810-5520	Id-II	Ly-6553
Charcoal	6830±85	5800-5630	Id-II	Ly-6554

21. Kraynitsi (Krainici, Krajnici)
1. Kyustendil district
2. Dzhubrena River, tributary of Struma River
3. 42°19'10"N, 23°13'02"E
4. The settlement lies on a low terrace on the right bank of river Dzhyubrena, at the south foot of Verila Mountain.

A
1. St. Chohadzhiev, A. Bakamska
2. 1986, 1990
3. 48 m²
4. –
5. Depending on the incline of the ground/area the thickness of the Early Neolithic layer varies between 1.50 and 2.40 m. There were distinguished three building horizons of the Early Neolithic period.

B
1. Around 10000 m²
2. One building horizon of I phase of the Monochrome Neolithic was distinguished; two building horizons which correspond to the I phase of the West Bulgarian painted pottery cultures

C
Čohadžiev & Bakamska 1990, Chohadzhiev et al. 2007

22. Kremenik (Sapareva Bania) (Sapareva Banja) [22]
1. Kyustendil district
2. Dzherman River, tributary of Struma River
3. 42°21'56"N, 23°03'55"E
4. The settlement lies on a high terrace on the left riverside of Dzherman River, on 720–730 m above the sea level

A
1. G. Georgiev
2. 1977–1983, 1987
3. 1850 m²
During 1977 the surveyed surface of the settlement is 250 m². In 1979 the settlement was excavated on a surface of 350 m². During 1980 the surveyed surface is 100 m². In 1983 investigations were carried on a surface of 750 m². In 1987 the surveyed surface is 400 m².
4. The remains of ovens were mainly discovered. In 1977 a base of an oven was revealed. The oven measures 1.60× 1.30 m. In 1983 the remains of a dwelling were investigated. The dwelling measures 10.40×5.15 m. It is comprised by two premises. The entrance is on the south side.
5. The Early Neolithic layer is 1.80–2.00 m thick. Within this layer four building horizons were distinguished. Late Neolithic layer has a thickness of 1.20–1.40 m. It is comprised by 3 building horizons.

Absolute dates see Table 9.
B
1. ~ 30 000 m²
2. Concerning the painted pottery, predominant are the vessels painted in brown and cream-colored. White painted vessels are also presented. Episodically polychrome ornamentation appears as wells as red painted and black painted decoration.

C
Čakalova & Sarbinska 1986; Georgiev et al. 1986; Ninov 1986; Vandova 2000a, b
[14]C dates: Görsdorf, Bojadžiev 1996, 127–128

23. Kremikovtsi
1. Sofia district
2. Kremikovska River, tributary of Iskar River
3. 42°21'56"N, 23°30'23"E
4. The settlement extends on the left bank of the Kremikovska River

A
1. G. Georgiev
2. 1958–1959
3. Four trenches were excavated – 100 m²
4. –
5. The Early Neolithic is presented by 7 building horizons of 3 m. thickness
The Early Neolithic layer comprises two phases: Ia and Ib. Ia is the inferior phase while Ib is the superior. Both phases are bounded by a layer of stones. In trench 4, phase Ia is marked by four building horizons.

B
1. There is lack of information
2. The settlement refers to the group of Kremikovtsi. It is characterized by its two phases:
Ia and Ib. The difference between the two phases consists of variation in the color of pottery decoration. Ia phase is comprised by four horizons. It is characterized by white painted pottery decoration. However black painted pottery also appears. Ib phase is assigned by red, black and brown ornamentation of the pottery. Three horizons of this phase were revealed. White painted pottery is predominant for the inferior horizons. Although in trench 4 white painted were and dark painted one appears together within the Neolithic layer.

C
Georgiev 1975

24. Krumovgrad
1. Kardzhali district

Table 9

Sample material	BP Data[years]	Cal BC [years]	Level	Provenance	Lab No
Charcoal	6620±100	5630-5480	II	qu. P12, floor (1,2)	Bln-2554
Charcoal	6460±60	5480-5370	II	qu. Q15, pithos (1,2)	Bln-2552
Charcoal	6840±60	5780-5660	III	qu. P14, floor (1,2)	Bln-2554
Charcoal	6660±60	5635-5535	III	qu. P15, oven (1,2)	Bln-2553
Charcoal	6530±50	5560-5460	III	qu. P15, house (1,2)	Bln-2105
Charcoal	6480±60	5490-5370	III	qu. P14, floor	Bln-2556
Charcoal	6475±40	5490-5370	III	qu. P15, house (1,2)	Bln-2106
Charcoal	6550±60	5610-5470	IV	qu. P16 (1,2)	Bln-2550
Charcoal	6450±100	5490-5310	IV	qu. P13, oven (1,2)	Bln-2551
Charcoal	6350±60	5470-5220	IV	qu. P16 (1,2)	Bln-2549

2. Krumovitsa River, tributary of Arda River
3. 41°28'23"N, 25°39'11"E
4. The settlemet is situated on a low terrace on the left bank Krumovitsa River

A

1. K. Kancev, M.Chohadzhiev
2. Excavations were carried out in 1974
3. Two trenches were done. The first one measures 3×4 m. The second trench measures 2×3 m.
4. The remains of several ovens were reveled. Well preserved is the oven of horizon VI. It has irregular round shape of maximal diameter of 1.40 m. A hearth has been also discovered in horizon VI. It measures 0.33×0.40 m.
5. The thickness of the cultural layer is 1.80 m.
   Six horizons of Karanovo I culture were reveled.
   Horizon I – together with a humus layer reaches a depth of 1.81 m
   Horizon II – from 1.81 to 2.10 m
   Horizon III – from 2.11 to 2.40 m
   Horizon IV – from 2.41 to 2.70 m
   Horizon V – from 2.71 to 3 m
   Horizon VI – from 3 to 3.35 m
   Karanovo I culture
   The Early Neolithic horizons of Karanovo I culture are characterized by white paited pottery. Decoration pattern consists of wide white bands as wells as of a lattice pattern. Vessels have hollow bases. The nuber of white painted sherds is different for each of the sixth horizons.
   Nine sherds of Karanavo I were discovered of horizon I, six sherds were found of horizon II. Two sherds were reveled of horizon II. Three sherds – in horizon IV, four sherds – in horizon IV, two sherds – in horizon II.
   According to the excavator, the settlement of Krumovgrad represents a local version of Karanovo I culture, which is synchronous to Starchevo culture II a-b as well as to the settlements Porodin, Zlenikovo, Anzabegovo, Vrashnik (Vrašnik) in Macedonia.

C

Kanchev & Chohadzhiev 1994

25. Kuklen

1. Plovdiv district
2. Maritsa River
3. 42°02'29"N, 24°47'15"E
4. The settlement spreads out on a low terrace on the right bank of Pranga River

B

1. 4800 m^2 (Field surveys, surface finds
2. Monochrom Neolithic – phase I

C

Detev 1976

26. Muldava

1. Asenovgrad district
2. Cheterideste izvora River, tributary of Maritsa River
3. 41°59'17"N, 24°56'23"E

A

1. P. Detev
2. 1965, 1966, 1967
3. The trench is localized in the East part of the settlement. It measures 5×6 m
4. No information was provided
5. EN

B

1. There is no information
2. Karanovo I culture

C

Detev 1968

27. Negovantsi (Negovanci)

1. Radomir district
2. Glavesh River, tributary of Struma River
3. 42°27'25"N, 22°56'59"E
4. The settlement is situated on the left riverside of Glavesh River

A

1. A. Bakamska and S. Chohadzhiev
2. 1996
3. 50 m^2
4. –
5. Four building horizons of the Early Neolithic period were distinguished.
   The deposits are of around 3 m. Three layers were revealed in the profile

B

1. Around 18000 m^2
2. There are two horizons which show similarities with the West Bulgarian painted pottery culture. To the second phase of the same culture could be assigned the also two horizons.

C

Dimitrov 1996

28. Nevestino

1. Kyustendil district
2. Struma River
3. 42°15'20"N, 22°51'15"E
4. The settlement was lies out on a small river terrace towers above the river basin of Struma

A

1. Y. Ivanov, St. Chohadzhiev, V. Genadieva
2. As a result of the field campaign of Yordan Ivanov of 1904–1906, the existing of the prehistoric settlement was registered. The first surveys were based on filed walking. They were carried out in 1939 by the American archaeologist J. H. Gaul. As a result of the surveys, an Early Neolithic settlement was discovered. Subsequently, archaeological surveys were undertaken in 1990 when cultural deposits were disturbed because of construction works. Lately in 1992 rescue excavations were continued.
3. –
4. –
5. The thickness of the Early Neolithic layer is 1.20 m. There were reveled two horizons of this period. The Late Neolithic is presented by one horizon with thickness of 0.70 m. Cultural deposits of the Early Bronze Age as well as of Antiquity and the Early Midlle Age are also presented.

B

1. The surface of the settlement is around 25000 m^2
2. West Bulgaraina painted pottery culture I/II phase? White painted pottery is predominant. However dark painted ware is also presented. Among the used colors of the decoration are: red, black and dark-brown color (Genadieva & Chohadzhiev 1994).

C

Chohadzhiev & Genadieva 2003; Genadieva 1991; Genadieva & Chohadzhiev 1994

29. Pernik

1. Sofia district
2. Struma River
3. 42°36'36"N, 23°01'55"E

4. The settlement is situated on a low terrace on the left bank of Struma River

A

1. M. Chohadzhiev
2. The settlement was excavated during the period 1975–1977
3. The surveyed surface during 1976 is 66 m². In 1977 two trenches were excavated. The first one measures 4×4m, while the second one measures 10×5 m.
4. –
5. The Early Neolithic layer is comprised by four horizons of about 1.50 m thicknesses. The lowest building horizons get under the subterranean waters. Life on this place continued also during the Late Neolithic period as well as during the Bronze Age, Iron Age, the Antiquity and the Middle age. This is confirmed by the discovered artifacts. The cultural deposits of enumerated periods are disturbed.

B

1. The settlement covered a surface of 10000–15000 m²
2. The pottery assemblage shows similarities to/ with the second stage of the West Bulgarian painted pottery cultures. Vessels of white, red and brown painted decoration are presented. Predominant in horizon I is the white painted pottery. In the upper horizons-dark painted ceramics is abundant.

C

Chohadzhiev 1978, 1983

30. Piperkov Chiflik (Piperkov Čiflik)

1. Kyustendil
2. Novoselska River, tributary of Struma River
3. 42°16'34"N, 22°45'11"E
4. The settlement is situated on the right bank of Novoselska (Suha) river, on a low river terrace

A

1. V. Vandova, R. Spasov
2. Drilling archaeological researches of the site were undertaken in 2003 they are not finished yet
3. Four trenches were excavated. They covered a surface of 29.50 m²
4. –
5. The Early Neolithic layer is 0.50–0.60 m. thick. The thickness of the cultural deposits of the Early Iron Age, The Antiquity and the Middle Age is 1.10–1.20 m.
Pottery assemblage shows common features with the II phase of West Bulgarian painted pottery culture. Vessels are characterized by dark painted vessels. Black and brown colors are presented in decoration.

C

Vandova & Spasov 2003; Vandova 2004, 2007

31. Priboy (Priboy)

1. Pernik district
2. Struma River
3. 42°30'19"N, 22°55'14"E
4. The settlement is situated close to the river, on an inclined in South direction terrace

A

The settlement has been discovered in 1939 by J. Gaul. Rescue archaeological excavations were undertaken in 1977
1. M. Chohadzhiev
2. Regular archaeological excavations were implemented in 1977. Three trenches were excavated.
3. 70 m²
4. Base of a furnace was discovered in the East profile of the third trench at a depth of 0.60–0.70 m
5. The thickness of the Early Neolithic deposits varies of

0.50 m to 1 m

B

1. Around 5000 m²
2. The pottery assemblage shows common features with the culture of West Bulgarian painted pottery culture. In trench 3 was distinguished one building horizon marked only by white painted pottery. In trench 1, where ceramics is mixed, white painted ware is presented together with red and black painted sherd.

C

Chohadzhiev 1986

32. Rakitovo

1. Pazardzhik district
2. Chepinska River, tributary of Maritsa River
3. 41°59'25"N, 24°05'13"E
4. The settlement is spreads out in the north-west part of the alley of Chepinska River. The valley is situated at the foot of Rodopa Mountain. It is surrounded by high mountain ranges and hills. According to the paleoecological and botanical dates in the past the settlement was extended on the waterside of the vast marshy area.

A

1. A. Raduncheva, V. Matsanova
2. 1974–1975
3. 3300 m²
4. In the first building horizon there were found 12 residential/building structures. The structures were single roomed, trapezium in shape.
In second horizon 6 buildings were discovered. The majority of them were still trapezium in plan. One of the particularities of/for the second horizon is the great number of pits.
5. The Early Neolithic layer is comprised by two horizons.

B

1. As a result of constructional works part of the settlement was damaged. The rest of the area that was not affected was investigated.
2. The site corresponds to Karanovo I culture, bearing some of the features of the culture of the Western Bulgarian painted pottery group of Anzabegovo-Vrashnik (Anzabegovo-Vrašnik)

C

Macanova 2000, 2002; Raduncheva *et al.* 2002

33. Slatina [33]

1. Town of Sofia
2. Slatina River, tributary of Iskar River
3. 42°41'18"N, 23°21'56"E
4. The settlement is situated on the right bank of Slatina River

A

1. V. Nikolov.
2. 1985–1995
Rescue archaeological excavations were undertaken in 1985 because of the construction works which have affected part of the prehistoric settlement
3. 2000 m²
4. Nine dwelling were revealed of horizon I. Buildings have rectangular shape. They are situated in two parallel rows. The distance between the two row of buildings varies of 5–15 m. Dwellings have wooden construction plastered by clay. In horizon IV a large house was discovered of 117 m².
5. The Early Neolithic layer is marked by 6 building horizons of 4 m. thickness.
Late Neolithic deposits are also presented.
Absolute dates see Table 10.

Table 10

Sample material	BP Data [years]	Cal BC [years]	Provenance	Lab No
Wood	6890±60	5780-5640	Post by/in the south wall	Bln-3434
Wood	6860± 50	5730-5635	Post by/in the West wall	Bln-3435
Wood	6840± 60	5720-5620	Wood presiding from the South-East part of the floor construction	Bln-3436
Wood	6810±50	5685-5610	Wood presiding from the South-West part of the floor construction	Bln-3437
Grain	6960± 60	5930-5910 5880-5730	Grain from grain-store 5	Bln-3438
Grain	6940±60	5930-5910 5850-5700	Grain from grain-store 1	Bln-3439
Grain	6840± 60	5730-5600	Grain from grain-store 3	Bln-3440
Grain	6960± 60	5930-5910 5880-5730	Grain from grain-store 2	Bln-3441
Grain	6780 ± 60	5675-5585	Grain from a ceramic vessel	Bln-3442
Grain	6840 ± 60	5730-5600	Grain from a ceramic vessel	Bln-3443
Wood	6970 ± 60	5930-5910 5860-5730	Wood upon the South-East part of the house	Bln-3504
Wood	6930 ± 60	5710-5610	Wood upon the North- West part of the house	Bln-3555

B

1. 80000 m².
   Culture and phase (based on typology):
2. I phase – Karanovo I culture. Horizons 6 and 5 are characterized only by white painted pottery. The maximal thickness of these horizons is 1.70 m.
   II phase – Western Bulgarian painted pottery culture. Horizons 4 and 3 The pottery assemblage of horizons 3 and 4 is marked by wine red painted decoration. The tradition of white painted vessels is carried on. In the upper two horizons dark brown-black paint decoration is presented, however white painted pottery is also presented along with wine red and yellowish-brown painted vessels. Polychrome ornamentation also appear.

C

Boyadzhiev 1994; Nikolov 1990, 1992, 2004b; Nikolov *et al.* 1991, 1992; Petkov 1959, 1960, 1961; Pernicheva 1993
[14]C dates: Görsdorf & Bojadžiev 1996

34. Slatina-Gradini

1. Town of Sofia
2. Slatina River, tributary of Iskar River.
3. 42°39'29"N, 23°22'36"E
A (trench)
1. N. Petkov
2. 1960
3. –
4.–
5. The I phase of the Early Neolithic is presented as well as the III one. There is a hiatus between the both phases. The existence on Late Neolithic deposits is also attested.
   The I phase of Monochrome Neolithic is presented.
   West Bulgarian painted pottery culture, II phase (Kremikovtsi group)
   The decoration patter shows similarities with this of Banitsa site. Above the white painted motifs there are motifs painted in dark colors.

C

Petkov 1961

35. Stara Zagora- Okrazhna bolnitsa (Okražna Bolnica)

1. Town of Stara Zagora district, the courtyard of the regional hospital

2. Maritsa River
3. 42°25'45"N, 25°36'18"E
4. The settlement is situated in the Thracian valley
A (trench surveys)
1. M.Dimitrov
2. 1967-1968, 1974-77, 1985
3.–
4. Remains of two dwellings structures were found in the Second layer, related to Karanovo II group.
   Relative chronology based on archaeological seriation; number of settlement phases
   Early Neolithic – 4 horizons of 2 m thickness
   Late Neolithic – 1 horizon of 0.40 m thickness
   Early Chalcolithic – 3 horizons of 1.00-1.20 m total thickness
   Late Chalcolithic – 1 horizon of 0.40 m thickness
   Absolute dates:
   horizon I – 7140 ± 65 bp (Bln-1587)
   horizon II – 6875 ± 65 bp (Bln-1586)

Absolute dates see Table 11.

B

1. There is lack of information
2. Two phases are presented in the settlement of Stara Zagora:
   Karanovo I culture – I phase
   Karanovo I culture, I phase (Karanovo II group)

C

Dimitrov 1985; Georgiev 1974
[14]C dates: Görsdorf & Bojadžiev 1996

36. Vaksevo

1. Kyustendil district
2. Eleshnitsa River, tributary of Struma River
3. 42°09'42"N, 22°51'16"E
4. The settlement extends over the left bank of Eleshnitsa River

A

1. S. Chohadzhiev
2. 1989–1996
3. 884 m²
4. Bases of ovens were revealed as a result of the excavations of 1993
5. The total thickness of the cultural deposits is 1.60–1.80 m. The Early Neolithic is presented by three horizons. The

Table 11

Sample material	BP Data [years]	Cal BC [years]	Level	Provenance	Lab No
Charcoal	7139±65	6070-5920	V	Horizon 2 sector 6	Bln-1587
Charcoal	6814±65	5750-5630	V	qu. A5	Bln-1586
Charcoal	6918±45	5840-5740	IV	Horizon 2	Bln-1589
Charcoal	6844±100	5840-5640	IV	House	Bln-1252
Charcoal	6820±100	5810-5620	IV	House	Bln-1250
Charcoal	6688±150	5730-5480	IV	House	Bln-1163
Charcoal	6750±60	5710-5620	IV	Horizon I, quadrant A1	Bln-1588
Charcoal	6723±100	5720-5550	IV	House 2, pithos	Bln-1164
Charcoal	6744±100	5740-5550	IV	House 2, pithos	Bln-1164

Late Neolithic is marked by one building horizon. The Late Chalcolithic is comprised by two horizons and the Early Bronze Age layer contains one horizon.

B

1. Around 10000 m^2
2. Horizons I and II are referred to the I phase (?) of the West Bulgarian painted pottery culture. Horizon III corresponds to the second phase (the end) of the West Bulgarian painted pottery culture.

C

Chohadzhev 2001

37. Yabalkovo

1. Haskovo
2. Maritsa River
3. 42°04'15"N, 25°26'32"E
4. –

A

1. K. Leshtakov
2. 2000–2008
   Excavations were undertaken in 2000 and they were carried on in 2001. In 2002 and 2003 rescue excavations were renewed/taken up again (because of the construction of a local road). Excavations were carried on in 2008.
4. The buildings are quadrangular in plan. Some of the dwellings are including dug-in structures. In several of this structures grain stores were revealed. Walls are clay-like. Stones were in used in the lower part of the construction of the buildings in order to make it stronger. In some cases the walls were raised in height with wooden structures of beams and clay, pressed in planks.
5. Three building horizons of the Early Neolithic were registered. Their average thickness is 1.50 m. Deposits of the Late Iron age were discovered as well as a settlement and necropolis of the Middle Age.

B

1. 25000 m^2
2. Karanovo I culture

C

Leshtakov 2004, 2006, 2007, Leshtakov *et al.* 2007, 2008

NORTHERN BULGARIA

38. Borovo-Chakmaktepe (Borovo-Čakmaktepe)

1. Ruse district
2. Batinsko dere, brook to the east of the Yantra River directly flowing into the Danube River
3. 43°29'15N, 25°48'36"E
4. Multilayered settlement mound on eroded leached chernosem.

A

1. Small trench surveys by V. Popov in the 1990ies. In 2000 field survey of the Römisch-Germanische Kommission of the German Archaeological Institute together with the National Archaeological Institute and Museum, BAS and the Historical Museum of Russe.
4. Tell-site with at least two overlaying horizons as reported by V. Popov

B

1. 36000 m^2
2. Lower Horizon belongs to the latest phase of the Early-Neolithic (Ovcharovo-Samovodene group) and is succeeded by a layer of the middle phase of the Late Neolithic (Hotnica I) (Popov 1996, 91; 118 and Krauß 2006, Kat. Nr. 142).

C

Krauß 2006c; Popov 1996

39. Devetashka peshtera (Devetaška peštera)

1. Lovech district
2. Osam River
3. 43°13'15"N, 24°53'25"E
4. The cave is situated on the left bank of Osam River

A

1. V. Mikov and G. Georgiev, M. Stoianov, V. Gergov and M. Hristov
2. The cave was discovered in1921. Excavations – 1950–1952; 1989–1993; 1998–1999.
3. The Early Neolithic layer was surveyed only at the cave's entrance up to the right-hand branch of the cave. Surveys were carried out also in the central hall. The surveyed aria is about 250 m^2.
4. The basis of six ovens was revealed. In the construction of the ovens were used pebbles and ceramic sherds. When ovens were constructed they were plastered by clay layer.
5. The cave used to be inhabited during the Early Neolithic, the Chaloclithic and the Early Iron Age. As a hole nine horizons were studied. Chronologically they refer to the: Early Neolithic period, Early Chalcolithic, Late Chalcolithic as well as of the transitional period of the Chaloclithic period to the Early Bronze Age. The nine horizons were registered near by the entrance of the cave, on the waterside of the river. A burial of the Iron Age was recorded, dating of the IV–III c. BC.

B

1. –
2. The pottery assemblage analysis shows common feature of Karanovo I culture as well as of the second phase of the Western Bulgarian painted pottery culture.
   The Early Neolithic layer of Devetashka peshtera contains red slipped white painted pottery. Black painted ceramic

Table 12

Sample material	BP Data [years]	Cal BC [years]	Level/horizon	Provenance	Lab No
Carbonized remains of a wooden construction	5590±100	4530-4340	XII	Sector 462	Bln-920
Posthole	5640±100	4570-4350	XII	Sector 462	Bln-920 A
Posthole	5515±100	4460-4250	IX	Sector 431	Bln-921
Posthole	5930±120	4950-4670 4640-4610	VII	Sector 954	Bln-922
Posthole	5970±100	4970-4720	V	Sector 362	Bln-923
Posthole	5780±100	4770-4520	IV	Sector 462	Bln-966
Posthole	5940±100	4950-4710	III	Sector 562	Bln-925

sherdes are also presented. Vessels are spherical in shape. Among the main shapes are dishes. The decoration consists of lattice pattern, triangle motifs, parallel lines, square motifs, S-motifs, circles etc.

C

Mikov & Dzhambazov 1960

40. Dzhulyunitsa-Smardesh (Dzuljunica Smardeš)
1. Veliko Tarnovo district
2. Yantra River
3. 43°07'19"N, 25°53'45"E
4. The settlement is situated on the first terrace of Yantra River, which does not get flooded. The western part of the terrace is the most elevated one. On the North the terrace is marked by a slope. It makes the impression of a plateau. At the foot of the slope there are four springs, which form a river.

A

1. N. Elenski
2. The first surveys took place in 1983–1984, when rescue excavations were undertaken. Subsequently, within the period 2001–2005 excavations were carried on/ continued.
3. During the period 2001–2005 the site was surveyed on a surface of 84 m2. Six trenches were made. Two trenches were excavated on a maximum depth of 2.30 m. Trench XII measures 6x5 m while trench XIII is 9x6 m. Both trenches are rectangular in plan. They are situated on the west outskirts of the terrace.
4. Partially excavated dug-in house and two pits were discovered. The dug-in house is oval-shaped. Within the dwelling were reveled four pits. A heart was localized in the east part of the dug-in house. The heart measures 1.20× 0.90 m and is oval-shaped.
Relative chronology based on archaeological seriation; number of settlement phases:
Because of trench surveys approach as wells as of difference of stratigraphic deposits thickness in each trenche, a certain information concerning the thickness of cultural layer of the single epochs could not be pointed. However cultural deposits of the Early Neolithic, Early Chalcolithic, Late Chalcolithic, Early Bronze Age, Early Iron Age and Antiquity were registered.

B

1. During the Early Neolithic period the settlement covered a surface of around 10000 m²
2. Three phases were distinguished in the settlement of Dzhulyunitsa-Smardesh
Monochrome Neolithic phase I is characterized by black-grey dark brown and brown polished were.
Monochrome Neolithic phase II. White painted pottery also appears.

Ovcharovo culture. The pottery of this phase is presented by plates and semi-spherical bowls, cups with vertical handles, tulip-shaped vessels and short necked spherical jars.

C

Elenski 2006

41. Golyamo Delchevo (Goljamo Delčevo) [41]
1. Varna district
2. Luda Kamchia River
3. 43°01'51"N, 27°24'30"E
4. The settlement is situated on the left bank of the Luda Kamchia River

A

1. H. Todorova
2. 1968–1969. In 1970 and 1971 the necropolis of the settlement was surveyed
3. Settlement was entirely surveyed on a surface of 1500 m²
4. Within the Early Neolithic horizon were revealed the remains of three large dug-in houses, four small semi dug-in houses, a dug-in corridor and a pit. The semi dug-in houses reach the depth of 0.40–0.50 m.
5. The Early Neolithic is presented by 1 building horizon. The layer of the Early Chalcolithic is contains 3 horizons. The Late Chalcolithic layer is marked by 13 building horizons.
Absolute dates: The seven obtain absolute dates concern mainly the Chalcolithic period.
Absolute dates see Table 12.
B
1. –
2. Golyamo Delchevo corresponds to the final of the Early Neolithic – Tsonevo group.
The Early Neolithic horizon 1 is characterized by slipped dark (grey-black) pottery surface.
C
Todorova *et al.* 1975
[14]*C dates:* dates Görsdorf & Boyadžiev 1996, 146–147

42, Gradeshnitsa – Malo pole (Gradešnica – Malo pole)
1. Vratsa district
2. Ogosta River
3. 43°29'10"N, 23°28'52"E
A
1. B. Nikolov
2. The settlement was discovered in 1965. Excavations were carried on during 1971–1974.
3. 2800 m²
4. As a result of the excavations were revealed the remains of 16 destroyed by fire houses: 3 from layer A, 5 from layer B and 8 from layer C. The houses measure 6–7×4–5 m nearby the houses were localized pits, used to extract clay. On

several of the floors were revealed the remains of ovens. Relative chronology based on archaeological seriation; number of settlement phases:
Three horizons of the Early Neolithic period were revealed.

B

1. The settlement expands over surface of 400×250 m
2. The pottery assemblage shows common features with the West Bulgarian painted pottery culture – II phase (Gradeshnica-Karcha group).
Horizon A is characterized by red slipped were. Vessels are spherical and semispherical in shape. Decoration pattern is presented by geometrical motifs of white or black paint. Some of the vessels bear only white paint decoration while others are decorated by both white and black paint. Among the decoration pattern are white painted rhomboid motifs, chess-boarded pattern, curvilinear lines, parallel bands motifs of crossed parallel lines, forming rectangular fields.
Horizon B: tulip-shaped vessels on a hollow base, polychrome ornamentation – black and light brown motifs upon an orange surface.
Horizon C is characterized by vessels with cylindrical upper part and spherical lower part. Polychrome decoration is presented. Among the used colors are brown, black, red and orange colors.

C

Nikolov 1974, 1975

43. Koprivets (Koprivec)

1. Ruse district
2. Baniski Lom River, tributary of Rusenski Lom River
3. 43°24'29"N, 25°52'51"E
4. The settlement is situated on a loess terrace slightly inclined to Baniski Lom River

A (trench surveys)

1. V. Popov, I. Vaisov
2. 1990–1994
3. 205 m²
4. The excavations in an area that slopes down to the Baniski Lom, comprised three trenches that cannot be connected stratigraphically. They brought forth a cultural sequence that spans the early to the late Neolithic.
5. In trench B, relevant to the early Neolithic, Popov discovered a settlement of the early Neolithic comprising a total of four successive layers. However, the archaeological material found in these layers was presented all together and not according to individual layers. Likewise problematic is the small size of the excavated surface, for it cannot be excluded that the absence of painted pottery in the oldest layer in Koprivec is merely due to excavation circumstances. The uppermost Horizon I corresponds to the final stage of the Early Neolithic and the beginning of the late Neolithic in Danube valley. Horizon I corresponds to the earliest horizons of Samovodene. Horizon II –The Late Neolithic (presents analogy with Hotnitsa culture) Horizon III – final phase of the Late Neolithic and the beginning of the Early Chalcolithic.

C

Krauß 2006c; Popov & Mateva 1993; Popov 1994, 1996

44. Malak Preslavets (Malak Preslavec)

1. Silistra district
2. Danube River
3. 44°03'48"N, 26°50'53"E
4. The settlement is situated on a terrace near by the Danube river, on the bank of lake 'Malak Preslavets

A

1. Ivan Panayotov
2. In 1985–1986 rescue excavations were undertaken. Throughout the years 1987–1988 excavations were carried on.
3. –
4. –
5. An Early Neolithic layer was distinguished as well as an layer of the transitional period of the Early Neolithic to the Late Neolithic
The lower layer shows common features with Gradeshnica-Karcha (Gradešnica Kîrča) group (second phase of culture of the Western Bulgarian painted pottery). There are common features also with Krish (Criš) culture. The upper layer shows common features with Dudeshti (Dudesti) culture.

C

Panayotov *et al.* 1992; Yordanov & Dimitrova 1996

45. Ohoden

1. Vratsa district
2. Skat River, tributary of Ogosta River
3. 43°23'08"N, 23°42'50"E
4. The settlement is situated on the left bank of river Skat

A

1. G. Ganetsovski
2. The excavations were undertaken in 2002 and still continue
3. 425 m²
4. Dwellings are dug into ancient terrain at a depth of 0.60–0.70 m. They are oval in shape. Dwellings used to have a massif construction. There is a span roof.
5. Concerning the typical features of pottery assemblage, two phases are presented at the site of Ohoden: Monochrome Neolithic; West Bulgarian painted pottery culture.
Absolute dates: KN5655: 6830±45 BP

B

1. The settlement used to spread on a surface of around 10000 m²
2. Monochrome Neolithic-II phase. Red or brown slipped pottery is presented. Vessels are spherical in shape. They have ring-shaped bases, vertical handles. Decoration consists of nail impression, plastic decoration. In some cases white painted decoration is presented. WBPC 22 phase

C

Ganetsovski 2007a, b, 2008a, b

46. Orlovets (Orlovec)

1. Veliko Tarnovo
2. Baninski Lom River, tributary of Rusenski Lom River
3. 43°21'38"N, 25°44'32"E
4. The settlement is situated on the second unflooded terrace near by a spring, feeder of Baninski Lom River.

A

1. P. Stanev.
2. 1993–1994
3. Around 10000 m²
4. As a result of the fild campaign of 1992 was reveled dug-in houses.
5. The Early Neolithic layer is 1.20 m thick. It is comprised by 3 horizons. The Late Neolithic refers to Hotnitsa culture.

B

1. During the maximum expansion of the settlement, it covers a surface of 60000 m²
2. Two horizons of the Monochrome Neolithic, phase II were revealed.

A1 – shards of white painted pottery on a black surface.
A2 – is characterized by white linear ornament on a red slipped surface.
The end of the Early Neolithic is characterized by pottery of black painted decoration. Parallels could be found within/in the culture of the Western Bulgarian painted pottery (Gradeshnitsa-Karcha group) and Karanovo II group.

C

Stanev *et al.* 1994; Stanev 1995

47. Ovcharovo – gorata (Ruec – Ruets) (Ovčarovo – gorata)
1. Targovishte
2. Oteki dere River, tributary of Golyama Kamchia River
3. 43°11'05"N, 26°39'36"E

A

1. I. Angelova
2. 1974–1979
3. Surveyed surface. The settlement is excavated on a surface of 4000 m²
4. According to I. Angelova thirteen buildings were reveled of horizon I. Eleven of the dwellings are orientated in northeast-southwest direction. Two of them are orientated in east-west direction and two of them – north-south. The majority of the houses are with one premise. Only dwelling 8 has is with two premises. This building has two ovens. In Dwellings 14 and 15 no ovens were found. Buildings are rectangular in plan. They have a width of 4–6.50 m and length 3–5 m. Typical feature for the building is the existence of barred wall in order to separate the oven of the entrance. Dwellings stand in two rows. Houses are parallel to each other and stand on both sides of a street. The settlement is surrounded by a back/rampart of small rocks. It is 80 m long, 5–6 m wide. It is 0.90 m high.
A new interpretation has been developed by R. Krauss and published (see the bibliography).
5. For the Early Neolithic four building horizons of a total thickness of 2.00 m were postulated.
Absolute dates see Table 13.
Through the series of 13 new AMS-datings on bone tools, which was achieved in the radiocarbon laboratory in Poznań, the date of the settlement can be placed in the second quarter of the 6th mill. BC (Krauß 2008a).

B

1. 4000 m²
2. Chronologically the settlement marks the end of Ovcharovo group as well as of the Early Neolithic. The settlement is assigned to the third phase of the Early Neolithic.

C

Angelova 1988, 1992; Angelova & Bin 1988; Krauß 2006a, b, 2007a, b, 2008a, b; Nobis 1986, 1988
¹⁴C dates: Görsdorf & Bojadziev 1996, 128–129

48. Ovcharovo – platoto 2 (Ovčarovo – platoto 2)
1. Targovishte district
2. Golyama Kamchia River
3. 43°11'39"N, 26°38'12"E
4. The site extends on the north sloop of a plateau, above a spring

A (small trench surveys were excavated)
1. –
2. –
3. There is no reliable data concerning the surface of the site because the cultural deposits of the settlement are disturbed by agricultural works
4. –
5. Two layers were reveled: Ovcharovo-platoto – Early Neolithic; Ovcharovo-platoto II – transitional period of the Late Chalcolithic to Early Bronze Age
Absolute dates: Bln-1356: 6480±60 BP

B

1. –
2. III phase of the Early Neolithic – Ovcharovo group

C

Todorova et al. 1983; Görsdorf & Boyadžiev 1996, 129

49. Ovcharovo – Zemnika (Ovčarovo – Zemnika)
1. Targovishte district
2. Golyama Kamchia River
3. 43°10'32"N, 26°38'22"E

A

1. H. Todorova
2. 1972
3. 60 m²
4. Two dug-in houses were revealed
5. Deposits of the Early Neolithic were registered

B

1. Around 10000 m²
2. Chronologically the site corresponds to Ovcharovo culture which is synchronous to Karanovo II in Thrace

C

Todorova *et al.* 1983

50. Peshterata – Iztok (Pešterata-Iztok)
1. Veliko Tarnovo district
2. Rositsa River, tributary of Yantra River
3. 43°09'13"N, 25°32'36"E
4. The settlement is situated on the first unflooded terrace

A

1. N. Elenski
2. 2001
3. Trench surveys were carried out. Eleven trenches were excavated. The length of the trenches varies between 3 and 5 m. while and the width is 1 m.
4. Semi dug-in houses were revealed.
5. Early Neolithic deposits were distinguished in trench IX,

Table 13

Sample material	BP Data [years]	Cal BC [years]	Horizon	Provenace	Lab No
Charcoal	6688± 60	5610-5480a	I		Bln-1544
Charcoal	6463±50	5435-5335a	I		Bln-1620
Charcoal	6125±45	5200-5180 5080-4950a	III	qu. 61	Bln-2030
Charcoal	5440±50	4340-4245a	III	qu. 61	Bln-2031
Charcoal	6555±70	5570-5430 5400-5380a	III	qu. 33	Bln-2032

trench X. Deposits of the Late Bronze Age, Iron Age and Antiquity (III–IV c.) are presented, too.
Monochrome Neolithic – phase II

C

Elenski 2002

51. Plochite (Pločite) [51]

1. Veliko Tarnovo district
2. Yantra River
3. 43°14'16"N, 25°42'17"E

A

1. P. Stanev
2. 1995–1998
3. –
4. –
5. Early Neolithic – phase I
   Two horizons of the Monochrome Neolithic – I phase were revealed.

C

Stanev 2008

52. Polyanitsa – platoto (Poljanica – platoto)

1. Targivishte district
2. Goliama Kamchia River
3. 43°12'49"N, 26°35'29"E

A

1. H. Todorova
2. 1975
3. 500 m²
4. Dwellings are rectangular in plan. They are constructed in wattle-and-daub technique. Houses measure 4×4 m or 3.5×3.5 m.
5. Deposits of the Early Neolithic and the Early Iron Age was distinguished as well as a Medieval village. Its layers are disturbed.

Absolute dates see Table 14.

B

1. The settlement measures 100x75 m.
2. Monochrome Neolithic – phase I

C

Todorova 1989
¹⁴C dates: Görsdorf & Boyadžiev 1996, 121–122

53. Pomosthitsa (Pomoštitsa, Pomoštica)

1. Popovsko
2. Malki Lom River, tributary of Rusenski Lom rRver
3. 43°28'23"N, 26°20'16"E
4. The settlement is situated near by the contemporaneous village of Pomosthitsa

A (trench surveys)

1. V. Nikolov, St. Stanev
2. 1995
3. Five trenches were excavated in 1995
4. –

5. The thickness of the cultural layer is 1.20 m. It is comprised of three layers. Early Neolithic pottery was discovered within the three layers.

B

1. The Early Neolithic layer covers a surface of 200/250 m²
2. Monochrome Neolithic – I and II phase

C

Nikolov 1997

54. Samovodene

1. Veliko Tarnovo district
2. Yantra River
3. 43°08'21"N, 25°36'37"E
4. The settlement is situated on a high terrsce on the left bank of Yantra River

A

1. P. Stanev
2. 1974–1994
3. 950 m². Sectors VI and VII in the North part of the tell cover a surface of 1900 m²
4. Dwellings are situated aglumerativly, in some cases wall by wall. Buildings have rectangular or square shape. One of the dwellings covers a surface of 132 m². A fortifying system was also registered. It consisted of wide and deep dich/foss and a palisade. It is 2.80 m and 12.50 m wide ditch. A bank and a signs of palisade were also registered.
5. The thickness of the Early Neolithic deposits is 1.50–1.60 m. In this layer are reveled horizons 11–9.
   The transitional period from the Early Neolithic to the Late Neolithic period is presented by horizons 8–7. The thickness of this layer is around 0.50 m.
   The Late Neolithic period is around 1.80 m thick. To this horizon could be refeared horizons 6–1.

B

1. At the end of the Early Neolithic period the settlement used to cover a surface of 6000–8000 m2.
   According to the excavator during the early phases (A; A-B1, B1, B2) the settlement spread out on a smaller surface in comparison with the late phases when the settlement coved surface of 60000 m² (Stanev 1997, 38).
2. Chronologically the settlement corresponds to the third phase of the Early Neolithic. On the ground of the typology of the artifacts P.Stanev differentiates the group of Samovodene. There are common features between group of Ovcharovo and Karanovo II.

C

Stanev 1997, 2002

55. Tlachene (Tlačene) [55]

1. Vratsa district
2. Skat River, tributary of Ogosta River
3. 43°20'30"N, 23°50'53"E

A

1. B. Nikolov

Table 14

Sample material	BP Data [years]	Cal BC [years]	Horizon	Provenance	Lab No
Organic - temper	7535±80	6420-6230	Hor.1	qu. 49	Bln-1571
Organic - temper	7140±80	6050-5860	Hor.1	qu. 153	Bln-1512
Organic - temper	7380±60	6340-6330 6300-6280 6240-6120 6090-6060	Hor.1	qu. 153	Bln-1613
Organic - temper	7275±60	6170-6020	Hor.1	qu. 153	Bln-1613 A

2. 1967

3. In 1967 small trench was excavated. It covered a surface of 200 m²

4. The remains of two dwelling were revealed. They measure 4.5×3.5 m. Basis of ovens was also excavated together with household utilities.

5. The thickness of the Early Neolithic layer is 1.40 m. Four building horizons of the Early Neolithic were distinguished. West Bulgarian painted pottery cultures group of Gradeshnitsa-Karcha (Gradešnitsa Kîrča).
The pottery is presented by red slipped were and white painted ornamentation. Black and wine – red painted decoration is also presented.
During the second stage of the Early Neolithic, polychrome ceramics is prevalent. The pottery assemblage of Tlachene corresponds to the second stage of Gradeshnitsa.

C

Kanchev & Nikolov 1981; Nikolov 1992

About the settlements Borovo-Chakmaktepe, Ovcharovo-gorata and Koprivets information has been given by Dr. R. Krauß. Thank you to Dr. R. Krauß for the information provided.

REFERENCES

Angelova I. 1988. Predvaritelni rezultati ot razkopkite na neolitnoto selishte "Ovcharovo-gorata". In Yordanov K. (ed.), *Terra Antiqua Balcanica* III. Sofia, 31–36.

Angelova I. 1992. Predvaritnie rezultaty razkopok neoliticheskovo poseleniya Ovcharovo – gorata. *Studia Praehistorica* 11-12, 41–50.

Angelova I. & Bin. N. V. 1988. Kremnevay artefaktay iz neoticheskovo poseleniya Ovcharovo – gorata. *Studia Praehistorica* 9, 16–33.

Bakamska A. 2007. The Galabnik. Architecture and Site Planning. In Todorova H., Stefanovich M. & Ivanov G. (eds.), *Strymon Praehistoricus*. Sofia, 175–180.

Boyadzhiev Ya. 1994. Datirane po radiovaglerodnia metod na rannoneolitno zhilishte ot Slatina (Sofia). *Arheologia* 2, 19-23.

Chohadzhiev M. 1978. Selishta ot rannia neolit v Pernishki okrag. *Thracia Antique* 3, 29–44.

Chohadzhiev M. 1983. Die Ausgrabungen der neolitischen Siedlung in Pernik. *Nachrichten aus Niedersachsens Urgeschichte* 32, 29–68.

Chohadzhiev M. 1986. Prouchvane na rannoneolitnoto selishte kray s. Priboy-Pernishki okrag. *Arheologia* 3, 41–49.

Chohadzhiev S. 2001. *Vaksevo. Praistricheski selishta*. Veliko Tarnovo. 1–253.

Chohadzhiev S. & Bakamska A. 1990. Etude du site neolithique ancien de Krainitsi dans le departement de Kustendil. *Studia Praehistorica* 10, 51–76.

Tchohadzhiev S., Bakamska A. & Ninov L. 2007. Kraynitsi – rannokeramichno selishte ot baseyna na reka Struma. In Todorova H., Stefanovich M. & Ivanov G. (eds.), *Strymon Praehistoricus*. Sofia, 181–190.

Chohadzhiev S. & Genadieva V. 2003. Kam prouchvaniata na neolitnoto selishte v Nevestino, Kyustendilsko. *Izvestia na istoricheskia muzey Kyustendil* 9, 21–30.

Detev P. 1950. Selishtnata mogila Baniata pri Kapitan Dimitrievo, *Godishnik na Narodnia arheologicheski musey Plovdiv* II, 1–21.

Detev P. 1968. Praistoricheskoto selishte pri s. Muldava. *Godishnik na narodnia arheologicheski muzey Plovdiv* VI, 9-48.

Detev P. 1976. Rannoneolitno selishte pri s. Kuklen. *Rodopi* 6, 35–36.

Detev P. & Yovchev I. 1978. Razkopki na selishtnata mogila "Manastirya" pri s. Chernichevo, Plovdivski okrag. *Arheologicheski otkritia i razkopki prez 1977 g.* XXXIII, 23–24.

Dimitrov D. 1996. Novootkriti rannoneolititni selishta ot dolinata na Gorna Struma. *Godishnik na Departament Arheologia, Nov Balgarski Universitet* II–III, 97–105.

Dimitrov M. 1985. Razkopki na selishtnata mogila v rayona na Okrazhna Bolnitsa. *Arheologicheski otkritia i razkopki za 1984 g.* Sliven, 23–26.

Čakalova E. & Sarbinska E. 1986. Pflanzenreste aus der neolithische Siedlung Kremenik bei Sapareva Banja. *Studia Praehistorica* 8, 156–159.

Elenski N. 2002. Sondagni prouchvania na neolitno selishte pri s. Hotnitsa – "Peshterata-iztok", Velikotarnovsko prez 2001g. *Arheologicheski otkritia i razkopki prez 2001 g.*, 28–29.

Elenski N. 2006. Sondazhni prouchvania na rannoneolitnoto seliste Dzhulyunitsa-Smardesh, Velikotarnovsko (predvaritelno saobshtenie). *Archeologia* 1-4, 96–117.

Ganetsovski G. 2007a. Arheologicheski razkopki na rannoneolitnoto selishte v m. Valoga (Dolnite laki) kray Ohoden. *Arheologicheski otkritia i razkopki prez 2006 g.*, 30–35.

Ganetsovski G. 2007b. Novi danni za rannia neolit v Severozapadna Balgaria.In Todorova H. & Stefanovich M., Ivanov G. (eds.). *Strymon Praehistoricus*, 147–164.

Ganetsovski G. 2008a. Rannoneoliten grob ot Ohoden, Vrachansko. In Gurova M. (ed.), *Praistoricheski prouchvania v Balgaria: novite predizvikateslstva*. Sofia, 106–119.

Ganetsovski G. 2008b. Arheologicheski razkopki na rannoneolitnoto selishte v m. Valoga (Dolnite Laki) kray s.Ohoden, obshtina Vratsa. *Arheologichski otkritia i razkopki prez 2007*, 30–35.

Genadieva V.1991. Arheologicheski danni za poselishte zhivot v mestnostta "Moshteni", kray selo Nevestino, Kyustendilsko. *Izvestia na istoricheskia muzey Kyustendil 3*, 5–18.

Genadieva V. & Chohadzhiev S. 1994. Arheologichesko prouchvane na praistoricheskoto selishte kray s. Nevestino, Kyustendilsko. *Arheologicheski otkritia i razkopki prez 1994 g.*, 7–9.

Georgiev G. 1961a. Azmashkata selishtna mogila kray Stara Zagora. *Arheologia* 1, 59–65.

Georgiev G. 1961b. Kulturgruppen der Jungstein- und der Kupferzeit in der Ebene von Thrazien (Südbulgarien). *L'Europe à la fin de l'âge de la pierre*. Praha, 45–100.

Georgiev G. 1963. Glavni rezultati ot razkopkite na Azmashkata mogila prez 1961 g. *Izvestia na Arheologicheskia Institut* 26, 157–163.

Georgiev G. 1965. The Azmak Mound in Southern Bulgaria. *Antiquity* 39, 6–8.

Georgiev G. 1969. Die äneolithische Kultur in Südbulgarien im Lichte der Ausgrabungen vom Tell Azmak bei Stara Zagora. *Studijne Zvesti Archeologichevo Ustavu Slovenskej Akademie Vied* 17, 141–158.

Georgiev G. 1974. Stratigrafia i periodizatsia na neolita i halkolita v dneshnite balgarski zemi. *Arheologia* 4, 1–19.

Georiev G. 1975. Stratigrafia i harakter na praistoricheskoto selishte v s. Kremikovtsi, Sofiysko. *Arheologia* 2, 17–30.

Georgiev G. 1981. Die neolitische Siedlung bei Cavdar, Bez. Sofia. Cultures prehistoriques en Bulgarie. *Izvestia na Arheologicheskia Institut* 36, (= Cultures prehistoriques en Bulgarie), 63–109.

Georgiev G., Nikolov V., Nikolova V. & Ĉohadziev S. 1986. Die neolithische Siedlung Kremenik bei Sapareva Banja, Bezirk Kjustendil. *Studia Praehistorica* 8, 108–151.

Görsdorf J. & Bojadziev Ya. 1996. Zur absoluten Chronologie der bulgarischen Urgeschichte. *Eurasia Antiqua* 2, 123–124.

Görsdorf J. & Weninger B. 1993. Berliner ^{14}C-Alterbestimmungen von Datierungsmaterialien aus dem Tell Karanovo. *Tell Karanovo 1992.* Vorläufiger Bericht. Salzburg, 20–4.

Grebska-Kulova M. 2007. Arheologisheski razkopki na praistoricheskoto selishte kray s. Ilindentsi, m. Masovets, obshtina Strumiani. *Arheologicheski otkritia i razkopki prez 2006 g.*, 34–36.

Grebska-Kulova M. 2008. Rannoneolitnata kultura na Sredna Struma, Yugozapadna Balgaria. In Ě. Gurova (ed.), *Praistoricheski prouchvania v Balgaria: novite predizvikatelstva.* Natsionalen Arheologicheski Institute s Muzey, Istoricheski muzey Peshtera, 56–65.

Hiller S. 1990. Neue Ausgrabungen in Karanovo. In Srejović D. & Tasić N. (eds.), *Vinča and its world.* Belgrad, 197–206.

Hiller S. 2004. Razvitie na selishtnata struktura v tel Karanovo. In Nikolov V., Bačvarov K. & Kalchev P. (eds.), *Praistoricheska Trakia.* Sofia-Stara-Zagora, 298–310.

Hiller S. & Nikolov V. (eds.) 1997. *Karanovo. Die Ausgrabungen im Südsektor 1984-1992. Österreichisch-Bulgarische Ausgrabungen und Forschungen in Karanovo.* bd. I. Salzburg.

Hiller S. & Nikolov V. (eds.) 2002. *Karanovo. Die Ausgrabungen in O19. (Karanovo II. Beiträge zum Neolithikum in Südosteuropa.)* Wien.

Kanchev K. 1995. Stratigrafsko razpredelenie na risuvanata keramika v mnogosloynoto rannoneolitno selishte Chavdar, Pirdopsko. *Archeologia* 2, 1–4.

Kanchev M. & Chohadzhiev M. 1994. Neolitno selishte v Krumovgrad. In Panayotov I.(ed.), *Maritsa-Iztok. Arheologicheski prouchvania* 2, 13–38.

Kanchev K. & Nikolov B. 1981. Oradia na truda i stopanskia zhivot v selishtata ot staria i srednia neolit pri s. Gradeshnitsa i s. Tlachene, Vrachansko. *Izvestia na muzeyte v Severozapadna Balgaria* 5, 9–36.

Kohl G. & Quitta H. 1966. Berlin Radiocarbon measurements II. *Radiocarbon* 8, 27–45.

Kovacheva M. 1995. Bulgarian archeomagnetic studies. In Bailey D. & Panayotov I. (eds.), *Prehistoric Bulgaria.* Monographs in World Archaeology 22. Madison Wisconsin, Prehistory Press, 209–224.

Krauß R. 2006a. Ovčarovo-gorata: Aufarbeitung der Altgrabung auf einer frühneolithischen Siedlung in Nordbulgarien. In Hansen S. & Wagner M. (eds.), *Forschungsprojekte der Eurasien-Abteilung.* Berlin, 26–27.

Krauß R. 2006b. Ovčarovo-gorata, Kreis Targovište (Bulgarien). *Jahresbericht 2005 des Deutschen Archäologischen Instituts.* Arch. Anz. 2, 334–337.

Krauß R. 2006c. Die prähistorische Besiedlung am Unterlauf der Jantra vor dem Hintergrund der Kulturgeschichte Nordbulgariens. *PAS* 20. Rahden, 342–343.

Krauß R. 2007a. Ovcharovo-gorata: Evaluation of previous excavations at an early Neolithic settlement in north Bulgaria. In Hansen S. & Wagner M. (eds.), *Current Research Projects of the Eurasia Department.* Berlin, 16–17.

Krauß R. 2007b. Ovčarovo-gorata, Kreis Targovište (Bulgarien). *Jahresbericht 2006 des Deutschen Archäologischen Instituts.* Berlin, 227–229.

Krauß R. 2008a. Karanovo und das südosteuropäische Chronologiesystem aus heutiger Sicht. *Eurasia Antiqua* 14, 115–147.

Krauß R. 2008b. Ovčarovo-gorata, Kreis Targovište (Bulgarien). *Jahresbericht 2007 des Deutschen Archäologischen Instituts.* Berlin, 323–325.

Leshtakov K. 2004. Keramika s vriazana i kanelirana ukrasa ot rannoneolitnoto selishte Yabalkovo na r. Maritsa. In: Nikolov V., Bačvarov K. & Kalchev P. (eds.), *Prehistoric Thrace.* So-

fia-Stara Zagora, 80–84.

Leshtakov K. 2006. Arheologicheski razkopki do selo Yabalkovo, Dimitrovgradsko. Rannoneolitno selishte. Spasitelni razkopki po traseto na zhelezopatnata linia Plovdiv-Svilengrad prez 2004. Veliko Tarnovo.

Leshtakov K. 2007. Spasitelni razkopki na rannoneolitnoto selishte Yabalkovo prez 2006 g. *Arheologicheski otkritia i razkopki* prez 2006 g., 39–41.

Leshtakov K., Petrova V, Todorova N.,.Borisova I., Katsarov G., Spasov N. & Zlateva V. 2008. Spasitelni razkopki na obekt Yabalkovo-praistorichesko selishte sektori yugozapad i sever v rayona na stroezha na zhp linia Plovdiv-Svilengrad i na AM "Maritsa". *Arheologicheski otkritia i razkopki* prez 2007 g., 38–41.

Leshtakov K., Todorova N., Petrova V., Zlateva-Uzunova R., Özbek O., Popova Tz., Spassov N. & Iliev N. 2007. Preliminary report on the salvage archaeological excavations at the Early Neolithic site Yabalkovo in the Maritsa valley, 2000-2005 field seasons. *Anatolica* XXXIII, 185–234.

Lichardus-Itten M., Demoule J.-P., Perničeva L., Grebska-Kulova M. &. Kulov Il. 2000. Zur bemalten Keramik aus der früneolithische Siedlung von Kovačevo (SW-Bulgarien). In Hiller S. & Nikolov V. (eds.), *Karanovo III. Beiträge zum Neolithikum in Südosteuropa.* Wien, 27–59.

Lichardus-Itten M., Demoule J.-P., Perničeva L., Grebska-Kulova M. &. Kulov Il. 2002. The Site of Kovacevo and the Beginnings of the Neolithic Period in Southwestern Bulgaria. In Lichardus-Itten M., Lichardus J. & Nikolov V. (eds.), *Beiträge zu jungsteinzeitlichen Forschungen in Bulgarien.* Bohn, Saarbrüker Beiträge zur Alterkumskunde 74, 99–158.

Lichardus-Itten M., Demoule J.-P., Perničeva L., Grebska-Kulova M. &. Kulov Il. 2006. Kovačevo an Early Neolithic site in South-West Bulgaria and its importance for European Neolithization. In Gatsov I. & Schwarzberg H. (eds.), *Aegean-Marmara-Black Sea: the Present State of Research on the Early Neolithic.* Schriften des Zentrums für Archäologie und Kulturgeschichte des Schwarzmeerraumes 5. Beier & Beran, 83–94.

Macanova V. 2000. Neolithische Siedlung bei Rakitovo. Stratigraphie und Chronologie. In Hiller S. & Nikolov V. (eds.), *Karanovo III.* Beiträge zum Neolithikum in Südosteuropa. Wien, 59–73.

Macanova V. 2002. Keramik aus der neolithischen Siedlung bei Rakitovo. In Lichardus-Itten M., Lichardus J. & Nikolov V. (eds.), *Beiträge zu jungsteinzeitlichen Forschungen in Bulgarien.* Bonn, Saarbücker Beiträge zur Altertumkunde 74, 191–223.

Mikov V. & Dzhambazov N. 1960. *Devetashkata peshtera.* Sofia. 199 pp.

Nikolov B. 1974. *Gradeshnitsa.* Sofia. 124 pp.

Nikolov B. 1975. Selishte ot staria neolit pri s. Gradeshnitsa, Vrachanski okrag. *Arheologia* 1-4, 25–40.

Nikolov V. 1990. Die neolitische Siedlung Slatina in Sofia (Ausgrabungen aus dem Jahre 1985). *Studia Praehistorica* 10, 77–85.

Nikolov B. 1992. Periodizatsia na neolitinite kulturi v Severna Balgaria – ot Yantra do Timok. *Izvestia na muzeyte v Severozapadna Balgaria* 18, 13–14.

Nikolov V. 1992. Rannoneolitnoto zhilishte ot Slatina. *Razkopki i Prouchvania* XXV. Sofia, 163 pp.

Nikolov V.1996. Yugozapaden variant na kultura Karanovo I. *Arheologia* 2-3, 1–8.

Nikolov V. 1997. Sondazhni prouchvania na praistoricheskoto selishte v m. "Izgoryalata niva" kray s. Pomoshtitsa, Popovsko prez 1995 a. *Popovo v minaloto* II, 33–37.

Nikolov V. 2004a. Dinamika na kulturnite procesi v neolitna Trakia. In Nikolov V., Bačvarov K. & Kalchev P. (eds.), *Praistoricheska Trakia*, 13–17.

Nikolov V. 2004b. Rannoneolitnoto zhilishte Slatina v Sofia: vtori stroitelen horizont (predvaritelno saobshtenie, I chast). *Arheologia* 1-2, 5–14.

Nikolov V., Grigorova K. & Sirakova E. 1991. Rannoneolitnoto selishte Slatina v Sofia: parvi stroitelen horizont (predvaritelno saobshtenie). *Arheologia* 3, 13–26.

Nikolov V. Grigorova K. & Sirakova E. 1992. Die Ausgrabungen in der frühneolithischen Siedlung von Sofia - Slatina, Bulgarien, in den Jahren 1985-1988. *Acta Praehistorica et Archaeologica* 24, 221–233.

Nikolov V. & Karastoyanova D. 2003. Risuvanata ornamentatsia kato sistema za komunikatsia megdu pokoleniata (po materiali ot ranno i srednoneolitnia plast na tel Kazanlak). *Archeologia* 2, 5–14.

Nikolov V., Matsanova V., Stefanova T., Bozhilov B., Bachvarov K., Gatsov I., Marinova L. & Ninov L. 1999. *Selishtnata mogila Kapitan Dimitrievo. Razkopki 1998–1999*. Sofia, Peshtera. 141 pp.

Nikolov V. & Maslarov K. 1987. *Drevni selishta kray Eleshnitsa*. Sofia, 36 pp.

Nikolov V. & Radeva M. 1992. Sondazhni prouchvania na rannoneolitnoto selishte v Dobrinishte, Razlozhko. *Arheologia* 1, 1–14.

Nikolova L. 1998. Neolithic sequence: the upper Stryama valley in western Thrace. *Documenta Praehistorica* XXV, 99–131.

Nikolova L. & Madzhev N. 1994. Sondazhno prouchvane na rannoneolitni mnogosloyni selishta pri s. Kliment i s. Dabene, Karlovsko. *Arheologisheski razkopki na praistoricheski obekti prez 1992 g.* Sofia, 10–11.

Ninov L. 1986. Tierknochen aus der prähistorischen Siedlung Kremenik. *Studia Praehistorica* 8, 152-155.

Nobis G. 1986. Zur Fauna der frühneolithischen Siedlung Ovčarovo gorata, Bez. Târgovište (NO-Bulgarien). *Bonn. zool. Beitr.* 37, 1–22.

Nobis G. 1988. Zur Fauna der frühneolithischen Siedlung Ovčarovo-gorata bei Târgovište (NO-Bulgarien). *Studia Praehistorica* 9, 37–53.

Panayotov I., Gatsov I. & Popova Ts. 1992. "Pompena stancia" blizo do s. Malak Preslavets – rannoeneolitischeskoe poselenie s intramuralnami pogrebeniyami. *Studia Praehistorica* 11–12, 51–61.

Pavuk J. & Bakamska A. 1989. Beitrag der Ausgrabung in Galabnik zur Erforschung des Neolithikums in Südosteuropa. Neolithic of South-Eastern Europe and its Near Eastern connections. *Varia Archeologica Hungarica* 2. Budapest, 223–231.

Pavuk J. & Čohadžiev M. 1984. Neolithische Tellsiedlung bei Galabnik in Westbulgarien. *Slovenska Archeologia* XXXII-1, 195–228.

Pernitcheva L. 1990. Le site de Kovachevo, néolithique ancient, dans le department de Blagovgrad. *Studia Praehistorica* 10, 142–196.

Pernicheva L.1993. Prinos kam prouchvaneto na rannia neolit v Slatina, Sofia. *Arheologia* 4, 1–14.

Pernicheva L. 1995. Prehistoric Cultures in the Middle Struma Valley: Neolithic and Eneolithic. In Bailey D. & Panayotov I. (eds.), *Prehistoric Bulgaria*. Monographs in World Archaeology 22. Madison Wisconsin, Prehistory Press, 99–140.

Perničeva L. 2002. Die prähistorische Siedlung Balgarčevo, Kreis Blagoevgrad. In Lichardus-Itten M., Lichardus J. & Nikolov V. (eds.), *Beiträge zu jungsteinzeitlichen Forschungen in Bulgarien*. Bonn, Saarbücker Beiträge zur Alterkumkunde 74, 271–324.

Perničeva L, Kulov Il. &. Grebska-Kulova M. 2000. Early Neolithic house from Balgarchevo. *Archaeologia Bulgarica* IV 3, 1–10.

Petkov N. 1948. Selishtnata mogila do Chelopech. *Naroden Arheologicheski Muzey v Plovdiv* I, 159-171.

Petkov N. 1959. Neolitno selishte pri s. Slatina. *Arheologia* 1-2, 100–105.

Petkov N. 1960. Prinos kam izuchavane na praistoriata na Sofiyskoto pole. *Arheologia* 4, 44–54.

Petkov N. 1961. Novi danni za neolitnata kultura kray Sofia. *Arheologia* 3, 64–73.

Peykov A. 1973. Razkopkina neolitnoto selishte v Kardzhali prezç 1972 a. *Rezyumeta na otcheti za razkopki prez 1972 g.* Sofia, 13–15.

Peykov A. 1978. Sondazhni razkopki na neolitnoto selishte v Kardzhali prez 1972 g. *Ahrida* 1, 7–44.

Popov V. 1994. Prouchvane na rannoneolitnoto selishte Koprivets, obshtina Byala. In Nikolov V. (ed.), *Archeologicheski razkopki na praistoricheski obekti prez 1992 g.*, 9–10.

Popov V. 1996. *Periodizatsia i hronologia na neolitnite i halkolitnite kulturi ot porechieto na r. Rusenski Lom*. Ruse. 308 pp.

Popov B. & Mateva B. 1993. Neolitno selishte pri s. Koprivets. *Godisnik na Muzeyte ot Severna Balgaria* IX, 23–31.

Quitta H. & Kohl G. 1969. Neue Radiocarbondaten zum Neolithikum und zur frühen Bronzezeit Südosteuropas und der Sowjetunion. *Zeitschrift für Archäologie* 3, N 2, 233–255.

Radunčeva A. 2002. Eine neolitische Siedlung am Ufer der Marica bei Simeonovgrad. In Lichardus-Itten M., Lichardus J. & Nikolov V. (eds.), *Beiträge zu jungsteinzeitlichen Forschungen in Bulgarien*. Bohn, Saarbrüker Beiträge zur Alterkumskunde 74, 225–243.

Raduncheva A., Matsanova V., Gatsov I., Kovachev G., Georgiev G., Chakalova E. & Bozhilova E. 2002. Neolitno selishte do grad Rakitovo. *Pazkopki i Prouchvania* XXIX. Sofia. 207 pp.

Stanev P. 1995. Topografia i stratigrafia na neoliten kompleks Orlovets. Zhilishta arhitektura na rannoneolitnoto selishte. *Izvestia na Istoricheski muzey-Veliko Tarnovo* X, 57–66.

Stanev P. 1997. Neolitna selishtna mogila Samovodene – rezultati ot dosegashnite prouchvania. *Izvestia na Istoricheski muzey – Veliko Tarnovo* XII, 38–70.

Stanev P. 2002. Der neolitische Siedlungshügel Samovodene: Einige Ergebnisse der bisherigen Forschungen. In Lichardus-Itten M., Lichardus J. & Nikolov V. (eds.), *Beiträge zu jungsteinzeitlichen Forschungen in Bulgarien*. Bonn, Saarbücker Beiträge zur Altertumkunde 74, 411–436.

Stanev P. 2008. *Orlovets. Neoliten kompleks*. Veliko Tarnovo. 379 pp.

Stanev P., Naydenova E. & Elenski N. 1994. Arheologicheski prouchvania v zemlishteto na s. Orlovets, Polskotrambeshka obshtina. *Izvestia na Istoricheski muzey-Veliko Tarnovo* IX, 89–95.

Tao M. 2000. The Early Neolithic Pottery from Delnicite near Elešnica. In: S. Hiller, V. Nikolov (eds.), *Karanovo III. Beiträge zum Neolithikum in Südosteuropa*. Wien, 51–57.

Todorova H. 1989. Das Frühneolithikum Nordostbulgariens im Kontext des Ostbalkanischen Neolithikums. Tell Karanovo und das Balkan Neolithikum. Salzburg, 9–25.

Todorova H., Ivanov S., Vasilev V., Hoph M., Quita X. & Kol G. 1975. Selishtata mogila pri Goliamo Delchevo. *Razkopki i Prouchvania* V. Sofia. 244 pp.

Todorova H., Vasilev V., Yanushevich Z., Kovacheva M. & Valev P. 1983. Ovcharovo. *Razkopki i Prouchvania* VIII, 10–11.

Vandova V. 2000a. Keramichniat kompleks na IV stroitelen horizont v neolitnoto selishte Kremenik kray Sapareva Bania. *Izvestia na istoricheskia muzey Kyustendil, Prilozhenie I,*

36–50.

Vandova V. 2000b. Keramikata "black topped" ot neolitnoto selishte Kremenik kray Sapareva Bania. In Nikolov V. (ed.), Trakia i sasednite rayoni prez neolita i halkolita. *Karanoski konferentsii za praistoriata na Balkanite* 1. Sofia, 43–50.

Vandova V. 2004. Sondazhni arheologicheski prouchvania v s. Piperkov Chiflik, obshtina Kyustendil prez 2003. *Arheologicheski otkritia i razkopki prez 2003 g.*, 27.

Vandova V. 2007a. Sondazhni arheologicheski prouchvania na neolitnoto selishte v s. Bersin, obshtina Kyustendil. *Arheologicheski otkritia i razkopki prez 2007g.*, 42–46.

Vandova V. 2007b. The Early Neolithic Site at Piperkov Čiflik, Near Kjustendil (Season 2004). In Todorova H., Stefanovich M. & Ivanov G. (eds.), *Strymon Praehistoricus*, 91–200.

Vandova V. & Spasov R. 2003. Terenni obhozhdania v obshtina Kyustendil prez 2002. *Arhaologicheski otkritia i razkopki prez 2002 g.*, 18–19.

Yordanov Y. & Dimitrova B. 1996. Antropological data about buried individuals in an Intramural necropolis in a settlementfrom the Early Neolithic- the village of Maluk Preslavets, Silistra region. *Godishnik na Departament Arheologia, Nov Balgarski Universitet* II-III, 106–118.

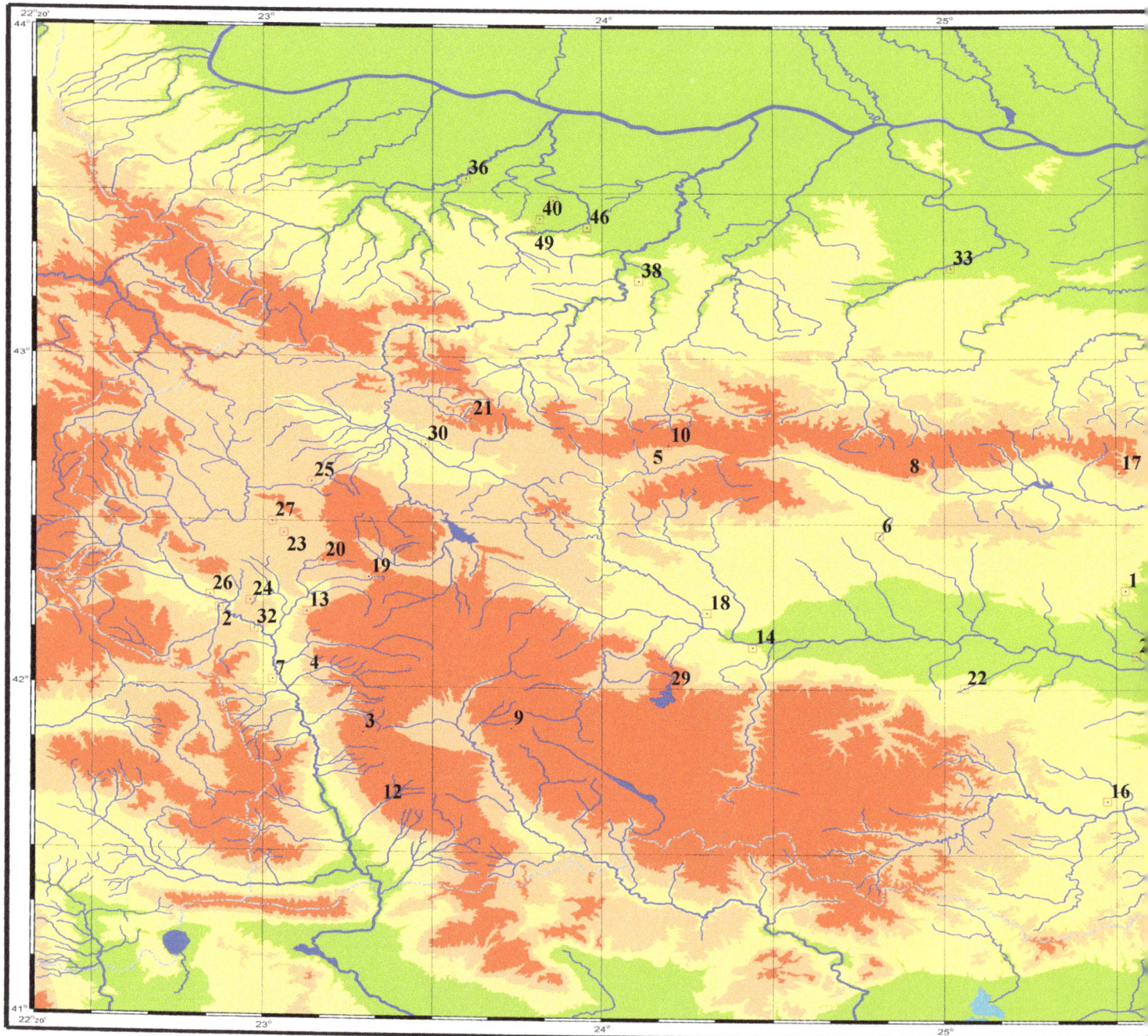

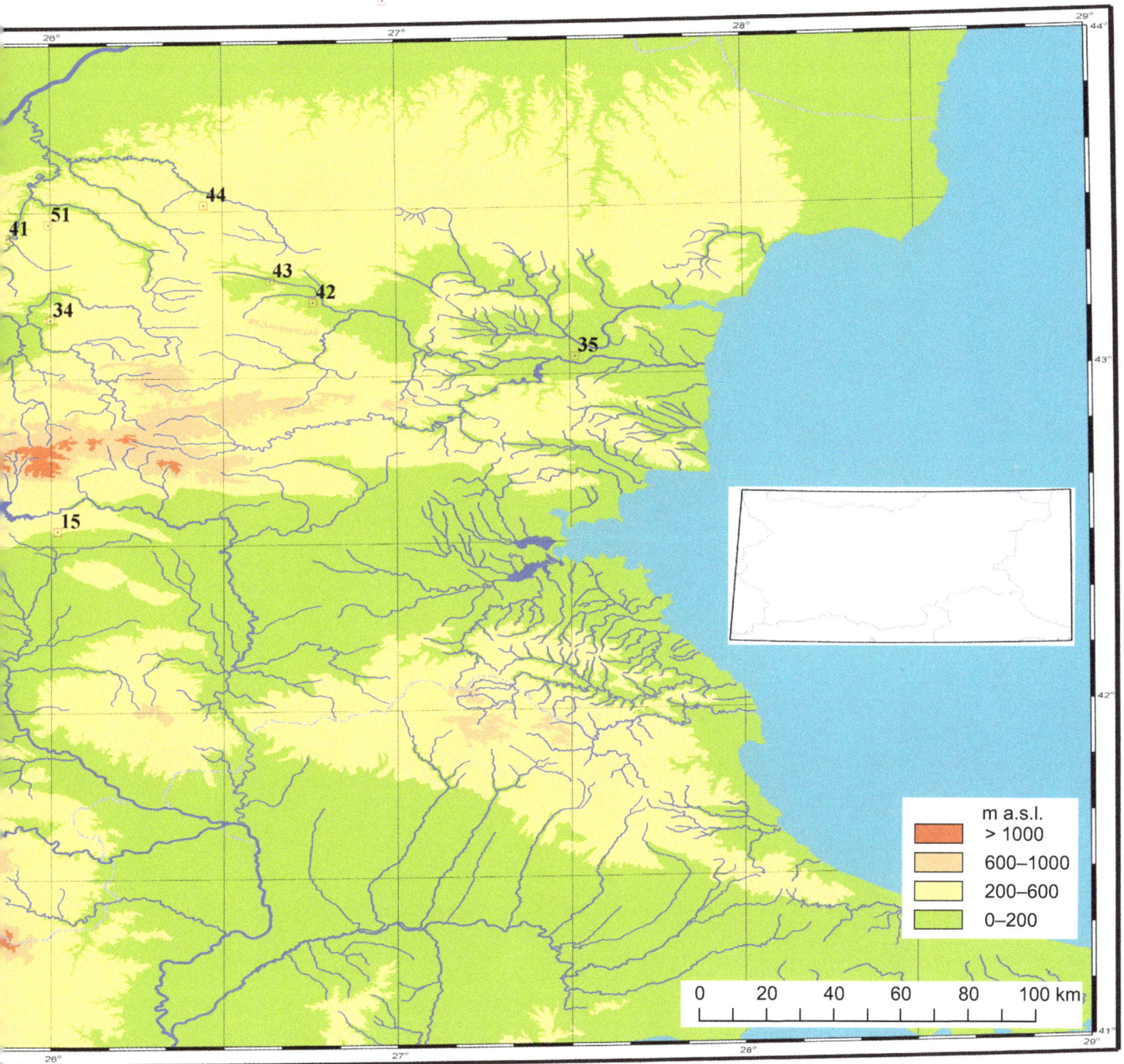

26° 27° 28° 29°
44°

41
51
44

34
43
42

35

43°

15

42°

m a.s.l.
> 1000
600–1000
200–600
0–200

| 0 | 20 | 40 | 60 | 80 | 100 km |

26° 27° 28° 29°
41°